Augsburg Commentary on the New Testament

I-II TIMOTHY, TITUS

Arland J. Hultgren

II THESSALONIANS

Roger Aus

Augsburg Publishing House

Minneapolis, Minnesota

AUGSBURG COMMENTARY ON THE NEW TESTAMENT
1-2 Timothy, Titus, 2 Thessalonians

Library of Congress Cataloging in Publication Data

Hultgren, Arland J.
   1-2 TIMOTHY, TITUS.

   (Augsburg commentary on the New Testament)
   Includes bibliographies.
   1. Bible. N.T. Pastoral Epistles—Commentaries.
2. Bible. N.T. Thessalonians, 2nd—Commentaries.
I. Aus, Roger, 1940-   . 2 Thessalonians. 1984.
II. Title. III. Title: 2 Thessalonians. IV. Series.
BS2735.3.H84   1984   227'.8   83-72126
ISBN 0-8066-8874-2 (pbk.)

Manufactured in the U.S.A.   APH 10-9032

1 2 3 4 5 6 7 8 9 0 1 2 3 4 5 6 7 8 9

CONTENTS

ABBREVIATIONS

BAGD   Walter Bauer, *A Greek-English Lexicon of the New Testament and Other Early Christian Literature*, trans. and adapted by W. F. Arndt, F. W. Gingrich, and F. W. Danker (2nd ed.; Chicago: University of Chicago, 1979).

BDF   F. Blass and A. Debrunner, *A Greek Grammar of the New Testament and Other Early Christian Literature*, trans. and rev. by R. W. Funk (Chicago: University of Chicago, 1968).

Bib   *Biblica*

BJRL   *Bulletin of the John Rylands University Library of Manchester*

BSac   *Bibliothea Sacra*

CBQ   *Catholic Biblical Quarterly*

ExpTim   *Expository Times*

IDB   *The Interpreter's Dictionary of the Bible*, ed. G. Buttrick (4 vols.; Nashville: Abingdon, 1962).

IDBSup   *The Interpreter's Dictionary of the Bible, Supplementary Volume*, ed. K. Crim (Nashville: Abingdon, 1976).

4

JB	Jerusalem Bible
JBL	*Journal of Biblical Literature*
JRelS	*Journal of Religious Studies*
KD	*Kerygma und Dogma*
KJV	King James Version
LXX	The Septuagint
NAB	New American Bible
NEB	New English Bible
NIV	New International Version
NTS	*New Testament Studies*
RSV	Revised Standard Version
RevThom	*Revue Thomiste*
TDNT	*Theological Dictionary of the New Testament,* ed. G. Kittel and G. Friedrich, trans. G. Bromiley (10 vols.; Grand Rapids: Eerdmans, 1964-1976).
TEV	Today's English Version
TQ	*Theologische Quartalschrift*

FOREWORD

The AUGSBURG COMMENTARY ON THE NEW TES-
TAMENT is written for laypeople, students, and pastors.
Laypeople will use it as a resource for Bible study at home and
at church. Students and instructors will read it to probe the
basic message of the books of the New Testament. And pastors
will find it to be a valuable aid for sermon and lesson prepara-
tion.

The plan of each commentary is designed to enhance its
usefulness. The Introduction presents a topical overview of the
biblical book to be discussed and provides information on the
historical circumstances in which that book was written. It
may also contain a summary of the biblical writer's thought.
In the body of the commentary, the interpreter sets forth in
brief compass the meaning of the biblical text. The procedure
is to explain the text section by section. Care has also been
taken to avoid scholarly jargon and the heavy use of technical
terms. Because the readers of the commentary will have their
Bibles at hand, the biblical text itself has not been printed
out. In general, the editors recommend the use of the Revised
Standard Version of the Bible.

The authors of this commentary series are professors at
seminaries and universities and are themselves ordained clergy-
persons. They have been selected both because of their exper-
tise and because they worship in the same congregations as the

people for whom they are writing. In elucidating the text of
Scripture, therefore, they attest to their belief that central to
the faith and life of the church of God is the Word of God.

The Editorial Committee

Roy A. Harrisville
Luther Northwestern Theological
Seminary
St. Paul, Minnesota

Jack Dean Kingsbury
Union Theological Seminary
Richmond, Virginia

Gerhard A. Krodel
Lutheran Theological Seminary
Gettysburg, Pennsylvania

I-II TIMOTHY, TITUS

Arland J. Hultgren

INTRODUCTION TO 1-2 TIMOTHY AND TITUS

1 Timothy, 2 Timothy, and Titus are traditionally called the "Pastoral Epistles," a term first used by the German scholar Paul Anton in lectures delivered in 1726-1727. The designation is due to their aims and contents: they provide instructions for pastoral oversight of congregations, giving considerable attention to the qualifications and duties of congregational leaders who function as pastors, although the term "pastor" itself does not appear in the letters.

Some scholars have judged the Pastorals harshly, claiming that these letters reflect a "bourgeois Christianity," which is mainly concerned about its own organizational structures, orthodoxy, and getting along in the world. These letters are said to lack the earlier zeal for the gospel, the freedom of life in the Spirit, and the sense of the church as the dynamic people of God in pilgrimage.

But, as it is hoped this commentary will show, the Pastorals should be judged much more positively. They are the work of a faithful witness to the gospel, setting forth a fine synthesis of Christian doctrine and moral teaching which was necessary at the time they were written, aiding the cause of keeping the church faithful to its calling under the lordship of Jesus Christ. Moreover, the Pastorals are of major importance for the church today. They are primary documents for studies in the doctrine of the church and its ministry. They call upon the church to be concerned about, pray for, and act charitably toward all persons, whether Christian or not. They also have a positive attitude toward the creation. God has created the world and all that is in it, and through God's continuing work of creation, all humankind is sustained. Christians do not despise the world but live and serve in it. Into this world God's grace has appeared in Christ for salvation.

1. Authorship of the Pastorals

The letters open with reference to Paul as their author. Nevertheless, the question of Pauline authorship is debated in modern scholarship (see Bibliography, p. 177). There are some commentators who affirm that the letters were indeed written by Paul (J. Bernard, C. Spicq, and D. Guthrie). Others contend they are Paul's work in the sense that they contain his message, even if these letters were drafted in their present form through the cooperation of a secretary (J. Jeremias, G. Holtz, and J. N. D. Kelly). But most commentators deny Pauline authorship of the Pastorals (e.g., F. Gealy, C. K. Barrett, M. Dibelius and H. Conzelmann, and A. T. Hanson). Some think that the Pastorals may contain some genuine fragments of letters by Paul—a question to be pursued below—but the Pastorals are taken in their present form to be pseudonymous (i.e., written by someone else in the name of Paul).

Before entering the debate about authorship, the matter of pseudonymous writing ought to be addressed. In modern times pseudonymous writing would be considered immoral and illegal. One may use a "pen name," but one dare not write a document today and attribute it to someone else, either living or dead. In the ancient world, however, pseudonymous writing was frequent and acceptable. In the pre-Christian Graeco-Roman world, for example, certain letters of Plato were written under his name, which are considered pseudonymous.[1] Jewish tradition also contains pseudonymous writings. The book of Daniel, for example, is attributed to a person by that name (8:15, 27; 10:2; 12:5, etc.) who lived in the sixth century B.C. As studies have shown, however, the book in its present form must have been written in the second century B.C., since it alludes to events of that century. The Wisdom of Solomon is attributed to Solomon (10th century B.C.), whom it impersonates, but today it is thought to have been composed in the Greek language in the first century B.C.

Pseudonymous writing is therefore common in the ancient world and also occurs in the case of some books of the Bible. If a book is judged to be pseudonymous, its value as Scripture is in no way diminished. Pseudonymous writings can be explained on the grounds that the person or persons writing them thought that they were being loyal to the figure who was impersonated, and, given the present circumstances, this is what that person would have said.

In the case of the Pastoral Epistles, the reasons for attributing them to a pseudonymous writer are several and weighty. These have to do with (1) ancient evidence; (2) vocabulary and style; (3) theological outlook and the form of church organization presupposed; and (4) problems of Pauline chronology. We shall review each of these.

First, the ancient evidence of Pauline authorship of the Pastorals is tenuous. When Marcion (fl., Rome, A.D. 150) compiled his canon, he did not include the Pastoral Epistles. Moreover, the earliest collection of Paul's letters in book form, known as p46 (dated by some as early as A.D. 200), does not include the Pastorals. The earliest evidence for the existence of the Pastorals within the body of Pauline letters is all from the second half of the second century (the Muratorian Canon, A.D. 175-200, and the late second century writers Irenaeus, Tertullian, and Clement of Alexandria). This relatively late attribution of the Pastorals to Paul is clearly at variance with both Marcion and p46.

The second line of investigation, concerning language and style, is even more significant. The total list of words used at least once in the Greek text of the Pastorals is 901. Of these 901, there are 52 which can be designated as proper nouns (persons and places). Once these are set aside, there remains a list of 849 words used at least once in these three letters. Of these 849, there are 306 (36.04%) which are not found in the other ten letters attributed to Paul, which of course is very high. Furthermore, of these 306 words not found in the other Paulines, no less than 121 (or 14.13% of the 849 words in the Pastorals) appear in the writings of the second century Apostolic Fathers and Apologists.[2]

It can be argued, of course, that Paul might have used these additional 306 words in addressing particular issues at a later stage of his ministry. But there is more to the issue than these statistics alone. Many stylistic words found in Paul's letters, such as certain particles, conjunctions, pronouns, and prepositions—words belonging to the "connective tissue" of Paul's writing habits—are lacking in the Pastorals. There are 77 such words.[3]

One may go even further. There is a growing consensus among many in the field of Pauline studies that there are only seven letters (Romans, 1 and 2 Corinthians, Galatians, Philippians, 1 Thessalonians, and Philemon), rather than 10, which can surely be said to have been written by Paul. If one compares the language of the Pastorals with that of these seven alone, the differences become even clearer. There are 20 additional words which appear in the Pastorals and in Ephesians, Colossians, and 2 Thessalonians, but not in the seven letters which are universally thought to be by Paul. The words distinctive to the Pastorals, but not found in the undisputed seven letters of Paul, now number 326 (38.4% of the 849).

Matters of style become even more striking in this comparison. For example, Paul uses the Greek conjunction *hōste* ("so that") 37 times in his undisputed letters, but it does not appear in the Pastorals (nor in Ephesians and Colossians; 2 Thessalonians has it twice). Or again, Paul uses two different Greek prepositions to express "with." These are *syn* plus the dative (28 times) and *meta* plus the genitive (37 times). But the writer of the Pastorals never uses the former; he uses only the latter expression (18 times). The former appears twice in Ephesians and seven times in Colossians. Taking these matters of vocabulary and style together, the evidence against Pauline authorship appears strong.

An examination of theological concepts and the type of church order presupposed by the Pastorals also calls Pauline authorship into question. Theological themes associated with Paul, such as Christian existence as life "in Christ" and an expected imminent parousia, are lacking in the Pastorals. The term *faith* means "the Christian faith" in the Pastorals (1 Tim. 1:2; 3:9, 13; 4:1; 2 Tim. 4:7; Titus 1:13, etc.) or a Christian virtue (1 Tim. 1:5, 19; 4:12; 6:11; 2 Tim. 2:22; Titus 2:2, etc.), whereas in Paul it has the basic meaning of "trust" in God, Christ, or the gospel (Rom. 1:17; 3:25, 30; 1 Cor. 13:2; 2 Cor. 5:7; Gal. 2:16; 3:26; Phil. 1:27; 3:9, etc., although in Gal. 1:23 and Phil. 1:25 Paul also speaks of "the faith"). The Greek term translated "godliness" or "religion" is found 10 times in the Pastorals (1 Tim. 2:2; 3:16; 4:7, 8; 6:3, 5, 6, 11; 2 Tim. 3:5; Titus 1:1), but it is never found in letters undisputedly attributed to Paul. The form of church order found in the Pastorals—which speaks of bishops, presbyters, and deacons—is not found in the letters definitely written by Paul; the church order of the Pastorals has similarities to those found in the second century Apostolic Fathers (see Part 4 of this Introduction for details).

Finally, a fourth line of investigation has examined matters of Pauline chronology. It is conceded by persons of various persuasions, including those who seek to maintain Pauline authorship, that the Pastorals will not fit into the career of

Paul as recounted in Acts. The only place at which these letters could be worked into a Pauline chronology would be a time after that covered by Acts. Acts closes with Paul imprisoned in Rome (28:30-31). It has been suggested that Paul was released from prison, traveled further, and was imprisoned again. According to this proposal, after the first imprisonment Paul wrote 1 Timothy and Titus and during the second imprisonment he wrote 2 Timothy. This is because in 1 Timothy and Titus the writer is portrayed as free (1 Tim. 3:14-15; 4:13; Titus 3:12), while in 2 Timothy he is portrayed as imprisoned in Rome (1:8, 16-17; 4:6-8). Those who advocate this view base it on additional sources as well. Clement of Rome (ca. A.D. 96) writes concerning Paul that, "reaching the limits of the West, he bore witness before rulers" (*1 Clement* 5.7). The Muratorian Canon (ca. A.D. 175-200) notes that in Acts Luke omits the account of "the journey of Paul, who from the city [of Rome] proceeded to Spain" (lines 38-39). Eusebius, a fourth century historian, writes that, after Paul's first trial in Rome and his vindication, the apostle set out again "on the ministry of preaching," was imprisoned a second time, and during that time "composed the Second Epistle to Timothy" (*Ecclesiastical History* 2.22).

This composite picture, while it is appealing in light of statements within the Pastorals themselves, has been rejected by many. It is clear that Paul, when he wrote the Epistle to the Romans from Corinth about A.D. 55, had hoped to travel to Rome and then on to Spain (15:24, 28). When he wrote these words, however, Paul expected to arrive in Rome a free person who could make such a journey westward. The fact of the matter is that he arrived in Rome as a prisoner. If Paul was in fact released, allowing for some subsequent missionary work, and was then imprisoned a second time, it is strange that Luke (writing ca. A.D. 80-90) does not mention that. In fact, as many have maintained, the inference can be drawn from Acts that, according to Luke, Paul met his death after a two-year imprisonment in Rome. Luke portrays Paul as giving a farewell speech at Ephesus which hints of a forthcoming martyrdom (20:24); the speech is then followed by the weeping and sorrow of the Ephesians because "they would see his face no more" (20:38). The story alludes to Paul's martyrdom which, for Luke, took place after Paul's imprisonment in Rome.

The composite picture of a subsequent release, travel, and second imprisonment can be explained readily. Clement's reference to the "limits of the West" is possibly a reference not to Spain, but to Rome itself, the place at which Paul "bore witness before rulers"; there is no need to assume a Spanish mission prior to this witnessing. The Muratorian tradition is late second century and could be based purely on the expressed hopes of Paul to visit Spain in Rom. 15:24, 28. The statement of Eusebius cites 2 Tim. 4:16-17, which speaks of a "first defense" of Paul and a consequent "rescue." From this Eusebius could have derived the idea that this letter was written during a second imprisonment after a period of intervening freedom. Yet the text does not say that. It speaks only of a first defense, which did not end in death ("I was rescued from the lion's mouth"). Paul is portrayed as still imprisoned (1:8, 12, 16-17; 2:9) and anticipating another, more ominous trial (4:6-8). There is no hint of a release between the two trials. If there had been a release, one would expect Paul to have traveled to Spain, as he intended, but not to Cyprus (far to the east), which Titus presupposes (1:5).

The cumulative weight of these four lines of investigation is so great that the Pastorals should be considered pseudonymous. That is the position taken in this commentary. Before leaving the question of authorship, however, two other proposals should be explored briefly. The first is the so-called fragment hypothesis, which grants that the Pastorals in their present form are pseudonymous but suggests that they contain fragments of genuine letters from Paul. These portions contain highly "personal" elements; yet it is difficult to isolate the extent of such fragments with certainty. Those who favor this hypothesis would include at least the following three passages as "fragments": (1) Titus 3:12-15; (2) 2 Tim. 1:15-18; and (3) 2 Tim. 4:9-17, 19-21.

Granted that these sections are more "personal," they appear to be little more than "postcard" messages. It is hard to believe, if they had been written as such, that they would have been preserved and incorporated in the Pastorals. They are not doctrinal or hortatory and they provide nothing in the way of nuclei around which the themes and concerns of the writer were developed. Furthermore, no one has ever succeeded in fitting them into a chronology of Paul's life. The position taken in this commentary is to reject the hypothesis, favoring the view that these "personal notes" are a device of the pseudonymous writer to add to the appearance of the genuineness of the Pastorals, as well as to show the intimacy of Paul with his co-workers.

Another more recent proposal concerning the origins of the Pastorals is that they were either actually written by Luke or compiled by him in their present form.[4] Advocates of this proposal highlight the commonality of vocabulary between the Pastorals and Luke-Acts and the fact that there are some significant theological similarities. But, granted certain similarities in language and theological outlook, the proposal is not finally convincing. Concerning language, one must recall that Luke-Acts is a relatively large and diversified body of literature.[5] Since Luke-Acts takes up about one-fifth of the New Testament and uses such a vast vocabulary (more than two words out of five), one could expect that many words in the Pastorals would appear in Luke-Acts as well. The Pastorals also share language with Paul, Hebrews, 1 Peter, and the Apostolic Fathers and Apologists. Similarities to Luke-Acts alone are not particularly striking and should not be unduly emphasized. Moreover, it is certainly possible that the author of the Pastorals was acquainted with Luke-Acts (cf. 2 Tim.

3:10-11) and would therefore use some elements of Luke's vocabulary and style.

In terms of theological outlook, there are some differences from Luke-Acts as well as the many similarities. For example, in regard to Christology the Pastorals affirm the preexistence of Christ (1 Tim. 1:15; 3:16; 2 Tim. 1:9-10; Titus 3:4), which is not a Lucan theme. While the title "Son of God" is found in Luke-Acts (Luke 1:32, 35; 3:22; 4:3, 9, 41; 8:28; 9:35; 10:22; 22:70; Acts 9:20; 13:33), it is lacking in the Pastorals altogether. Or, again, the role of the Spirit as a dynamic power in the ministry of Jesus and the life of the early church is pronounced in Luke-Acts (Luke 1:15; 4:1, 18; 10:21; 11:13; Acts 1:8; 2:38; 6:5; 8:29; 9:17; 13:2, 9; 19:21, etc.), but in the Pastorals the Spirit is mentioned only four times (1 Tim. 3:16; 4:1; 2 Tim. 1:14; Titus 3:5). Finally, Luke reserves the title "apostle" for the Twelve in Acts and considers Paul a missionary who is to some degree responsible to them (only at 14:14 does he call Paul an apostle), but in the Pastorals Paul is *the* apostle par excellence. The result is that there are aspects of commonality between the Pastorals and Luke-Acts, but there are differences as well. It is not likely that they are from the same author or compiler.

2. The Setting and Rise of the Pastoral Epistles

The letters are ostensibly written to Timothy and Titus. Nevertheless, it is clear that they are addressed to a congregation or congregations, for in fact the writer "talks past" Timothy and Titus to a broader audience. This becomes especially clear in instances in which the third person imperative in Greek is used. For example, at 1 Tim. 6:1 the writer says, "Let all who are under the yoke of slavery regard their masters worthy of all honor." This is a direct address to slaves, not to Timothy. Other instances of "talking past" to the community can be seen at 1 Tim. 2:8-11; 3:12; 5:3-8, 14-16; Titus 3:14, and elsewhere. Even sections which have to do with qualifications for congregational leaders (1 Tim. 3:1-13; 5:9-13; Titus 1:5-9), while they appear to be instructions given by Paul to Timothy and Titus, are actually regulations for the communities themselves. Once the writer even addresses the community itself concerning its relationship to its leaders (1 Tim. 5:17-19). Finally, each of the letters closes with "Grace be with you," and the Greek pronoun for "you" is plural each time (1 Tim. 6:21; 2 Tim. 4:22; Titus 3:15). As in the case of Paul's letters (cf. 1 Thess. 5:27), these are to be read to the community.

According to the contents of the letters, 1 Timothy is addressed to Timothy at Ephesus (1:3), and Titus is addressed to Titus on Crete (1:5). No explicit reference is made as to where the writer is supposed to be located. In the case of 2 Timothy the data is reversed. It is purportedly written from imprisonment at Rome (1:16-17; 4:6), but it is not said explicitly where the addressee is located. It is probable, however, that we are to think of it as addressed to Ephesus, since Onesiphorus, an Ephesian Christian (1:16-18), is greeted (4:19), as are Prisca and Aquila, who resided at Ephesus (1 Cor. 16:19; Acts 18:26); moreover, the association of this letter with 1 Timothy would also support the view that we are to think of it as addressed to Ephesus.

A critical examination raises questions. In the case of Titus, a slanderous remark about Cretans is recorded and even endorsed by the writer (1:12-13). It is unlikely that a writer would be so insensitive in a letter addressed to the churches on Crete, which are to be presided over by Cretan leaders. (The epithet about Cretans would actually preclude Cretan leaders.) The letters to Timothy, on the other hand, could have been addressed to Ephesus from outside, but in fact a strong case can be made for their origins in Ephesus, from which they were distributed. The discussion which follows will conclude that all three of the epistles were most likely composed in Ephesus, or its vicinity, around A.D. 100.

Introduction

A. The Ephesian Setting

A survey of persons mentioned in the Pastorals is instructive. Leaving aside names from the Old Testament (Adam, Moses, etc.), plus references to Jesus and Pontius Pilate, there are 28 persons to whom references are made. Are these persons associated with any particular community either as contemporaries or as persons of the community's history (e.g., Paul)? A survey of the names shows that 18 out of the 28 persons named have a definite, documented connection with Ephesus; of the 10 persons for whom no association with Ephesus can be documented, it is possible that even some of these would have been known there (as will be shown further on). Naturally, some have connections with other places too; for example, Prisca and Aquila resided at Corinth (Acts 18:2) as well as Ephesus (Acts 18:26; 1 Cor. 16:19). But what is common to the vast majority of the persons named is that they have resided at Ephesus or have traveled there as emissaries of Paul.

The charts which follow are based on certain critical assumptions: first, that 1 Corinthians was written from Ephesus, which is certain (cf. 16:8); second, that our present 2 Corinthians is made up of several letters, and that Chapters 10-13 comprise one of them, which Paul sent from Ephesus along with Titus; and third, that Philippians and Philemon were written by Paul when he was imprisoned at Ephesus (cf. 1 Cor. 15:32; 2 Cor. 1:8-10). The purpose of the charts is to establish an "Ephesian connection" with a large majority of persons named in the Pastorals.

1. Evidence in the Pastorals for an Ephesian association of certain persons

Name	Information from Pastorals
Timothy (1 Tim. 1:2, etc.)	At Ephesus (1 Tim. 1:3); cf. 2 Cor. 1:1 and Phil. 1:1 where Timothy is at Ephesus.

Hymenaeus (1 Tim. 1:20)	Heretic at Ephesus; cf. 2 Tim. 2:17.
Alexander (1 Tim. 1:20)	Heretic at Ephesus (possibly the Ephesian in Acts 19:33-34 by same name).
Phygelus (2 Tim. 1:15)	A person of Asia Minor who betrayed Paul.
Hermogenes (2 Tim. 1:15)	Ibid.
Philetus (2 Tim. 2:17)	Linked with Hymenaeus, heretical teacher at Ephesus (1 Tim. 1:20).
Tychicus (2 Tim. 4:12)	Emissary of Paul to Ephesus. Cf. also Eph. 6:21. At Acts 20:4 he is called an "Asian."
Onesiphorus (2 Tim. 1:16-18)	A Christian at Ephesus (cf. 4:19).

2. *Evidence in the Pauline Corpus (other than the Pastorals) for an Ephesian association*

Name	Information from Pauline Corpus
Paul (1 Tim. 1:1, etc.)	Resided at Ephesus (1 Cor. 16:8). Acts 20:31 claims he was there three years.
Titus (Titus 1:4)	Bearer of 2 Cor. 10–13 from Ephesus to Corinth (cf. 2 Cor. 8:16, 22).
Demas (2 Tim. 4:10)	Companion with imprisoned Paul at Ephesus (Philemon 24); cf. Col. 4:14.
Luke (2 Tim. 4:11)	Ibid.

Mark (2 Tim. 4:11)	Ibid.
Prisca and Aquila (2 Tim. 4:19)	With Paul at Ephesus (1 Cor. 16:19); cf. Acts 18:18-19, 26.
Apollos (Titus 3:13)	With Paul at Ephesus (1 Cor. 16:12); cf. Acts 18:24.

3. *Evidence in Acts for an Ephesian association*

Name	Information from Acts
Erastus (2 Tim. 4:20)	Emissary with Timothy from Ephesus to Macedonia (19: 22).
Trophimus (2 Tim. 4:20)	Called "the Ephesian" (21: 29).

4. *Persons having no known association with Ephesus in our sources*

Name	Information from Pastorals and other sources
Lois (2 Tim. 1:5)	Timothy's grandmother; no other information.
Eunice (2 Tim. 1:5)	Timothy's mother; of Jewish descent (Acts 16:1), but no further information.
Crescens (2 Tim. 4:10)	Has gone to Galatia; in Polycarp (*Phil.* 14:1) bearer of letter from Smyrna to Philippi.
Carpus (2 Tim. 4:13)	Resident at Troas.
Eubulus, Pudens, Linus, and Claudia (2 Tim. 4:21)	These are with Paul in Rome, and they send greetings to addressees of 2 Timothy.

Artemas (Titus 3:12)	Potential emissary from Paul (place unknown) to Crete.
Zenas (Titus 3:13)	Associate with Apollos on Crete.

Among those persons in group 4 it is possible that some would have been associated with the church at Ephesus. Artemas (Titus 3:12), a trusted emissary, can probably be considered a native Ephesian, since his name is derived from the name Artemis, the goddess and chief divinity of Ephesus (Acts 19:28, 34-35). Crescens (2 Tim. 4:10) may have been known in Ephesus too. Polycarp in the early second century sends a person by that name from Smyrna to Philippi (*Letter to the Philippians* 14.1). Smyrna was located about 35 miles (50 km.) north of Ephesus, and the two churches had contact with each other (cf. Ignatius, *Letter to the Ephesians* 1.3; 2.1; 5.1; 6.2; 9.1, whose letter was written to Ephesus from Smyrna, 21.1). Finally, Zenas may have been known at Ephesus in his association with Apollos, with whom he is linked in Titus (3:13). If these three persons were known to Christians at Ephesus, then at least 21 of the 28 persons named in the Pastorals were known there, although a definite link can only be documented for 18. As for other persons mentioned, neither an Ephesian association, nor a lack thereof, can be established.

That so many persons named in the Pastorals have an Ephesian association is striking. One has to assume that the persons named would be familiar to the community of the Pastorals, and that makes Ephesus and its vicinity their likely setting. According to Acts 20:31, Paul had spent three years there. Furthermore, both Timothy and Titus had been companions of Paul in Ephesus, from where he sent them as his emissaries.

To propose Ephesus as the setting does, however, pose a problem. In 1 Timothy (1:3), Timothy himself is supposed to be in Ephesus, so the letter is supposedly destined there, and one would not normally think therefore of its having originated from there. Yet this problem is taken care of nicely within the Pastorals themselves, since Timothy is called to join Paul in Rome (2 Tim. 1:4; 4:9, 11, 21). Likewise, of course, Titus—who is supposed to be on Crete (1:5)—is summoned to leave Crete (3:12). The picture which emerges is that both Timothy and Titus have been called away from their stations long ago. The hypothesis that the Pastorals were written at Ephesus can therefore be maintained, for the letters would have the appearance of being correspondence from an era now long gone. Timothy is gone from Ephesus, but the letters to him remain, as does the letter to Titus in the same collection. There are still other reasons to propose an Ephesian setting, which shall be given below.

B. The Rise of the Pastorals in Ephesus

Paul had worked in Ephesus. According to Luke's tradition, at the time of Paul's final farewell, the congregation at Ephesus had presbyters (Acts 20:17) who were charged by Paul to serve as "overseers" (*episkopoi*, 20:28) in that church. Whether this reflects actual conditions in the time of Paul can be disputed, but that such existed at the time Acts was written (A.D. 80-90) can be affirmed.

It is widely held today that, after the death of Paul, a "Pauline school" came into existence at Ephesus, which collected the letters of Paul and produced additional letters in his name, technically known as the deutero-Pauline letters.[6] It is likely that Colossians and Ephesians, considered deutero-Pauline, were produced there. Both were supposedly carried to their destinations by a certain Tychicus (Col. 4:7-8; Eph. 6:21-22), who was himself an Ephesian Christian (Acts 20:4), and who is also mentioned in the Pastorals as Paul's emissary (2 Tim. 4:11; Titus 3:12). One can hardly avoid concluding that this person was a leader of the Pauline school at Ephesus, although his role in the production of any of the deutero-Paulines is impossible to assess. At a minimum, however, it appears that Tychicus serves as a link between Paul and the Pauline school at Ephesus.

The earlier deutero-Pauline letters are concerned deeply about the unity of the church as the body of Christ, the head of which is Christ (Col. 2:19; Eph. 1:22; 5:23). Unity is through Christ in a common faith. Yet in the case of Ephesians (written later than Colossians) there are already hints of a need to shore up that unity and common faith through the exercise of the "gifts" given, by which there are apostles, prophets, evangelists, pastors, and teachers (4:11)—for the sake of unity, knowledge, and maturity (4:13)—for the church is built upon the "foundation of the apostles and prophets" (2:20). The Pastorals can be assigned to a time even later in which the writer—a person of the still-existing Pauline school, which has already composed pseudonymous works in Paul's name—writes these letters to meet a crisis in the Ephesian field. The way to meet that crisis now is to appeal to the role of the presbyters, particularly those recognized as bishops among them, and to assert that these persons are the true successors of Paul the apostle. Heretical teachers have arisen, who represent a form of Jewish-Christian Gnosticism (see Part 5, p. 44). These persons are repudiated in the name of the apostle Paul himself, while those who revere Paul as their teacher—persons aligned with the Pauline school and exercising leadership in the church already—are to be recognized by the community as the only legitimate leaders. The heretical teachers include Hymenaeus, Alexander, Phygelus, Hermogenes, and Philetus. With the possible exception of Alexander—if this person is to be identified with the Alexander of Ephesus at Acts 19:33-34, which cannot be known—these persons are not named in the earlier sources (Paul's letters, Acts, Colossians, and Ephesians). Yet each is associated with Ephesus (see chart, part 1, above). This raises a critical question. If these persons were in Ephesus at the time the Pastorals were written, it seems that the readers at that time would wonder how Paul could have attacked them in letters appearing to have been written a generation earlier. This problem cannot be settled adequately. It is a problem for any theory of the Pastorals which places them after the death of Paul. A plausible solution is that, since the readers are to avoid such persons, they will not inquire into the question of whether the historical Paul knew them, but will simply assume that they and Paul overlap chronologically. In fact it is not impossible that they did.

It is puzzling why three letters were written and why they were addressed to two persons (Timothy and Titus). We would also like to know the sequence in which they were written. The questions are interrelated, and there have been several proposals. While virtually every possible sequence has been proposed, only two have been argued vigorously. First, there is the proposal that they were written in the order of Titus, 1 Timothy, and 2 Timothy. This is the sequence listed in the Muratorian Canon. Jerome Quinn has adopted this sequence, pointing to the fact that the long introduction to Titus (1:1-4) can be taken as an introduction to the whole collection, and he suggests that 2 Timothy can be read as Paul's "last will and testament." [7] A second proposal is that they were written in the sequence of 2 Timothy, Titus, and 1 Timothy. This is the position of B. Easton. He observes that 2 Timothy is concerned about the selection of presbyter-bishops; Titus provides them with their technical titles and orders their installation; and 1 Timothy, taking their existence for granted, gives rules for their remuneration, duties, and discipline.[8]

One must entertain the possibility, however, that the letters were written at the same time and for complementary purposes. In the case of 1 Timothy the existence of a church order is taken for granted, and that letter may have functioned to give weight to the ecclesiastical officers, their duties, remuneration, authority, and discipline in Ephesus itself. Titus may have served to extend the Ephesian model beyond the city, since it calls for appointing office bearers on the Ephesian model (1:5-9), and 2 Timothy seeks to win sympathy for and loyalty to Paul. Contrary to Easton, the selection of office bearers is not a main theme in 2 Timothy, and even when this instruction does appear (only once, 2:2) the concern is that persons selected be competent instructors, faithful to Pauline tradition. The letter, in fact, is about doctrinal matters (especially at 1:13; 2:15; 3:10, 16; 4:3), and its character is summarized in the exhortation to "continue in what you have learned and have firmly believed, knowing from whom you learned it" (3:14). Right doctrine and loyalty to Paul are identical. It is sufficient to hold that the letters were written at approximately the same time and that they were circulated in and from Ephesus. Their present sequence in the New Testament is probably based on their length (longest to shortest). The extent to which they were to be circulated (the Ephesian vicinity alone, or the whole Pauline field, extending through Greece and Macedonia and even to Rome) cannot be determined exactly. Why the letters should be addressed to two persons remains a puzzle. Of course, both Timothy and Titus were Paul's representatives and associates in travel. But perhaps more can be conjectured. Timothy is associated with Paul at the head of certain letters (2 Cor. 1:1; Phil. 1:1; 1 Thess. 1:1), which establishes him as like-minded and faithful to Paul and enjoying special authority. Titus, a Gentile (Gal. 2:3), is singled out by Paul as an "ecumenical" co-worker: "he has been appointed by the churches to travel with us" (2 Cor. 8:19). Whether he actually traveled to Crete cannot be known, but his role as a traveling emissary is well established, and his standing in the churches far and wide equips him for representing Pauline tradition in those areas where the Ephesian model has yet to be established. What would be required at Crete would presumably be required also within the circumference around the Ephesus-Crete radius, which includes Asia Minor, Greece, and Macedonia—the Pauline field of the east and the extent of Ephesian influence.

C. Date of the Pastorals

The date of these letters is probably the turn of the century (ca. A.D. 100). The heretical teachers represent an early form of Jewish-Christian Gnosticism (see Part 5, p. 44) which is not yet to be identified with the later Gnosticism of Basilides (active in Alexandria and Rome, A.D. 115-145) and Valentinus (active in Rome, A.D. 140-160). Therefore a date earlier can be given. Can we be more precise? On the one hand, the Pauline letters have been collected in a corpus, including Colossians and Ephesians, and the book of Acts (A.D. 80-90) appears to be known to the author (cf. especially 2 Tim. 3:11; information on Timothy, Tychicus, Trophimus, Erastus, Apollos, and Prisca and Aquila in Acts also appears to inform the writer). On the other hand, the *Letter to the Ephesians* by Ignatius and Polycarp's *Letter to the Philippians* are instructive. Ignatius (d. A.D. 117), writing from Smyrna, makes reference to a bishop at Ephesus named Onesimus (1.3), speaks of the presbytery there as "closely tied to the bishop as strings to a harp" (4.1), and names a certain deacon (Burrhus, 2.1) as well. Further, he says, "I have heard that some strangers came your way with a wicked teaching. But you did not let them sow it among you. You stopped up your ears to prevent admitting what they disseminated" (9:1). Thus, by the time that Ignatius writes to Ephesus, both church order and orthodoxy have been stabilized. Further, when Polycarp, bishop of Smyrna, writes to the Philippians during the first quarter of the second century, he shows an acquaintance with the Pastorals at several places and on one occasion appears to quote 1 Tim. 6:7, 10 (*Letter to the Philippians* 4.1). B. Easton has provided a list of passages showing probable dependence of Polycarp on the Pastorals.[9] Ephesus at the turn of the century, then, appears to be the most probable setting for the Pastorals.

D. The Pastorals and the Pauline Corpus

The setting and date proposed cohere with other data. As indicated earlier, Marcion did not include the Pastorals in his canon, but they are referred to in the Muratorian Canon and, by A.D. 200, they are known as letters of Paul by Irenaeus, Tertullian, and Clement of Alexandria. It is probable that the letters of Paul were collected in three stages.

The first collection of Paul's authentic letters would have been made near the end of his life or after his death (ca. A.D. 60-64) but prior to the writing of Colossians and Ephesians, which are dependent on that collection.[10] This first collection was probably undertaken at Ephesus, where Colossians and Ephesians were composed, in the generation following Paul's death (A.D. 65-90).

The second stage in the process would have been the incorporation of the three deutero-Paulines (Ephesians, Colossians, 2 Thessalonians) by the Pauline school at Ephesus near the turn of the century. This new corpus of 10 letters would have been that available to the writer of the Pastorals and known to Marcion (Rome, A.D. 150). Polycarp is an exception, since he appears to be familiar with the Pastorals early in the second century. Yet, as indicated, Smyrna is close by Ephesus, and after the Pastorals were written, they would have had a limited circulation.

The third stage would have been the addition of the Pastorals, creating an expanded Pauline corpus of 13 letters. This could not be done until the Pastorals had received wide circulation and acceptance, which was after Marcion (A.D. 150) but by the time of the Muratorian Canon (A.D. 175-200).

A problem with this dating, however, is codex p46. Although written around A.D. 200, it does not contain the Pastorals. There are some scholars who believe that the Pastorals could have been contained on 18 leaves missing from the codex,[11] but most conclude that there would not have been room for them,[12] which is the view of certain major text critics as well.[13] It would appear then that this codex provides witness to the earlier tradition (our second stage above), which does not yet contain the Pastorals.

3. Theology of the Pastoral Epistles

The Pastorals are heir to a rich theological tradition which includes elements of both Pauline theology and common Christian teaching. They also contain accents of their own, which contribute to the theological heritage of the church. Some of these distinctive accents will be summarized here, including God and creation, sin and salvation, and Christology.

A. God and Creation

There is one God (1 Tim. 2:5), or God the Father (1 Tim. 1:2; 2 Tim. 1:2; Titus 1:4), who has created all things. The writer emphasizes that God has created everything good (1 Tim. 4:3-4; cf. Titus 1:15). The Christian does not despise the creation, flee from it, or consider material things as evil. The author does not look upon the world as a mere stage upon which people live or a prison from which they must be delivered. His concern is rather the right use of the creation and right conduct within the world. He speaks against an asceticism which forbids certain foods and marriage (1 Tim. 4:3). While love of wealth is a vice (1 Tim. 6:9-10; 2 Tim. 3:2), the author takes for granted that some Christians have wealth; his concern is that they be generous and rich in good deeds (1 Tim. 6:17-18) and that every Christian be content with basic needs (1 Tim. 6:8). Marriage and having children are considered a positive good (1 Tim. 3:2-5; 5:10, 14; Titus 2:4) and the care of the elderly by their children and grandchildren is considered a religious duty (1 Tim. 5:4).

God has created the world but has not withdrawn from it. God continues to "give life to all things" (1 Tim. 6:13) and "richly furnishes us with everything to enjoy" (6:17). The writer teaches a doctrine of continuing creation that is rooted in the Old Testament (Job 10:8-9; 33:4; 37:1-13; Ps. 139:13; Isa. 40:28-29; 44:24; 45:5-7, 9-11), the teaching of Jesus (Luke 12:22-31; Matt. 5:45; 6:25-33; 10:29), and elsewhere in the New Testament (1 Cor. 8:6; Col. 1:15-17; cf. John 5:17).

Because God has created the world and sustains it yet, the Christian is to live within the context of the social order, which is also a part of God's ordering of creation. Instructions are given concerning the conduct of wives and children within the family (1 Tim. 2:9-10, 15; 5:14; Titus 2:4); no corresponding duties are given for husbands in general, but they are given to congregational leaders in regard to their families (1 Tim. 3:2-4, 12; Titus 1:6), and these persons are to serve as models for others (1 Tim. 4:12; 5:19-22, 25; 2 Tim. 2:24). It is assumed that some Christians are slaves (1 Tim. 6:1; Titus 2:9-10), and they are to be exemplary in conduct. Christians are to be submissive to governmental authorities (Titus 3:1-2), offer prayers for them (1 Tim. 2:1-2), and serve human needs within the secular community (not only among Christians, Titus 3:2, 8, 14). In sum, the Pastorals have a broad and sympathetic view toward the world. It is recognized that there is evil in the world (1 Tim. 1:9-10; 2 Tim. 3:13), and that Christians will be persecuted. The persecutions envisioned, however, are not those of the state but of unbelievers and heretical antagonists (2 Tim. 3:12-13). The church of the Pastorals does not have a sense of being besieged by a hostile world, nor does it withdraw from the world as a sect. It lives as a witnessing community within the world, showing courtesy toward all (Titus 3:2) and praying for the good of all humankind.

B. Sin and Salvation

Standing within the Pauline tradition, indeed that of Christianity generally, the writer of the Pastorals affirms that the whole human race is sinful. But there is a slight shift away from Paul. In Paul's writings sin (singular) is a power which exercises dominion over all persons (Rom. 3:9; 5:12, 21; 7:14; Gal. 3:22). Within the Pastorals this concept is not found explicitly. Human sinfulness tends to be treated in terms of particular "sins" which people commit (1 Tim. 5:22, 24; 2 Tim. 3:6). Yet even in the Pastorals it is taken for granted that "sins" are the fruit of the natural life (or human condition), which is alienated from God. The many vices listed (e.g., at 2 Tim. 3:2-5) are the result of a life disoriented toward serving the self and its passions (Titus 2:12).

The thinking appears akin to elements in Jewish and Hellenistic thought of the era. In Jewish thought of the time sin was understood to be rooted in the "evil impulse" *(yeṣer ha-ra')*, which is in perpetual conflict with the "good impulse" *(yeṣer ha-ṭob)*. The concept of the "evil impulse" is rooted in Gen. 6:5; 8:21, but it is developed further in texts of the pre-Christian era (Sirach 15:11-20, especially 15:14), other texts contemporary with the rise of Christianity (4 Ezra 3:21; 4:30-31), and in later rabbinic texts.[14] In such texts the "evil impulse" is manifested in passions at war with the "good impulse," and the struggle goes on within the human heart. So in the Pastorals, persons are led about by passions leading to vices. But Christians are called to purity of heart (1 Tim. 1:5; 2 Tim. 2:22) in order that they may serve God aright and practice love.

Likewise, in Stoic thought it was believed that one must

learn to exercise control over passions—ever prone to vices—by renouncing them and striving for "self-sufficiency" *(autarkeia)*. The latter term appears in the Pastorals (1 Tim. 6:6), but there is a difference. The term is properly translated "contentment." The writer does not teach "self-sufficiency," but "contentment" due to "godliness," which is rooted in faith. Furthermore, the ideal is not contentment itself, for there is to be a struggle toward righteousness and godliness (1 Tim. 6:11; 2 Tim. 2:22).

In the final analysis, it must be said that the writer looks upon the human condition differently than Paul. His analysis is closer to these elements of Jewish and Stoic thought. But he stands along with Paul, on the other hand, in considering all persons to be in need of salvation.

In the Pastorals, salvation itself does not come through a victory of a "good impulse" over the "evil impulse," nor through one's own righteousness or effort, but purely through the mercy and grace of God (Titus 2:11; 3:5-7). This is of course Pauline. Christ came into the world to save sinners (1 Tim. 1:15), and God desires all to be saved (1 Tim. 2:4; Titus 2:11). Although no doctrine of the atonement is spelled out explicitly, the Pastorals stress the "objectivity" and "universality" of Christ's saving work. In his death Christ gave himself as a "ransom" for all persons (1 Tim. 2:6); therefore he is the one who sets humankind free from the punishment deserved at the final judgment. Through his death and resurrection he has "abolished death and brought life and immortality to light" (2 Tim. 1:10). Yet, as indicated in both passages, it is the gospel which alone attests this "objective" event. The "universal" grace of God, which has appeared in Christ, is for all, but it must be proclaimed if it is to be effective. The writer can say that God is "the Savior of all persons, especially of those who believe" (1 Tim. 4:10). Thus both the universality of grace and the particularity of faith are held together. The work of Christ for the redemption of the world is finished.

The gospel proclaims his saving work. Faith is the acceptance of the "gospel" (or "Christian message") as true, and such acceptance is at the same time a grasping on to the salvation offered (1 Tim. 6:12, 19; 2 Tim. 4:7-8). Salvation is finally the divine rescue of persons from mortality, with its ignorance and unbelief, to life in the eternal kingdom (2 Tim. 1:10; 4:18).

Salvation is portrayed as both present and future. The accent is on future salvation, a future hope, life in the age to come, which will be inaugurated with the coming of Christ (1 Tim. 4:16; 6:12; 2 Tim. 2:10-11; 3:15; 4:18; Titus 1:2; 2:13; 3:7). This is taught by Paul as well (Rom. 10:9; 13:11; Phil. 2:12; 3:20; 1 Thess. 5:8-9). But the writer can also speak of salvation as having been given already (2 Tim. 1:9; Titus 3:5); it can be "taken hold of" in the present (1 Tim. 6:12, 19). This too is taught in Pauline theology whenever he speaks of the "already" of salvation and newness in Christ (1 Cor. 1:18; 2 Cor. 2:15; 5:17; 6:2). The Christian lives in expectation of final salvation, but also lives a transformed existence in the present world. This becomes the basis for ethics in the Pastorals. As the commentary will show, there are many virtues used in the Pastorals which are common to the ethical teaching of the time. But these virtues are not valued purely for their own sake. They serve to map out the life of the Christian and give it content. The basis for the moral teaching is that Christians belong to Christ and are therefore "a people of his own who are zealous for good deeds" (Titus 2:14).

In keeping with Paul's teaching, the Pastorals assert that salvation is a gift from God and that no one contributes to it through good works (2 Tim. 1:9; Titus 3:5). Justification is purely an act of God's grace (Titus 3:7). The Pauline accent of faith as trust in the gospel proclaimed (Rom. 4:24; 10:17; Gal. 2:16; Phil. 1:27) is not found explicitly in the Pastorals, however. The relationship of faith to justification and salvation has become more formalized. Faith now has more of the character of accepting what is true and holding on to it (1

Tim. 4:16; 6:12). It is the means of a right standing before God, which will be certified at the judgment (1 Tim. 4:6-8, 16; 2 Tim. 3:15; 4:7-8). The word *faith* generally refers to "the faith" (the Christian religion, 1 Tim. 1:2; 3:9; 4:1, 6; 5:8; 6:10, 21; 2 Tim. 4:7; Titus 1:13; 3:15).

One final matter of interest in the Pastorals concerning salvation is that the word *Savior* appears no less than 10 times. On six occasions it is God (the Father) who is designated as Savior (1 Tim. 1:1; 2:3; 4:10; Titus 1:3; 2:10; 3:4); at four other places Jesus Christ is spoken of as Savior (2 Tim. 1:10; Titus 1:4; 2:13; 3:6). Paul refers to Jesus Christ as Savior only once (Phil. 3:20). Only two other times in the New Testament is God designated as Savior (Luke 1:47; Jude 25). The background for speaking of God as Savior is of course the Old Testament (e.g., Isa. 45:15, 21; Ps. 62:2, 6). By using the term for both the Father and Jesus Christ, the writer asserts that salvation is willed by God (1 Tim. 2:4; 4:10; Titus 2:11) and made possible through the sending of Christ (2 Tim. 1:9-10; Titus 2:11; 3:4-6). Christ is the decisive manifestation of the "goodness and lovingkindness of God our Savior" (Titus 3:4).

C. Christology

The Christological titles appearing in the Pastorals are Christ, Lord, Savior, and Mediator. The term *Christ* is the most common (used 32 times). The term *Lord* is also common, being used in connection with Jesus Christ (1 Tim. 1:2, 12; 6:3, 14; 2 Tim. 1:2), with God the Father (1 Tim. 6:15; 2 Tim. 1:18b; 2:19 [twice]), and in reference to Christ (2 Tim. 1:18a; 4:8). The term appears 12 more times (1 Tim. 1:14; 2 Tim. 1:8, 16; 2:7, 14, 22, 24; 3:11; 4:14, 17, 18, 22) in a more ambiguous way, but even in these instances it appears to function as a Christological title (especially at 2 Tim. 4:22, and as a comparison of 2 Tim. 1:16 with 1:18a shows). The term *Savior* is applied to Christ four times (references above), and *Mediator* appears once (1 Tim. 2:5). Notable by its complete absence is the fact that the title *Son of God* is never used in the Pastorals.

The titles of exaltation (Christ, Lord, and Savior) affirm his divine regency and status, but the humanity of Christ is also affirmed (1 Tim. 2:5; 6:13; 2 Tim. 2:8). When he is spoken of as "Mediator" (1 Tim. 2:5), the term does not speak of his nature so much as his function: there is but one Mediator (not many); he is the "man Christ Jesus" whose atoning work in lowliness and death ("man") reconciled the human race to God, since his work was the work of God's Messiah. It is he who will also appear at the end of time (1 Tim. 6:14; 2 Tim. 4:8) and who will judge the living and the dead (2 Tim. 1:18; 4:1, 8).

The Pastorals reflect a "three-stage Christology" of an implied preexistence, incarnation, and exaltation (following crucifixion). Nowhere does the writer speak of an eternal *logos* or Son of God existing before the creation of the world, so an explicit statement of Christ's preexistence is lacking. In his own way, however, he speaks of what can be called "preexistent grace" in Christ, which is functionally equivalent to a doctrine of preexistence. At 2 Tim. 1:9 he speaks of the grace which God gave in Christ Jesus "before the ages" (of temporal time), and at Titus 2:11 he speaks of the (eternal) grace of God, which has appeared. Furthermore, since Christ "was manifested in the flesh" (1 Tim. 3:16), preexistence is presupposed. Even more significant, the earthly life of Jesus is the result of the Christ's coming into the world (1 Tim. 1:15; 2:6; Titus 2:14), the manifestation of the Savior (2 Tim. 1:10; Titus 3:4). His death is alluded to at 1 Tim. 2:6; 2 Tim. 2:11; Titus 2:14. Finally, the crucified Christ has been exalted to divine status (1 Tim. 3:16; 2 Tim. 1:10; 2:12) and can therefore be called Lord. The consequent picture is that the Pastorals have a "high" Christology, portraying a thoroughgoing union of Christ with God. The concept of a "subordination" of Christ to the Father is almost lacking (except at 1 Tim. 2:5 where "Mediator" is used). This may explain the absence of the Son of God terminology, which implies subordinationism. Christ the Lord is "our great God and Savior" (Titus 2:13) who manifests the "goodness and loving kindness of God our Savior" (3:4). He is the visible manifestation of the invisible God who opens the way to eternal salvation and who will appear bearing the divine glory. In the Pastorals we therefore reach a high point in New Testament Christology.

4. Church Order in the Pastorals

Church order is important in the Pastorals, but it is not of the same rank as teaching and proclamation. It is true that in the Pastorals there emerges a picture of clerical ranks (bishops, presbyters, and deacons), but those offices are not clearly defined. They do not appear at all in 2 Timothy; there the writer simply calls for entrusting the Pauline tradition to "faithful persons" who are able to teach others (2:2).

The clerical offices exist for the sake of the gospel, apostolic interpretation of it, and good order.[15] The offices are therefore considered necessary, and it is important that the officeholders are orthodox before they are installed into them. Thus doctrine and order are not played off against each other, but are held together. In Titus 1:5 the writer calls for the appointment of presbyters in every city where they do not yet exist. Because for this writer the act of ordination bestows a "gift" (*charisma*, 1 Tim. 4:14; 2 Tim. 1:6) upon those who exercise offices in the church, great care must be taken in choosing persons for the offices (1 Tim. 5:22).

The offices of bishop (1 Tim. 3:1-7; Titus 1:7-9), presbyter (1 Tim. 5:17-19; Titus 1:5), and deacon (1 Tim. 3:8-12) are referred to, and there is also a recognizable body of "widows," into which certain women are enrolled (1 Tim. 5:3-16).

The offices of bishop and presbyter appear to overlap both in the Pastorals and in Luke's Acts. At Acts 20:17 Luke refers to Ephesian "presbyters" ("elders" in RSV; the Greek term *presbyteros* can be translated as such, but we shall retain "presbyter" for reasons stated below). Then at 20:28 these same persons are called "bishops" (*episkopoi;* "guardians" in RSV), who are to "shepherd the church of God." Likewise in the Pastorals the terms overlap. Titus is to appoint "presbyters" (1:5), but the writer goes on to speak of the qualifications of a "bishop" for such persons (1:8-9). It has sometimes been suggested, therefore, that the terms are virtual synonyms, referring to the same persons. Yet this is probably not accurate. Throughout the Pastorals the term "bishop" appears in the singular, while there is a plurality of "presbyters." At 1 Tim. 4:14 there is a reference to a "presbytery" or "council of presbyters." Given the data, it appears that the order presupposed consists of a council of presbyters, from whose midst arises a singular, recognized "bishop" who is distinguished from the rest by having a supervisory function, as the Greek word for bishop, *episkopos,* "overseer," denotes. Because the bishop comes from the ranks of the presbyters, the overlap of terms at Titus 1:5-7 can be explained: only those who can qualify for the office of bishop should be selected as presbyters. The functions of the various offices are as follows.

A. Presbyters

The Greek word *(presbyteros)* and its Hebrew equivalent *(zaqen)* can mean simply an "older" person. The Hebrew term is found already in the Old Testament, however, to designate persons who, while being the more mature of the communities, were office bearers (Num. 11:16-17, 24-25). In the New Testament era both the Jerusalem Sanhedrin (Matt. 16:21) and the councils of local synagogues (Luke 7:3) were composed in part of "elders." This Jewish pattern had an affect on early Christianity. In Acts (15:2, 4, 6, 22-23; 16:4) the "apostles and presbyters" form a central council for the church in Jerusalem, somewhat analogous to the Sanhedrin, and there are indications that some local congregations were governed by councils of presbyters (James 5:14; 1 Peter 5:1-4). This is not the case, however, with the churches founded by Paul.

The churches to which the Pastorals are directed either have presbyters already (1 Tim. 5:17-19), or they should have them (Titus 1:5). The presbyters have a "ruling" function (1 Tim. 5:17). While at times the term *presbyteros* still has the connotation of "older man" (1 Tim. 5:1; Titus 2:2), it is primarily a title for an office. Age is never listed as a prerequisite for the office. On the contrary, it is routinely assumed that the presbyter will have children at home (Titus 1:6; cf. 1 Tim. 3:4). The presbyters form a council (1 Tim. 4:14) within the congregation. Each must be capable of preaching and teaching, sharing the qualifications of the bishop, but not all are engaged in these (1 Tim. 5:17).

Since "presbyter" has become a technical title, it has been preserved (rather than "elder") in the commentary. The English word "priest" is derived from it. By retaining the link in our language between bishop and presbyter, we are able to sense the historic link which has existed between bishop and priest.

B. Bishop

The Greek term *(episkopos)* means "overseer." It appears in secular Greek, but its New Testament usage is based on Jewish models. It is found in the Old Testament, although not frequently (Num. 4:16; Neh. 11:9, 14, 22), in Philo (*Who Is the Heir* 30, applied to Moses as "one who knows souls"), and in Josephus (*Antiquities* 10.4 for "overseers" of justice and law). Furthermore, at Qumran the title of *mebaqqer* ("overseer") appears, and this person's role is that of presiding over the community, admitting persons to it, giving instruction, settling disputes, and caring for the poor.[16] Many of these functions are parallel to those of the bishop in various Christian communities.

In the Pastorals the bishop has three main functions. First, with the presbyters he supervises the life of the community as though it were his extended household (1 Tim. 3:5). He provides leadership in all matters, whether spiritual, temporal, or organizational. As a model of Christian virtue (1 Tim. 3:2-7; Titus 1:6-9), he leads the congregation in realizing what it is to be a Christian community. Second, he combats false teaching and preserves what is sound (Titus 1:9). Finally, the bishop must be an apt teacher (1 Tim. 3:2; Titus 1:9), and we can infer that he was engaged in teaching regularly. He and those presbyters engaged in preaching and teaching are paid officers (1 Tim. 5:17-18), but they should not be lovers of money (1 Tim. 3:3; Titus 1:7).

C. Deacon

The Greek term *(diakonos)* means "servant." The earliest usage of the term is found in Paul's letters (Phil: 1:1) and in the Pastorals, where the office of deacon is closely linked in work with that of the bishop. The precise duties of the deacon, however, are not clearly delineated there. In 1 Tim. 3:8-13, for example, it is only their qualities, not their duties, which are treated. From later sources (see Part 4, F) it becomes clear that they were engaged in administrative and practical service in the communities. On the question whether there were female deaconesses, see the commentary at 1 Tim. 3:11.

D. Widows

A recognized group of widows is spoken of at 1 Tim. 5:3-16. Widows over the age of 60 can qualify, if they do not have children or grandchildren to support them (5:4, 8, 16). They are supported by the congregation (5:5, 16). Their main service is intercessory prayer (5:5) and relief of those in need through visitation (5:10, 13) — and probably bringing these needs to the attention of the community leaders. Ignatius (*Letter to the Smyrnaeans* 13.1, *Letter to Polycarp* 4.1) and Polycarp (*Letter to the Philippians* 4.3) refer to a recognized body of "widows" in the church of the second century as well, but provide no further information than what is given in the Pastorals.

E. Ordering the Community

The Pastorals disclose little concerning how persons were selected for the offices of bishop, presbyter, and deacon, except that Titus is to appoint presbyters at Crete (1:5), and Timothy is supposed to have a leading role in choosing leaders at Ephesus (1 Tim. 5:22; 2 Tim. 2:2). But this picture is idealized. Assuming that the Pastorals were written at the turn of the century, Timothy and Titus have passed from the scene; the offices have been in existence for some time already; and they have been filled by recognized and recognizable persons. Furthermore, one can actually "aspire to the office of bishop" (1 Tim. 3:1).

The writer "talks past" Timothy and Titus to the community. His words indicate that, in fact, persons are instructed for the clerical offices (2 Tim. 3:14-17) and some form of testing is required (1 Tim. 5:22; 2 Tim. 2:2). When the presbytery (including the bishop) is satisfied, which itself is seen to be a moment of prophecy (1 Tim. 1:18; 4:14), the laying on of hands by the presbytery takes place, which bestows a "gift" (*charisma*) for the work of ministry (4:14). It is not clear whether such a ceremony took place for all three clerical offices, whether a person could move from deacon to presbyter, or whether, if such were possible, another ceremony would have been required. Nor can we know whether another ceremony of laying on of hands was conducted when a presbyter took up the office of bishop.

The silence of the Pastorals suggests that the move was only a change in function, becoming first among equals.

F. The Pastorals in Context

There is no uniform development of church order in the New Testament. Even within the letters of Paul there is variety. In his first letter he called upon his readers to "respect those who labor among you and are over you in the Lord and admonish you" (1 Thess. 5:12). Elsewhere he spoke of persons appointed by God as apostles, prophets, teachers, and for other functions (1 Cor. 14:28-30; cf. Rom. 12:6-8). In still another place he referred to "bishops and deacons" (Phil. 1:1). In all such places we must conclude that certain recognized and recognizable persons filled the various offices. By the time that the Pastorals were written, the offices have become standardized under the titles of bishop, presbyter, and deacon.

Yet it is clear that even when the Pastorals were written, as well as subsequently, no single pattern had yet evolved. In *1 Clement* (Rome, ca. A.D. 96) no distinction is made between the offices of bishop and presbyter; in fact they appear to be equivalent (44.4-5), which is also the case in the mid-second century book called *The Shepherd of Hermas* (2.4; 9.26-27) and in the works of Irenaeus, bishop of Lyons, near the end of the second century (*Against Heresies* 3.3.4; 4.26.2). Among the Apostolic Fathers it is with Ignatius (bishop of Antioch, Syria, early second century) that the bishop becomes clearly a leading figure in the church. In his writings the bishop is in charge of worship (*Letter to the Smyrnaeans* 8.1-2) and administration (*Letter to the Trallians* 7.2), and he is considered a prophet (*Letter to the Philadelphians* 7.1). The bishop represents God, the presbyters represent the apostolic council, and the deacons are entrusted with the ministry of Christ (*Magnesians* 6.1). The bishop is not yet the head of a district (diocese) but of a local congregation. It is interesting to note that in his letter to Rome, however, Ignatius does not refer to its bishop, probably because (as *1 Clement* indicates) there was yet no distinct, singular bishop there (monepiscopacy).

During the second and third centuries the pattern of three clerical offices provided by the Pastorals and Ignatius became standardized, but there were further developments. While the bishop was originally the leader of a congregation, he became the leader of congregations within a city, and then those in outlying districts (Cyprian, *Unity of the Church* 5 and *Epistle* 67.5). Presbyters became local leaders serving congregations under the supervision of the bishop (Tertullian, *On Baptism* 17) and deacons served under the bishop in charitable work and temporal concerns (Hippolytus, *Apostolic Tradition* 9).

Thus the organization of the church developed in these early centuries, and it has been maintained in major branches of the church to the present day. During the Reformation the organization was challenged, however, since the Roman Catholic bishops refused to ordain ministers for the Protestant churches. The Reformers therefore appealed to the Pastoral Epistles (Titus 1:5-7) and early Christian writers, particularly Jerome, to argue that the distinction between bishop and pastor is by human, not divine, authority. Therefore the rite of ordination, they maintained, could be performed by pastors.[17] As a consequence, a "presbyterial" form of ordination—rather than "episcopal"—was instituted in several Protestant churches on the basis of the Pastorals (cf. also 1 Tim. 4:14, which speaks of the laying on of hands by the presbytery).

5. The False Teachers and Their Teaching

The following portrait of the heretical teachers emerges from the Pastorals.[18] They are portrayed as persons whose consciences are under the power of Satan and debased (1 Tim. 4:2; Titus 1:15). They are therefore greedy and lovers of pleasure (1 Tim. 6:15; 2 Tim. 3:2, 4; Titus 1:11), puffed up with conceit (1 Tim. 6:4; 2 Tim. 3:2, 4), deceptive (1 Tim. 4:1; 2 Tim. 3:13), professing religion but not living it (2 Tim. 3:5; Titus 1:16), prone to engage in senseless controversies (1 Tim. 1:6; 6:4, 20; 2 Tim. 2:14-17, 23) and speculations (1 Tim. 1:4, 6; 4:7; 2 Tim. 4:4; Titus 1:14; 3:9), and ever seeking to make converts (2 Tim. 3:6; 4:3; Titus 1:11). Their many vices are listed at 2 Tim. 3:2-5.

Their teaching is not fully described or refuted in the Pastorals, and controversy with them is discouraged (1 Tim. 4:7; 6:20; Titus 3:9). The tactic of the writer is to attack the false teachers more on moral than doctrinal grounds. In a few places (e.g., 1 Tim. 1:4-11; 4:1-5), however, he begins to describe their teachings and to refute them, and certain features of the heretical teachings emerge.

As suggested in the commentary at 1 Tim. 1:3b-5, the heretics are involved in speculative exegesis of the Old Testament leading to esoteric and fanciful interpretations (cf. also 1 Tim. 4:7; Titus 1:14; 3:9). The issue between the writer and the heretics is not whether the Old Testament is to be used as Scripture, but who has the proper interpretation (cf. 1 Tim. 1:8-11; 2 Tim. 3:14-17). The heretics claim to be teachers of the law (1 Tim. 1:7; Titus 3:9), but with their speculative interpretations they develop elaborate "Jewish myths" (Titus 1:14; 1 Tim. 1:4; 4:7; 2 Tim. 4:4) and "genealogies" (1 Tim. 1:4; Titus 3:9). This method ignores the plain sense of the Torah (cf. commentary at 1 Tim. 1:8-11 and 4:4-5) and wanders away from the true function of Scripture (2 Tim. 3:14-17) and apostolic teaching (1 Tim. 1:4-5; 2 Tim. 4:4; Titus 1:9-16).

The writer speaks of certain opponents as belonging to the "circumcision party" (Titus 1:10). Whether that means that they actually teach circumcision is not clear, since the writer may be using a Pauline epithet (Gal. 2:12; cf. Acts 11:2; Col.

4:11). This may be an instance of "name-calling" by which the writer caricatures his opponents, but it also indicates that in the writer's mind these persons think they belong to an inner core of true Christians who despise others. The heretical teachers forbid marriage, teach abstinence from certain foods (1 Tim. 4:3), and claim that "the resurrection has taken place already" (2 Tim. 2:18).

The teaching reflected here, as well as in other references to it, appears to have features of an early form of Jewish-Christian Gnosticism. Gnosticism was a heretical movement of the second and succeeding centuries which arose out of an attempt to express the Christian faith in Hellenistic philosophical categories. Today many scholars think that a gnostic "attitude" or "outlook" existed already within pre-Christian Jewish groups. Fundamental to this outlook in all its forms was the conviction that the human race lives in a sphere of ignorance or illusion, but that one can attain salvation (or liberation) through *gnōsis* (knowledge, insight). A central insight was that God is absolutely transcendent, and the world is entirely evil. Therefore God did not create the world; the world was created by a lesser god. Only those who are "spiritual"—persons capable of receiving *gnōsis*—can be saved from this world. Such persons realize that they are children of God and enjoy union with him. The consequent way of life may be that of asceticism, leaving the earthly behind. On the other hand, it may be libertinism, asserting that the true self is above earthly pleasures enjoyed by the body and unaffected by them.

The Gnostic outlook came to expression in Christianity in various times and places of the ancient world, represented by such persons as Basilides (fl., Alexandria and Rome, A.D. 115-45), Valentinus (fl., Rome, A.D. 140-60), and those persons who produced the Nag Hammadi tractates (an extensive collection of Gnostic writings in Coptic discovered near

Introduction

Nag Hammadi in upper Egypt, dated ca. A.D. 150-400). That the writer of the Pastorals appears to have combated a Gnostic interpretation of Christianity can be asserted with confidence, although one would hesitate to identify his opponents with any particular, known Gnostic group. The writer charges Timothy to avoid "the godless chatter and contradictions of what is falsely called *gnōsis*" (1 Tim. 6:20; cf. Titus 1:16). He affirms that there is but "one God" (1 Tim. 2:5) and that the creation is good (1 Tim. 4:4; 6:17). Salvation is not available only to a few through *gnōsis*, for God desires all persons to be saved (1 Tim. 2:4; 4:10). The God who has created all things is himself the Savior (1 Tim. 1:1; 2:3; 4:10; Titus 1:3; 2:10; 3:4) who has sent his Son into the world "in the flesh" (1 Tim. 3:16) and "has abolished death and brought life and immortality to light through the gospel" (2 Tim. 1:10), which is to be received by faith (1 Tim. 4:10, 16). While Christian Gnosticism denies the humanity of Jesus, our writer affirms it (1 Tim. 3:16; 2 Tim. 2:8). He rejects asceticism on the one hand (1 Tim. 4:3) and libertinism on the other (2 Tim. 3:2-5). The battle against false scriptural interpretation (speculations, myths, genealogies) can also be seen as directed against midrashic exegesis by Gnostics; various Gnostic groups (especially Valentinus and writers of the Nag Hammadi tractates) made use of the Old Testament to develop or justify their teachings. Even the false teaching that "the resurrection has taken place already" (2 Tim. 2:18) appears to be rooted in Christian Gnosticism, reflecting the views of the Gnostics that (1) there can be no resurrection of the flesh, since matter is evil, and (2) therefore the traditional Christian term "resurrection" must be a symbol for spiritual union with the divine. The Nag Hammadi *Treatise on the Resurrection* (1.4.48-49) from the second half of the second century has developed an interpretation of the resurrection precisely in this way:

47

> The resurrection . . . is the revelation of what is, and the trans-
> formation of things, and a transition into newness. For imper-
> ishability [descends] upon the perishable; the light flows
> down upon the darkness, swallowing it up. . . . Therefore do
> not . . . live in conformity with the flesh . . . but flee from the
> divisions and the fetters, and already you have the resurrec-
> tion. . . . Why not consider yourself as risen and (already)
> brought to this? [19]

Over against the Gnostic interpreters of the Christian faith,
the writer of the Pastorals launches criticism in the name of
the apostle Paul. He is not interested in refutation as much as
he is in silencing them (Titus 1:11). Later the Gnostic teachers
themselves used Paul's letters, excluding the Pastorals, for
their own purposes.[20] But at the time of the Pastorals, Paul can
either (1) be safely appealed to as apostle of the orthodox, or
(2) be portrayed as such, rescuing him from the hands of the
Gnostic Christians. Given the fact that the writer of the Pastorals does not do exegesis of Paul's letters, providing an orthodox treatment of disputed passages, gives support for the former alternative and suggests that these letters were written before the rise of Gnostic literature. In sum, the opponents appear
to be Jewish-Christian Gnostics at the turn of the first and
second centuries A.D.

I TIMOTHY

Arland J. Hultgren

OUTLINE OF 1 TIMOTHY

I. Opening (1:1-2)
II. Body (1:3—6:21a)
    A. Charge to Timothy (1:3-20).
        1. Aim of the Charge: (1:3-11)
        2. Paul as an Example of One Entrusted (1:12-17)
        3. Timothy as Paul's Emissary at Ephesus (1:18-20)
    B. Instructions for Worship (2:1-15)
        1. Instructions for Prayer (2:1-7)
        2. Instructions for Conduct at Worship (2:8-15)
    C. Instructions Concerning Bishops and Deacons (3:1-13)
        1. The Pattern of Life for a Bishop (3:1-7)
        2. The Pattern of Life for a Deacon (3:8-13)
    D. The Church and Its Confession (3:14-16)
    E. Expectations and Duties of Ministry (4:1—5:2)
        1. False Teaching and Apostasy to Be Expected (4:1-5)
        2. Duties of Ministry (4:6-10)
        3. Practice of Ministry (4:11—5:2)
    F. Order and Duties in the Congregation (5:3—6:2)
        1. Instructions Concerning Widows (5:3-16)
        2. Duties toward, Disciplining, and Selecting of Presbyters (5:17-25)
        3. Duties of the Christian Slave (6:1-2)
    G. True and False Teaching (6:2b-21a)
        1. False Teaching and Its Consequences (6:2b-5)
        2. Two Ways (6:6-10)
        3. Exhortation to True Christianity (6:11-16)
        4. Ministry to the Wealthy (6:17-19)
        5. Call to Fidelity (6:20-21a)
III. Closing Benediction (6:21b)

COMMENTARY

■ Opening (1:1-2)

The letter opens with a greeting from Paul to Timothy. If that were all that these verses contained ("Paul to Timothy, Greetings"), the greeting would be no different from the usual beginning of a letter in the Greek-speaking world from 200 B.C. to at least A.D. 200. But there is more. The entire opening is modeled after the form of opening which Paul had used in his letters. Paul transformed the traditional greeting of the Greek-speaking world in two ways: (1) rather than using the word "greetings" *(chairein),* he used the word "grace" *(charis);* and (2) he added the common greeting from Jewish tradition, "peace" *(shalom* in Hebrew). So Paul's letters always contain the phrase "grace to you and peace" (Rom. 1:7; 1 Cor. 1:3; 2 Cor. 1:2; Gal. 1:3; Phil. 1:2; 1 Thess. 1:1; Philemon 3), as do other letters as well (2 Thess. 1:2; Eph. 1:2; Col. 1:2; 1 Peter 1:2; 2 Peter 1:2).

1 Timothy contains yet another word in the greeting, however. The words are **grace,** *mercy,* **and peace** (1:2), which is also found at 2 Tim. 1:2 (Titus 1:4 reverts to "grace and peace") and at 2 John 3. The phrase "mercy and peace" is found at least once in Jewish writings (*2 Baruch* 78:2), and it also appears as the form of greeting in Jude 2 (cf. also Gal. 6:16).

The greeting here, as in the letters of Paul, differs in one important respect from conventional secular greetings. While the conventional form conveys greetings from the sender to the addressee, the Christian form goes beyond that to an announcement of **grace, mercy, and peace from God the Father and Christ Jesus our Lord.** The writer thereby acts as a herald of good things. The unity of writer and addressee is underscored, and the writer establishes that he conveys good tidings from God and Christ. It consists of God's unde-served favor (**grace**), God's help for the helpless (**mercy**), and God's power to establish well-being (**peace**). The writer as-sumes the authority to declare that God, as he is known in Christ, is favorably disposed to those who belong to him through their common confession of Jesus as Lord.

Paul is spoken of as an **apostle of Christ Jesus** in the very first sentence, which corresponds exactly with the first line of 2 Cor. 1:1, and which is used again in 2 Tim. 1:1. The term **apostle** signifies one who has been commissioned by the resurrected Christ, and Paul claimed this title for him-self (cf. Gal. 1:1, 11-12). Moreover, he is an apostle by the **command** of God and Christ. That he is an apostle by **com-mand** is said only here and at Titus 1:3. In the genuine letters Paul is an apostle by "call" (Gal. 1:15) or the will of God (1 Cor. 1:1; 2 Cor. 1:1; cf. Eph. 1:1; Col. 1:1; 2 Tim. 1:1). By such usage Paul thinks of himself as one "called" in the sense of the Old Testament prophets (Isa. 49:1-6; Jer. 1:4-5). That here in the Pastorals Paul is thought of as an apostle by **command** connotes a Graeco-Roman understanding of apostle-ship, in which one is ordered into service as the formal rep-resentative of an emperor. He is less one called and sent in the Pauline sense, and more one who is a guardian or trustee of the Christian tradition (1 Tim. 1:11-12; 2 Tim. 1:11-13; Titus 1:1-3), and one who commands that Timothy and Titus guard the same (1 Tim. 6:20; 2 Tim. 1:13-14; 2:1-2; Titus 1:9; 2:1, 15; 3:8).

The title **apostle** is not applied to Timothy or Titus in the Pastorals. Timothy had served as an emissary of Paul (1 Thess. 3:2, 6; 1 Cor. 4:17; 16:10; Phil. 2:19, 23; Acts 16:1; 18:5; 19:22), but nowhere does he bear a formal title. Here he is spoken of as Paul's **true child in the faith,** and at 2 Tim. 1:2 as the apostle's "beloved child." Both designations are rooted in Paul's own designation of Timothy in 1 Cor. 4:17 as "my beloved and faithful child in the Lord" (see also Phil. 2:22). What the RSV translates as **true child** can also be translated "genuine" or "legitimate child." Timothy is thus portrayed as Paul's legitimate, authoritative successor, as is Titus too (Titus 1:4).

Within this brief greeting there appear confessional formulae which already disclose elements of the theology of the Pastorals. The writer speaks of **God our Savior** and **Christ Jesus our hope.** God is spoken of as **Savior** six times in the Pastorals (see Introduction, Part 3, B). God has drawn near in mercy (Titus 3:4-5) by sending Christ into the world (2 Tim. 1:9; Titus 2:11) to abolish death and bring life and immortality to light to all who accept the gospel (2 Tim. 1:10). God saves his people from iniquity and its consequence, death; Christ has been given—indeed gave himself—"to redeem us from all iniquity and to purify for himself a people of his own who are zealous for good deeds" (Titus 2:14). The designation of Christ as **our hope** is the only such instance in the New Testament. His coming appearance is "our blessed hope" (Titus 2:13), and his grace is the basis of our "hope of eternal life" (Titus 3:7). Christ is also called **our Lord** (1:2), which is common in the Pastorals (see Introduction Part 3, C). Finally, the writer refers to **the faith** (1:2), which is the Christian faith in the Pastorals (1 Tim. 3:8; 4:1, 6; 5:8; 6:10, 21; 2 Tim. 4:7; Titus 1:13; 3:15). Since Timothy is a **true child in the faith,** he is considered one who has been taught the faith correctly from the apostle Paul, and who has maintained it up to the present time.

■ Body (1:3–6:21a)

The seven genuine letters of Paul have a fairly common structure of five parts. It consists of (1) opening, (2) thanksgiving or blessing, (3) body, (4) paraenesis (exhortation), and (5) closing (greetings and/or benediction).[1] Some variations appear; e.g., Galatians has no thanksgiving section and a distinction between the body and the paraenesis is not always clear. But the fivefold structure is typical and can be seen when the letters are placed side-by-side in parallel columns.

The Pastorals do not share this fivefold structure. A thanksgiving following the opening, for example, can be found only in 2 Timothy (1:3-7). Furthermore, one cannot make a distinction between the body and the paraenetic, or exhortative, section in these letters. Much of the body is paraenetic; in fact, the Pastorals have appropriately been classified as paraenetic letters.[2] One can only speak, in the case of 1 Timothy, of an opening (1:1-2), a body (1:3—6:21a), and a closing benediction (6:21b).

Charge to Timothy (1:3-20)

Timothy is to remain at Ephesus (1:3), order people to refrain from false doctrine (1:3-4), hold the apostolic aim in view (1:5), look to Paul as an example (1:16), and carry out his duties as a successor to Paul (1:18-19).

1. Aim of the Charge: Purity, Good Conscience, and Faith (1:3-11)

3a—Timothy had been ordered to remain at Ephesus as Paul went to Macedonia. As indicated (see Introduction, Part 1), this detail cannot be made to coincide with information from Acts and Paul's genuine letters. The intent of the verse is to provide an "occasion" for the letter. The letter appears to have been written by Paul to a trusted emissary and now, at the turn of the century (see Introduction, Part 2, C), is to be read in the churches of the Pauline field. At the end of 2 Timothy (4:9, 13, 21), Timothy is called away from Ephesus. The readers are to assume that the letters were left behind.

3b-5—Timothy is to **charge** (or command) certain persons various things. First, they are not **to teach any different doc-**

trine *(heterodidaskalein)*, a verb found only here and at 6:3 in
the New Testament. Its antithesis in the Pastorals is "sound
doctrine" (1 Tim. 1:10; 2 Tim. 4:3; Titus 1:9; 2:1) or "good
doctrine" (1 Tim. 4:6). That which is "sound" or "good" has
to do with both correct belief (1 Tim. 4:6; 2 Tim. 1:13; 4:3;
Titus 1:9) and Christian morality (1 Tim. 1:10; 6:3; Titus 2:1,
10). Faith (as correct belief) and good works are therefore
integral and cannot be separated (cf. especially Titus 2:10).

Second, persons are not to be preoccupied with **myths** and
endless genealogies which give rise to speculations rather
than the **divine training that is in faith** (1:4). The writer
refers to "Jewish myths" in another context (Titus 1:14), and
at Titus 3:9 he refers to "genealogies" again (along with
"quarrels over the law"—meaning Jewish law). The writer
has in mind a strain of unorthodox, speculative Christianity
which makes use of the Old Testament and Jewish tradition,
and which is a threat to sound teaching (see Introduction,
Part 5). Already in the Judaism of the time stories from the Old
Testament were taken and expanded by a process known
as "midrash" (from the Hebrew verb *dārash*, "to investigate").
The presupposition was that the Scriptures are not simply a
record of the past, but also God's revelation for every age.
The interpreter therefore seeks out meanings for the present
and future through meditation upon even the most minor details (e.g., numerals, the spelling of words, and incidents
within stories).[3] The writer of the Pastorals does not name
any particulars or refute them, but opposes preoccupation
with theological and cosmological constructions arising out
of midrashic exegesis, particularly those which result in **myths**
(cf. also 1 Tim. 4:7; 2 Tim. 4:4; 2 Peter 1:16) and attention to
genealogies. The reason for doing so is that these activities do
not lead to **divine training that is in faith.** The words **divine
training** stand for the Greek *oikonomia theou*, which the NEB
renders "God's plan" (of salvation). The RSV is closer to the
intended meaning. The contrast is not between error and

God's plan, but between error and the way of life which is proper (**divine training**), which comes by way of true **faith.**

Over against such misguided preoccupations, the writer says that the **aim** (or "goal," *telos*) of his charge is **love that issues from a pure heart and a good conscience and sincere faith** (1:5). Elsewhere in the New Testament love *(agapē)* can be commanded (Mark 12:28-31; John 15:12; Rom. 13:9; Gal. 5:14; 1 John 3:23) or can be spoken of as a "fruit of the Spirit" (Gal. 5:22). It is the basis from which all Christian thought and action flow. In the Pastorals, however, **love** becomes a virtue (cf. 1 Tim. 2:15; 4:12; 6:11; 2 Tim. 1:7; 3:10; Titus 2:2) or, as in this verse, a "goal," flowing from a well-ordered and virtuous inner life. In this sense it becomes the summation of all virtues working together, particularly the triad of a **pure heart, good conscience,** and **sincere faith.** The term for **pure heart** is found in the Old Testament (LXX, Gen. 20:5; Ps. 50:12–51:10 in the Hebrew and RSV; cf. also Matt. 5:8) and also at 2 Tim. 2:22. Generally the **heart** is the center of volition, thought, and religious response in biblical anthropology; a **pure heart** is a heart undivided in such matters. It is therefore the basis for right worship (2 Tim. 2:22) and genuine love. **Good conscience** (cf. 1:19; Acts 23:1; 1 Peter 3:21) is a concept not found in Paul. For Paul, conscience is the center of making moral judgments (Rom. 13:5; 1 Cor. 8:7, 10, 12; 2 Cor. 4:2; 5:11), and it also has an accusing or excusing function (Rom. 2:15; 9:1; 2 Cor. 1:12). In the Pastorals, however, **conscience** is a center which gives directives to thought and activity. When it is **good,** it directs a person to think and do what is right without duplicity (cf. 3:9). **Sincere faith** is faith which is free from hypocrisy *(anhypokritos).* Taken together, all these terms within the triad present the Christian life as one of virtue and genuine faith, which then brings forth love as its fruit.

8-10a—The writer makes a defense of the law (Pentateuchal law) on its own terms, understood in its plain sense without midrashic interpretation. The law is **good** (cf. Rom. 7:12, 16), if one uses it "lawfully," i.e., according to its true nature (as law). In what follows (1:9) it is clear that the writer has no sense of the law as that which exposes sin—a concept found in Paul (Rom. 3:20; 5:20; 7:8; Gal. 3:13). In rather un-Pauline fashion, in fact, he assumes that certain persons are righteous before the law. The function of the law is to curb the attitudes and actions of evildoers. The writer gives a lengthy list of persons whom the law is to hold in check (1:9b-10). The list consists of categories of persons, and their evils correspond sequentially to things prohibited in the Decalogue (Exod. 20:1-16): (1) the **lawless and disobedient** do not heed the words of God (Exod. 20:1); (2) the **ungodly and sinners** do not honor God as the Lord (Exod. 20:2); (3) the **unholy and profane** do not keep the commandment concerning God's name (Exod. 20:7); (4) the **murderers of fathers and murderers of mothers** do not keep the commandment concerning parents (Exod. 20:12); (5) the **manslayers** do not abide by the commandment against murder (Exod. 20:13); (6) the **immoral persons** and **sodomites** do not keep the commandment concerning the prohibition against adultery (Exod. 20:14, interpreted in reference to sexual morality in general); (7) the **kidnappers** are the worst of thieves (so Philo, *On the Special Laws* 4.13) and therefore violate the commandment against stealing (Exod. 20:15); and (8) the **liars** and **perjurers** do not keep the commandment against false witness (Exod. 20:16). It has been suggested that the passage represents a "Hellenistic transformation of Jewish ethics." [4] While that is probably true, it can be seen that the Decalogue actually provides the framework and essential contents of the passage.

10b-11—At 10b a shift takes place. While in 8-10a the writer speaks of categories of persons against whom the law has been set, in 10b he turns to vices themselves (**and whatever else**) which are against **sound doctrine.** Then again at 1:11 there is another abrupt shift into a prepositional phrase, **in accordance**

with the . . . gospel. The **sound doctrine** being spoken of is that which is conformed to (or "accords with") the gospel—specifically the gospel with which the apostle Paul had been entrusted (cf. 1 Thess. 2:4). The verse also provides a transition to what follows.

2. *Paul as an Example of One Entrusted (1:12-17)*

12a—Although the writer does not have a thanksgiving section, he does give an expression of thanks. The wording used (*charin echō,* "I am grateful" cf. also 2 Tim. 1:3) is not that of the genuine Pauline letters (*eucharistō tō theō,* "I thank God," Rom. 1:8; 1 Cor. 1:4; Phil. 1:3; Philemon 4; cf. variations at 2 Cor. 1:3; 1 Thess. 1:2). Moreover, Paul's thanksgiving is always directed toward God, but here it is to Christ (at 2 Tim. 1:3, to God).

12b-14—The thanksgiving is to Christ for his judging Paul **faithful, appointing** him to **his service** (*diakonia,* which can also mean "ministry"), in spite of the fact that Paul had formerly been a persecutor. Paul speaks of his persecuting activities in his own letters (1 Cor. 15:9; Gal. 1:13-14, 23; Phil. 3:6), and Acts relates stories about them too (8:3; 9:1-5; 22:3-5; 26:4-11). There are some contrasts to be seen, however, between Paul's own statements and what is portrayed here. First, Paul indicates that his persecuting of "the church" was carried on because he was pro-Torah (hence, he persecuted Jewish Christians, seeking to bring them back into right belief and conduct);[5] but in the Pastorals he is said to have persecuted Christ, not "the church," and that the basis of his action was ignorance, i.e., not knowing the truth. Second, the change which came about in Paul is treated differently. Paul speaks of the event as a "call" (Gal. 1:15) or "revelation" (Gal. 1:16; cf. 1 Cor. 15:8). But here it is more definitely a "conversion," since it involved a move from ignorance and unbelief to knowledge and belief. Grace **overflowed** for him with **faith and love** as a result (1:14). The **faith and love that are in Christ** are not faith and love from Christ, but the faith and love which distinguish the Christian life (cf. 1 Tim. 2:15; 4:12; 6:11; 2 Tim. 1:13; 2:22; 3:10; Titus 2:2), and which now characterize the life of the one converted. The **foremost of sinners** had received **mercy** (1:15-16) and is now the exemplary Christian.

15a—The verse contains two stylized features. First, **the saying is sure** *(pistos ho logos)* is a formula which appears elsewhere in the Pastorals (3:1; 4:9; 2 Tim. 2:11; Titus 3:8), but nowhere else in the New Testament. Within the Pastorals the formula is used in connection with certain maxims about salvation designated as "sound" and important for Christians.[6] Here the formula introduces the maxim: **Christ Jesus came into the world to save sinners.** This is a traditional saying which has similarities to sayings in the Gospels which express the purpose of Jesus' "coming" into the world (Mark 2:17b; 10:45; Luke 12:51; Matt. 10:34; Luke 12:49; 19:10; Matt. 5:17; cf. also John 18:37).

15b-16—Paul is portrayed as the **foremost** of sinners. In spite of the moralistic tone of the Pastorals generally, here the designation **foremost of sinners** is not due to immoral conduct, but is based on his opposition to Christ as the greatest known persecutor. This provided the "occasion" (NEB) for Christ to display his patience. The form of argument is the rabbinic *kal-wa-homer*, "from the greater to the less." If Christ has displayed his patience with Paul and granted him mercy, how much more will he not do so for others? The display of Christ's mercy toward Paul, who **had acted ignorantly and in unbelief** (1:13), was an example of the perfect patience of Christ, which was to extend then **to those who were to believe in him for eternal life,** i.e., subsequent Christians.

17—The section closes with a doxology. The shift is from Christ (1:12-16) to God, **the King of ages.** The doxology appears to be from a Hellenistic Jewish worship tradition. The attributes of God are found in Hellenistic Jewish sources: **King of ages** (LXX, Tobit 13:7, 11), **immortal** (Wis. 12:1; Philo, *Life* *of Moses* 3.171), and **invisible** (Philo, *Life of Moses* 2.65; Josephus, *Jewish War* 7.346). The latter two terms appear also in Paul (Rom. 1:20, 23).

3. *Timothy as Paul's Emissary at Ephesus (1:18-20)*

This charge, which is committed to Timothy, can refer only to what is to follow: to **wage the good warfare, holding faith and a good conscience** (1:18-19) in general and, in particular, devoting himself to the instructions beginning at 2:1 concerning worship, conduct, church order, and the opposing of heresy.

Timothy is spoken of as Paul's spiritual "child" (**son** in RSV and NEB), as also at 1:2 (and 1 Cor. 4:17; Phil. 2:22). Moreover, he has been designated for his work "according to the prophecies leading to you" (1:18, translated literally). The picture is one in which Timothy has been designated for this specific task as an emissary at Ephesus by divine guidance through the Spirit. It is not likely that the writer has in mind the initial call of Timothy. At Acts 16:3 it is said only that "Paul wanted Timothy to accompany him" after their first encounter. The present verse refers to an occasion on which Timothy had been set aside for his work at Ephesus in particular. At 4:14 it is said that Timothy received a gift *(charisma),* given by "prophecy" with the laying on of hands of the presbytery, and at 2 Tim. 1:6 it is said that Timothy possesses a gift *(charisma)* through the laying on of hands by Paul himself. There is a discrepancy here concerning who was involved in the laying on of hands, and there are three possible ways of trying to resolve it. First, it is possible to harmonize the data and conclude that, according to the writer, Timothy was set apart for the work at Ephesus through the laying on of hands by both the presbytery and Paul at the same time. Second, it is possible that at 2 Tim. 1:6 the writer refers to the initial calling of Timothy, with imposition of Paul's hands. 1 Tim. 4:14 will then refer to Timothy's being set apart for service at Ephesus in particular, with imposition of hands by the local presbytery. Third, it is possible that the writer has no unified picture in mind. If this is so, 1 Tim. 4:14 reflects the writer's aim to "speak past" Timothy to the present leadership, which has been ordained by an existing presbytery (see commentary at 4:14), while 2 Tim. 1:6 reflects the particular aim of that letter, which is to affirm more clearly the connection between Paul and Timothy and to appeal for sympathy with Paul (see Introduction, Part 2, B); one way to do that would be to claim that, after all, it was Paul who bestowed upon Timothy the *charisma* he possesses, a gift which Timothy is now to "rekindle"—the effect of which will be to remember Paul and to transmit his teachings. Which of these three most likely reflects the viewpoint of the writer is difficult to say. The last mentioned is the most satisfactory, however, given the data of the Pastorals and Acts and the purposes of these letters. In any case, the leadership at Ephesus, which Timothy idealizes, is grounded not merely in formal appointment. Selection of present leaders is itself based upon a "charismatic consent" of the community, and appointment is its certification. Cf. Acts 13:1-3 for an instance at Antioch in which "prophets and teachers," inspired by the Spirit, designate Paul and Silas for their mission and lay their hands upon them.

The writer commits a charge for a purpose: to **wage the good warfare.** This military imagery is rooted in the genuine letters of Paul (Rom. 13:12; 1 Cor. 9:7; 2 Cor. 6:7; 10:3-4; Phil. 2:25; 1 Thess. 5:8), and it appears also at Eph. 6:10-17 and elsewhere in the Pastorals (1 Tim. 6:12; 2 Tim. 2:3-4). The waging of this warfare will take place as Timothy (the present leadership) recalls the prophetic utterances and holds fast **faith and a good conscience** (for comment on these terms, see commentary at 1:5). Certain persons have rejected **a good conscience** and have thereby (literally translated) "suffered shipwreck with respect to the faith." Two such persons are named,

Hymenaeus and Alexander (mentioned also at 2 Tim. 2:17 and 4:14, respectively; Hymenaeus is otherwise not mentioned in the New Testament; an Alexander appears in Acts 19:33, but it is not clear whether the same person is meant). Both are heretics, and both must have been known to the community of Ephesus—at least in memory. It is said that Paul **delivered** both **to Satan** in order that **they may learn not to blaspheme.** The language recalls 1 Cor. 5:5, but the thought is different. In that case an immoral man is to be delivered to Satan by the community and the result is bodily death (cf. 11:30). Here the consignment to Satan is purportedly by Paul alone, and it is more in keeping with the thought of Job 2:6 in which "Satan is allowed to inflict any bodily suffering short of death on Job to test the sincerity of his religion." [7] This theme is found also at 2 Cor. 12:7 concerning Paul, who is assaulted by Satan, lest he be too elated. It is expected that Hymenaeus and Alexander will suffer at the hands of Satan and therefore **learn not to blaspheme.** A precise line between the realms of Christ and Satan is thereby presupposed. Those consigned to Satan's realm are subject to his power and are tormented already in this life. Yet there is held out for them the possibility of repentance as a result of learning from their experience. If repentance follows, it is possible for them to be restored. All of this serves to exhort Timothy, and therefore the leadership of the congregation, to fight the good fight, holding faith and a good conscience.

Instructions for Worship (2:1-15)

1. Instructions for Prayer (2:1-7)

1-2—Having begun his "charge" (1:18) with general admonitions, the writer now turns to more specific instructions. The phrase **first of all** (2:1) makes a transition to them. **Supplications, prayers, intercessions, and thanksgivings** are to be made for all persons. The terms need not be distinguished sharply, for they are but different aspects of prayer; the writer speaks of these aspects for fullness and emphasis. Paul uses similar terms in a series at Phil. 4:6: "by prayer and supplication and thanksgiving let your requests be made known to God." What is distinctive of 2:1, however, is the inclusion of the noun **intercessions** *(enteuxeis),* which is a term found only here and at 4:5 in the New Testament. With this term the accent of the verse is brought into the open. The congregation is to be involved in **intercessions** for all persons.

For all persons indicates that the Christian community is inclusive in its concerns. The church envisioned is "at home" in the world (unlike Gnostic groups, which were negative or indifferent to it). It is to pray for **kings and all who are in high positions.** This tradition of praying for civil authorities is rooted in the Old Testament and Judaism. During the Exile (587-539 B.C.) Jeremiah wrote from Jerusalem to his compatriots in Babylon to pray for that city, "for in its welfare you will find your welfare" (Jer. 29:7). Other instances of prayer for heathen rulers can be found in Jewish literature of various times and places (Ezra 6:10; 1 Macc. 7:33; Philo, *Flaccus* 49; and the Mishnah tractate *Pirke Aboth* 3.2). Thus prayer for those in authority came naturally into Christianity from this Jewish background. Christians could, and sometimes did, take a negative attitude toward the state and its authorities (as Revelation 13 shows). Moreover, it cannot be said that the writer of the Pastorals has a clearly positive attitude toward the state, nor that he reflects the teaching of Paul, for whom civil authorities have been appointed by God (Rom. 13:1-7). He stops short of that—perhaps because he is aware of persecutions to an extent not envisioned by Paul—and merely calls for prayer on their behalf "in order that" (a purpose clause is introduced) Christians **may lead a quiet and peaceable life.** In the welfare of the empire is the welfare of the Christian community. His thought here is more akin to Jeremiah's than Paul's (see also 1 Peter 2:13-17). Nevertheless, the church is truly "at home" in the world, and therefore prayers are to be made for all persons, including rulers, that peace may abound (cf. Titus 3:1-2).

The life hoped for on earth is **quiet, peaceable,** and attended "with all piety and reverence" (RSV, **godly and respectful in every way**). The church, it is hoped, will be free from persecution and be allowed to be itself both in its inner life and in its relationship to the broader social context. The term "piety" (or "godliness," *eusebeia*) appears 10 times in the Pastorals (1 Tim. 2:2; 3:16; 4:7, 8; 6:3, 5, 6, 11; 2 Tim. 3:5; Titus 1:1) as a virtue of those who are faithful in belief and conduct, and the term for "reverence" appears twice more (3:4; Titus 2:7), but nowhere else in the New Testament.

The call to Christians to make intercessions for all persons, particularly for those in authority, has had an enduring place in Christian worship. Instructions for such prayers, or allusions to them, are found in the second century Apostolic Fathers (*1 Clement* 61; Polycarp, *Letter to the Philippians* 12:3; Justin, *Apology* 1.17; and Tertullian, *Apology* 30.39). The practice continues in liturgical orders to the present day whenever congregations pray for their nation and its rulers, often making use of the phrase from 1 Tim. 2:2, **that we may lead a quiet and peaceable life.**

3-6—This is good refers to the practice of praying for all persons. Then the reason is given. **God our Savior** (on this term, see Introduction, Part 3, B) **desires all persons to be saved and come to the knowledge of the truth.** Here a shift of thinking takes place. In 2:1-2 the writer calls for intercessions, but at 2:4 the concern is for the salvation of all persons (the **for all persons** of 2:1 prompts the latter). It is probable that 2:4 is a creedal statement concerning **God our Savior,** which interrupts the section, for at 2:5 the writer picks up the theme of 2:1-3: it is good to pray for all persons, including rulers, for there is but **one God,** who is Lord and ruler over all creation, including the secular order.

Along with the concern for the created world (prayers for all, and for order and peace), teachings about Christ (Christology) and salvation (soteriology) are also interwoven. **God our Savior** desires the salvation of all persons and wills them **to come to the knowledge of the truth,** i.e., to know and accept true apostolic teaching (cf. 2 Tim. 2:25; 3:7; Titus 1:1). Verses 5 and 6 are a creedal or hymnic fragment. As there is **one God,** so there is **one mediator . . . the man Christ Jesus, who gave himself as a ransom for all.** Within these words lies a wealth of Christological affirmations. Against Gnostic systems, in which there are many angelic intermediaries, there is but **one mediator,** and he is a **man who gave himself** (on the cross) **as a ransom** *(antilytron)* for all. As a **ransom** Christ has provided the means of liberation from sin and its consequences in the final judgment (cf. Titus 2:14), which persons cannot do for themselves. This **ransom** is on behalf of **all** *(hyper pantōn);* therefore all persons are the object of God's saving purposes. The writer adds a difficult Greek phrase which reads (literally) "the testimony to [or "in"] its own times." Christ's giving himself as a ransom is a **testimony** or witness to God's redemptive work at the time determined by him. Christ crucified is the witness to God's saving purposes (so NEB, "so providing, at the fitting time, a proof of the divine purpose").

7—The section ends with an autobiographical note. Paul was appointed a "herald" *(kērux,* **preacher** in RSV), **apostle,** and **teacher** of the Gentiles. This triad appears also at 2 Tim. 1:11. While Paul frequently designates himself as an apostle in his own letters, he never uses the other two terms for himself. That his mission was to Gentiles is frequently affirmed (Rom. 1:13; 11:13; 15:16, 18; Gal. 1:16; 2:2, 8-9; 1 Thess. 2:16), and the aside (**I am telling the truth, I am not lying**) is based on similar statements in Rom. 9:1; 2 Cor. 11:31; and Gal. 1:20.

2. *Instructions for Conduct at Worship (2:8-15)*

8—**In every place** at which Christians gather for worship

(cf. 1 Cor. 1:2; 2 Cor. 2:14; 1 Thess. 1:8), **the men** (not "persons," but males, *andres*) should pray, **lifting holy hands without anger or quarreling.** This posture for prayer is rooted in Hebrew tradition (Neh. 8:6; Pss. 28:2; 134:2; 141:2; 143:6) and is not therefore an innovative badge of charismatic experience in the early church. It is also referred to by certain early Christian writers (*1 Clement* 29.1; Tertullian, *Apology* 30). The term **holy hands** is found in various sources, pagan and Jewish, but here Ps. 24:3-4 comes to mind ("Who shall ascend the hill of the Lord? . . . He who has clean hands and a pure heart." Cf. also Ps. 18:20, 29). The term has a ritual meaning in Judaism, but here (as in Ps. 24:3-4) it has a moral meaning—**without anger or quarreling.** True worship of God can take place only when those who participate are at peace with others (cf. Matt. 5:23-24; 1 Cor. 11:17-34).

9-10—The RSV (and other modern versions) separates these verses from 2:8 more than the Greek text warrants. The impression left can be that while 2:8 refers to conduct at worship, 2:9-10 takes up general conduct. But 2:9-10 continues the exhortation concerning public worship, this time speaking to and about women. The Greek for **seemly apparel** can also be translated "respectable deportment," and no doubt the double meaning is intended. Women are to avoid ostentatious dress and be "clothed" properly—both in terms of what they wear and in terms of conduct—adorned not by **costly attire but by good deeds.** The writer stands in the tradition of Old Testament (cf. Isa. 3:16—4:1), Jewish, pagan, and Christian (cf. 1 Peter 3:4-5) moral teaching concerning the "appearance" of women: they are to appear **seemly,** and that is a matter of conduct (which also includes avoiding ostentatious outward dress).

11-15—Often overlooked in this well-known and controversial passage is the positive emphasis in the first clause: that a woman, no less than a man, is to **learn.** The congregation addressed is not modeled on the synagogue, where instruction is primarily, sometimes solely, for men and boys. From the beginning, women were included in the worship and instruction of the church, and the author of the Pastorals assumes this as a matter of course. Nevertheless, a woman's learning is to take place in a particular way—**in silence with all submissiveness.** And the author will not **permit** a woman to (1) **teach** or (2) **have authority over** (literally) "a man" (RSV, **men**).

The writer goes on to give a basis for his position (2:13-14). The question arises whether there was an occasion for his teaching. The Pauline congregations had had female, as well as male, leaders. At 1 Cor. 11:5 Paul speaks, as a matter of course, of women leading in prayer (cf. also 11:13) and prophesying. At Phil. 4:2-3 Paul refers to two women who have labored with him "in the gospel," and in Romans 16 several congregational leaders are women (16:1, 3, 6, 12, 15), although it is impossible to know exactly what their leadership roles entailed. Furthermore, at Acts 18:26 Priscilla (with her husband Aquila) instructs Apollos. But it is clear that in the situation of the Pastorals a shift has taken place. There are hints in the Pastorals that the heretical teachers opposed by the writer had success especially among certain women (2 Tim. 3:6-7; 1 Tim. 5:13-15). Apparently the emancipation which Paul's gospel proclaimed (Gal. 3:28; 1 Cor. 11:11) led women to anticipate more than the church was willing to grant at the time the Pastorals were written. This can be explained as a reaction to present realities, in which the heretical teachers carried on a special mission among women (as 2 Tim. 3:6 indicates). Naturally there were men who followed the heretical teachers also, and the heretical teachers and opponents named are all men (2 Tim. 1:15; 2:17; 4:15). But the author apparently thought that great strides in the battle against heretics could be made, and as many people as possible be kept in the true faith, if at least one large segment (the women) could be excluded from teaching and exercising authority. By doing so, and by insisting that they learn in silence and with submissiveness, the author has effectively reduced the pool of possible heretical teachers. This section is similar to 1 Cor. 14:33b-36, a passage which is not likely to be from the hand of Paul, for, among other reasons, it is not consistent with 1 Cor. 11:5.[8] It appears to be a later interpolation, perhaps based on 1 Tim. 2:11-12, but in any case reflecting a similar view.

In order to maintain his position, the author provides a "proof" in 2:13-14 based on a particular interpretation of Genesis. This proof has a bearing on both prohibitions: (1) a woman is not to have authority over a man, because Adam was prior in creation (Gen. 2:7, 21-22); and (2) a woman should not be allowed to teach because **the woman was deceived** (cf. Gen. 3:1-6). The first point—the priority of Adam, and therefore the subjection of woman to man—is found in Paul (1 Cor. 11:8-9; cf. also 11:3). The author could also have alluded to Gen. 3:16 (and Isa. 3:12), but does not do so. Other New Testament passages on the subordination of women to their husbands are found at Eph. 5:22-24; Col. 3:18; 1 Peter 3:1-2, 5. Yet these have to do with domestic relationships, not with the issue of authority within the congregation. Paul himself makes a significant "qualification" to his statements when at 1 Cor. 11:11 he says that, in spite of the subordination of woman to man in creation, "in the Lord" both are mutually dependent. In principle, then, the question of subordination of one to the other no longer maintains in the new age and, by implication, in the church (cf. Gal. 3:28). Concerning the second issue, the writer says that **Adam was not deceived, but the woman was deceived and became a transgressor.** At Gen. 3:6 the woman "gave some [of the fruit] to her husband, and he ate." In a sense, of course, Adam was deceived or tricked, but not in the sense of "being led astray" or "beguiled" (which the verb *apataō* connotes; cf. LXX, Gen. 3:13; Sir. 14:16; Eph. 5:6; James 1:26). Eve, however, was "beguiled" by the serpent (Gen. 3:13). The author reflects a stream of Jewish-Christian tradition which claims that it is through Eve that the human race has fallen. This tradition appears in Sir. 25:24 from the second century B.C. ("From a woman sin had its beginning, and because of her we all die"), and then appears subsequently in Paul at 2 Cor. 11:3 ("the serpent deceived Eve") and in the second century apocryphal *Gospel of the Egyptians,* as quoted by Clement of Alexandria (*Stromata* 3.9.63, "I came to destroy the works of the woman"). But the author falls short of affirming the other tradition, dominant in Paul's thinking, that Adam was the first transgressor, whose fall brings death to all persons (Rom. 5:12-21; 1 Cor. 15:21-22, 45-59). The reason for following the one tradition rather than the other is clear. The writer wants to exclude women (whom he considers susceptible to the influence of deceptive heretics; cf. 2 Tim. 3:6-7) from teaching and assuming authority, so he picks up and develops the tradition of the deception of Eve as a basis for his position.

The final verse of this chapter (2:15) causes problems for translation, exegesis, and theology. In the first part of the sentence the Greek reads, "But [she] will be saved" *(sōthēsetai de).* Left alone, the antecedent to "she" could be assumed to be Eve (2:13-14). But the RSV and other modern translations are surely correct in translating, **Yet woman will be saved,** referring to any woman (2:11). The second part of the sentence is also problematic, for the Greek has a plural verb ("if *they* continue"; RSV, "if *she* continues"), which results in a mixing of singular and plural ("woman"/"they"). This mixing happens also at 2:9-12, although not in the same sentence. There have been attempts to overcome the theological problem which the verse causes. It has been suggested, for example, that **through bearing children** cannot refer to bearing children in general, but must refer to the birth of the Savior through Mary, which has undone the work of Eve. This is an idea appearing in some Latin fathers, but not in any of the Greek fathers.[9] One would expect that if this was intended, the author would have been more explicit; the term *teknogenia* ("giving birth to children") is general, and its verb form (*teknogeneō*, "to give birth to children") is used at 5:14 in reference to women in the community. Given the outlook of the writer concerning the role of women (1 Tim. 4:3; 5:9-16; Titus 2:3-4), he must have the same in mind here as well. But how can he say that their salvation will come through childbearing? Salvation, for this writer, is based on the redemptive work of Christ, and that is effective for all, male and female (2:6; 2 Tim. 1:9; Titus 3:5). But for him both male and female have their own "place" in the divine order. Good deeds (1 Tim. 2:10; 5:10, 25; 6:18; 2 Tim. 3:17; Titus 2:7, 14) and piety (1 Tim. 2:2; 4:7-8; 6:11) must issue forth from the life of every Christian. In the case of women, that means to bear children and—in what appears to be an attempt to make the statement more orthodox—to maintain her virtues, **faith and love and holiness with modesty,** rather than to teach publicly or to exercise authority in the congregation. The author does not make a definitive soteriological statement concerning women that even he would raise to a dogmatic level. He is more practical here and is concerned that women carry out what he takes to be their divinely given role, attended with the proper virtues, and thereby live the life which issues in salvation. Anything else is a sign of being led astray and its consequent peril.

This section (2:11-15) must be evaluated in terms of other parts of the New Testament, including those cited above concerning the leadership of women in the Pauline congregations. One can understand the writer's aim in his own time and place. Given the fact that heretical teachers had a following among women as well as men, he thinks that he can reduce the opportunities for their success by having women silenced, bereft of authority, and subject to trusted, authorized, orthodox male leaders. Although that may have been prudent strategy for that time, place, and situation, this passage cannot be considered binding on Christian doctrine and practice for all times and places; its teaching is contradicted within the New Testament itself.

Instructions Concerning Bishops and Deacons (3:1-13)

1. The Bishop's Qualifications and Pattern of Life (3:1-7)

The section appears to provide criteria for selection of persons for the office of bishop, but it functions also as exhortation concerning how a bishop as incumbent will conduct his life. On the office of the bishop, see Introduction, Part 4, B.

1—On **the saying is sure,** see commentary on 1:15. Some commentators think that this formula refers back to 2:15 as a conclusion. Given the fact that it is usually found in a soteriological context, there is some support for such a position, but the writer can just as well be introducing what follows. Some scribes substituted for it, "there is a human saying," to smooth out the difficulty of placing a saying about episcopacy on a par with soteriological teachings introduced by the phrase (e.g., at 1:15; 4:9; 2 Tim. 2:11; Titus 3:8). The NEB follows this reading, rendering it, "there is a popular saying," but the RSV follows the stronger textual evidence. Difficult as it is, one must conclude that (1) **sure** (or "faithful," but not "human" or "popular") is the correct reading, and (2) the saying introduces what follows—a saying about episcopacy which is proverbial, but also trustworthy. Translated literally, it begins, "if anyone aspires to episcopacy" (RSV, **the office of bishop**). "Episcopacy" (oversight) need not mean strictly the office of bishop, as though 3:1 were being directed to presbyters preparing to become bishops. More likely it refers to the overseeing function of both presbyters and the bishop, who arises from among the presbyters as their "first among equals." Therefore the qualifications will apply for those seeking to be presbyters no less than those aspiring to be a bishop. (See Titus 1:5-7 and commentary on these verses.) But in the next verse (3:2) the term **bishop** is used for the first time in this letter.

2-7—What follows is mostly a list of moral qualifications. There are, however, some exceptions which are "professional" qualifications. The person must be **an apt teacher,** since preaching, teaching sound doctrine, and refuting heretics are central to his function (cf. 5:17; Titus 1:9). He must be able to manage his own household well; only then can one be sure that he will be able to **care for God's church.** This means that administrative skills and a concern for order are essential to his role. Finally, he must not be a **recent convert** (*neophytos,* "a newly planted one"). This implies that the person aspiring to leadership should be one who has learned, and made his own, that which is sound doctrine and appropriate behavior (cf. 2 Tim. 3:14-17).

Other qualifications reflect essentially an ethic of "moderation in all things." Most of the terms appearing as virtues in 3:2-7 are found only in the Pastorals in the New Testament, but they are found in Hellenistic literature as part of common moral teaching.[10] Only a few items in the list require comment. The bishop must be the **husband of one wife.** This phrase is ambiguous, but certain interpretations can be excluded. It is not meant to preclude from office (1) single persons (for the concern is for "one" wife; the phrase does not require marriage as such), although the context does take marriage for granted; (2) persons in polygamous marriages (such persons would of course be precluded, but since polygamy was prohibited for all Christians, no special point would have to be made of it here in reference to a bishop); [11] and (3) widowers who have remarried (cf. 5:14, at which young widows are urged to remarry; the remarriage of widows and widowers was not looked upon as wrong). Later on such persons were indeed precluded. Tertullian (ca. A.D. 200) indicates that persons cannot serve as priests if they have been widowed and marry again (*Exhortation to Chastity* 7).[12]

There are two possible meanings of the phrase **husband of one wife.** It may simply mean that the bishop is to be devoted to his wife, i.e., not be unfaithful.[13] But more likely it means that the bishop must not only be devoted to his wife, but—as the emphatic **one** implies—must therefore not be a person who has divorced his wife and married another.[14] This meaning, of course, would include the former, i.e., lifelong fidelity to one wife. Remarriage after divorce was prohibited for all followers in the teachings of Jesus (Matt. 19:9; Mark 10:11-12; Luke 6:18) and Paul (1 Cor. 7:10-11). If that prohibition applies to all, much more does it apply in the Pastorals to those in positions of leadership. That the bishop will have a wife and children indicates that the writer is not ascetic; in fact, he opposes heretics who would forbid marriage (4:3). That the bishop must be **well thought of by outsiders** indicates that the church has become an institution which is in public view, and its welfare is best served by having leaders who are not distrusted or held in suspicion by others, but are **well thought of** (literally, "have good testimony from those outside"). For a similar teaching in Paul, see 2 Cor. 8:21 and 1 Thess. 4:12 (cf. also Col. 4:5; 1 Peter 2:12). As indicated above, 3:2-7 provides not only a list of qualifications, but exhortations for those who are bishops as well.

2. The Deacon's Qualifications and Pattern of Life (3:8-13)

8-12—On the office of deacon, see Introduction, Part 4, C. The qualifications of deacons, as in the case of the bishop, are mostly moral ones. Yet there are some requirements which are specifically related to assuming this office. First, **they must hold the mystery of the faith with a clear conscience.** The Greek term *mystērion* is translated **mystery,** but it can have the meaning of "secret" as well (cf. Mark 4:11). In the LXX the term refers to mysteries (or "secret purposes") which are revealed by God (Dan. 2:18-19, 27-30, 45, representing Hebrew *rāz;* and Wisdom 2:22; 6:22). The Dead Sea Scrolls also speak of God's plan for the universe and history as a "mystery" *(rāz)* which is revealed to his servants at the proper time, but remains hidden to the wicked (*Habakkuk Commentary* 7:4-5, 14; *Hymn Scroll* 1:21; 5:25-26; 9:24; *Book of Mysteries* 1:3-4). This understanding of "mystery" is apparent in the writings of Paul, particularly at Rom. 16:25-26, which speaks of the "mystery which has been kept secret for long ages but is now disclosed" in the gospel (cf. also Rom. 11:25; 1 Cor. 2:7; 4:1; 15:51; in other writings, Eph. 1:9-10; 3:4-5, 9; Col. 1:26-27; 2:2-3). In the Pastorals, however, there is a different nuance. Here the **mystery of the faith** is the Christian faith as received and held by believers who stand in apostolic tradition—which is an understanding of the term appearing in the Apostolic Fathers also (cf. Ignatius, *Letter to the Trallians* 3.2; *Letter to the Ephesians* 19.1; *Letter to Diognetus* 4.6; 7.1; 10.7). It is essentially a Christological confession, as indicated in 3:16 ("the mystery of our religion," followed by a Christological hymn). Whoever would be a deacon must therefore have first given assent—**with a clear conscience** (without reservations)—to Christian teaching; moral qualities and a willingness to serve are not sufficient. Yet, as 3:10 indicates, deacons must also be **tested first; then if they prove themselves blameless let them serve as deacons.** It is not said who is to do the testing or how long the process is to take. Most likely all that is meant is that the candidate is to have a good reputation in the community. At one place Ignatius touches upon both themes (mysteries and reputation): "Those too who are deacons of Jesus Christ's 'mysteries' must give complete satisfaction to everyone. For they do not serve mere food and drink, but minister to God's church. They must therefore avoid leaving themselves open to criticism, as they would shun fire" (*Letter to the Trallians* 2.3).

11—It is unclear whether the author is speaking of deacons' wives or deaconesses. The Greek text reads, "women likewise [must be] serious, not slanderers, temperate, faithful in all things." The KJV, NEB, TEV, and NIV have made an exegetical decision, reading "their wives," while the RSV, JB, and NAB read simply **the women,** which leaves the question open. The Greek text has words for neither "their" nor "the" before "women." (The Greek *gynaikas,* an accusative plural, can be translated as either "women" or "wives.") No commentator is absolutely certain what is meant. Some tend to read 3:11 as a reference to deacons' wives; [15] others take it to refer to deaconnesses; [16] some leave the question open; [17] and finally there is the suggestion that we cannot detect here a "distinct order of deaconnesses," but nevertheless a ministry of women in visitation and attending women candidates for Baptism.[18] No certainty can be achieved, but there is reason to conclude that the writer is speaking of women who are involved in diaconal service rather than simply being closely associated with the work of their husbands (who are deacons). If so, some (hypothetically all) could in fact be single.

The term *diakonos* can apply to women (cf. Rom. 16:1) as well as men, and it may be that in 3:8-13 the writer speaks of (1) general qualifications for deacons/deaconnesses (3:8-10); (2) specific qualifications for deaconnesses (3:11); and (3) those for deacons (3:12-13). Yet this is doubtful for two reasons: (1) at 3:11 the author uses the term *hōsautōs* (**likewise**) which, as at 3:8, makes a shift to another group of persons, and (2) at 3:12 the term **deacons** is reintroduced (as though 3:11 interrupts the discussion), and it clearly refers now to men. Perhaps the best that we can conclude is that while *diakonos* applies to male deacons, there are also **women** (not "wives") involved in diaconal service, even if they do not bear the title in this community.[19]

13—The **good standing** which deacons who serve well gain **for themselves** is to be thought of in terms of their standing within the community, not before God. They also gain **great confidence** (the NEB translation "the right to speak openly" is to be dismissed) **in the faith.** That is, they gain a sense of certainty in the truth of the Christian faith.

The Church and Its Confession (3:14-16)

14-15a—Paul's letters sometimes speak of his intended coming to visit his various addressees (Rom. 1:10, 13; 15:23, 29, 32; 1 Cor. 4:18-19, 21; 11:34; 2 Cor. 12:14, 20-21; 13:1; Phil. 2:24), and also of his being hindered in doing so (Rom. 1:13; 15:22; 1 Thess. 2:18). The writer of the Pastorals has resorted to this feature of Paul's letters to stress that even in Paul's absence—indeed even if no one in the congregation could recall that Paul had ever given **these instructions** personally on location—they are to be followed (cf. 4:13). The words **if I am delayed** portend that Paul would not arrive to confirm the contents of this letter. The letter is sufficient to represent him. The verses do not presume that Paul is in prison. A prison setting is affirmed only in 2 Timothy (1:8, 16-17; 2:9; 4:6-9), but 1 Timothy and Titus (cf. 3:12) presume freedom to travel.

15b—Three phrases are used to describe the church. The first is **household of God** (RSV and NEB; KJV has "house of God," which suggests a place and is not accurate in this context), comparing it to an extended family in which God is head and each person a member (cf. Gal. 6:10; Eph. 2:19-22; Heb. 3:6; 1 Peter 2:5; 4:17). Further it is the **church of the living God. Church** represents *ekklēsia,* which appears in the LXX to represent the Hebrew *qahal,* "assembly." The term **living God** (cf. 4:10) appears in the Old Testament (Deut. 5:26; Pss. 42:2; 84:2; Isa. 37:4, 17; Jer. 10:10; 23:36; Dan. 6:20, 26; Hos. 1:10) and in the writings of Paul (2 Cor. 3:3; 6:16; 1 Thess. 1:9). But to speak of the church as the "assembly of the living God" is unique to this writer, who thereby stresses the role of responsiveness to God, which is to characterize the community. Finally, the church is the **pillar and bulwark of the truth.** The sense of the Greek is not so much that the church is a **bulwark,**

protecting the truth (as the RSV and NEB imply), but a "foundation" (*hedraiōma;* KJV, "ground"). At Qumram the instruction is given to "lay a foundation of truth for Israel" (*Rule of the Community* 5:5). So for this writer, the church is a **pillar** (in the sense of "support"; cf. Sir. 24:4; 36:24) and "foundation" of the truth in the midst of conflicting claims. The truth does not rest upon the church, as though the church can never err, but the church is ever seeking to uphold the truth.

16—The Christ-hymn, it has been said, is the "high-point of the whole letter." [20] The author recognizes its importance in his introduction to the hymn (translated literally): "undisputedly great is the mystery of our religion." The word "undisputedly" reflects the Greek *homologoumenōs,* an adverb found only here in the New Testament, and combines ideas of confession and common agreement in matters under dispute (RSV renders it as a clause, **we confess,** and NEB as "beyond all question"). On **mystery,** see commentary on 3:9. The fact that 3:16 goes far beyond the theological concerns of the immediate context indicates that the author is quoting a hymn from an earlier source; therefore, the verse is presented in poetic form.

The first word (*hos* in the earliest and best manuscript witnesses) is a masculine relative pronoun ("who" in English), which has no antecedent in the text of this letter, although it must refer to Christ. We can assume that it would have clearly referred to him in the original, fully-intact hymn. The same pronoun appears in the hymn quoted by Paul (Phil. 2:6); it too lacks an antecedent, except for that supplied by Paul himself prior to quoting it. Some Greek manuscripts of 1 Timothy read *theos* ("God") for the first word of the hymn and the KJV follows this reading, but this reading appears in Greek manuscripts no earlier than the eighth century. Still other Greek manuscripts read *ho* ("which," a neuter pronoun) to refer back to *mystērion* (a neuter noun). But the earliest and best read *hos* ("who") referring to Christ. Some modern translations (RSV, JB, TEV, NAB, and NIV) read **he,** referring to Christ, to supply a subject and thereby smooth out the awkward syntax (NEB reads, "he who," which is cumbersome).

In form the hymn consists of six lines. Each line contains a verb in the third person, singular, aorist (simple past tense), passive (**was manifested . . . vindicated . . . seen . . . proclaimed . . . believed on . . . taken up**) and a noun in the dative, usually preceded by **in** (**in the flesh . . . in the Spirit . . . by angels . . . in** [or among] **the nations . . . in the world . . . in glory**). Since comments to follow are rather detailed, it is necessary to place the hymn here, providing numerals for each line. The translation is our own.

1. Who was manifested in [the] flesh,
2. Vindicated by [the] Spirit,
3. Made visible to angels,
4. Proclaimed among [the] nations,
5. Believed on in [the] world,
6. Taken up in glory.

It has been suggested that the hymn consists of three couplets, each consisting of two lines (1 and 2 the first, 3 and 4 the second, 5 and 6 the third). Further, each couplet has to do with the "earthly" and "heavenly" spheres of Christ's destiny in the following pattern: earthly-heavenly (1 and 2), heavenly-earthly (3 and 4), earthly-heavenly (5 and 6). The hymnist, according to this view, affirmed that through Christ earth and heaven have been reunited; there is no longer any separation between God and his people.[21]

Attractive as this is, it is not without problems. It is not clear, for example, that line 2 speaks of the "heavenly" sphere. On the contrary, it appears that in the thought of the hymnist the vindication of Christ **in the Spirit** took place on earth (the resurrection/exaltation, as indicated in similar confessional formulations, e.g., Rom. 1:4; 8:11; 1 Peter 3:18; cf. Heb. 9:14), and that it is only at line 3, **made visible to angels,** that Christ is portrayed as entering the "heavenly" sphere (cf. Phil. 2:10).

Furthermore, lines 3 and 4 do not necessarily form a unity. In fact, a case can be made for a division of the six lines into two stanzas of three lines each, as some commentators claim.[22] In this case the first three lines have to do with Christ's life on earth (1 and 2) together with a refrain (3), and the next three have to do with his continued postresurrection life in the church (4 and 5) plus a refrain (6).

Both attempts at discerning a structure are plausible, but they may be artificial and the hymnist may have had neither in mind. It is more plausible that the hymnist composed lines 1 through 5 to recite in song the general course of events in the story of salvation through Christ: (1) incarnation, (2) exaltation, (3) heavenly reign of Christ, (4) proclamation in the world, and (5) the consequent emergence of the believing community. Line 6 **taken up in glory** serves as a final, doxological exclamation. Rooted in apocalyptic thought, **glory** signifies the status of the Son of man (Dan. 7:14; *2 Baruch* 30.1; Mark 8:38; 13:26, etc.). The term is also used more generally as an attribute of the risen Christ, who has entered into his glory (Luke 24:26; John 17:5; 2 Cor. 3:18; 4:4; 8:23; Heb. 1:3; 2:9; 1 Peter 1:21, etc.). If line 6 refers specifically to the ascension (cf. "taken up" in Acts 1:2), it should be placed between lines 2 and 3 for a strict chronological progression. But it need not have so specific a reference. Line 6 can best be seen as a doxological conclusion to the hymn, testifying that the Christ—who became incarnate and who has been vindicated, manifested to angels, proclaimed, and believed on—has been **taken up** and endowed with glory, sharing the heavenly glory of God. He will appear in glory at the close of the age (Titus 2:13), and believers will share his glory (2 Tim. 2:10). The line serves as a doxology, which is the appropriate conclusion of hymns (cf. Phil. 2:11), benedictions, blessings (Rom. 11:36; Gal. 1:5; Eph. 3:21; 1 Tim. 1:17; Rev. 1:16; *1 Clement* 5.7; 20.12), and prayers (*Didache* 8.2; cf. also the doxology to the Lord's Prayer, Matt. 6:13, found in later

manuscripts; it does not likely belong to the original text of
Matthew, but reflects early Christian liturgical practices). Although the line shares the same grammatical form as the
others, it serves as a doxological conclusion to the hymn.

The hymn reflects a theological outlook, but it does not
intend to be comprehensive. For example, there is no reference
in it to the death of Christ (on this, compare the short creedal
statement in Rom. 1:3-4 which also lacks such; but contrast
Phil. 2:8, at which Paul inserts an explicit reference to the
cross, and 1 Peter 3:18). The focus is upon Christ, who has
appeared on earth, has returned to heavenly glory, and is now
proclaimed and believed on in the community of faith. Nor
does one learn from this hymn what the contents of this proclamation would be, except the basic outline of the story of salvation given by the hymn itself. But a hymn need not offer so
much. The community gathered for worship, making use of
this hymn, recites in song the story of salvation: Christ has
appeared for the salvation of the world and now reigns in
heaven; Christ is **believed on** in the world as Savior as a
consequence of proclamation. Those who believe have come
under the lordship of the heavenly, reigning Christ and therefore belong to him eternally, even while **in the world.** The
writer of the Pastorals makes use of this hymn to express the
mystery of the Christian faith. For all his rather prosaic outlook elsewhere, he is able to sense that the **mystery** does not
consist merely of received doctrine. The closer one apprehends
the **mystery,** the more one senses how **great** it is (**great . . . is
the mystery of our faith),** and at that point the language of
the community at worship is the most appropriate vehicle of
expression.

Expectations and Duties of Ministry in the Church (4:1–5:2)

After providing instructions for conduct at worship (2:1-15),
recounting the qualifications of bishops and deacons (3:1-13),

and speaking of the church and its confession (3:14-16), the author discusses the problems and duties of those engaged in ministry. It appears for the most part that the instructions are for Timothy (4:6-7, 11-16). Nevertheless, the writer "talks past" Timothy to the leadership of the congregation addressed.

1. False Teaching and Apostasy to Be Expected (4:1-5)

1-2—The Spirit expressly says. Here the writer has in mind the utterances of the Spirit through inspired prophets, and it appears that he considers himself such. The phrase **in later times** is found nowhere else in the New Testament in the precise form appearing here, but it is equivalent to other expressions for the last days before the parousia (cf. 2 Tim. 3:1). In common with other New Testament writers, this writer claims that in the times before the end there will be false teachers who try to lead believers into apostasy (cf. Mark 13:22; Acts 20:29-30; 2 Thess. 2:3, 11-12; 2 Peter 2:1-3; 3:3-4; 1 John 2:18; 4:1; Jude 18). These heretical teachers are called **deceitful spirits** and their teachings are **doctrines of demons.** The heretics are not merely wrong; they are agents of Satan himself (cf. 2 Cor. 2:11; 4:4; 11:13-14; Eph. 6:12; James 3:15). They are **liars** whose **consciences are seared;** the Greek term for **seared** is also used for "branding" with a red-hot iron and suggests that in respect to conscience these persons are captivated and claimed by Satan (so NEB has, "whose own conscience is branded with the devil's sign"). Cf. 2 Tim. 2:26.

3-5—The author spells out two of the false teachings of the heretics: (1) they **forbid** persons to marry; and (2) they demand **abstinence from** certain **foods.** For more on their teachings, see the Introduction, Part 5. The heretics teach an asceticism which is contrary to the will of God. While at one place Paul had advised persons not to marry in light of the coming end (1 Cor. 7:8, 25-26), he did not forbid marriage, but assumed that most persons would and should marry (1 Cor. 7:2-6, 9, 36-38). The writer of the Pastorals has an even more positive view of marriage and holds it as the norm (1 Tim. 2:15; 5:14; Titus 2:4; cf. 1 Tim. 3:2, 12; Titus 1:6). Concerning **foods,** Jewish dietary laws prohibited eating certain foods (e.g., Lev. 11:1-47). Whether the heretics based their prohibitions on Jewish law or on other ascetic practices is unclear. In any case, the Gospels indicate that according to the teachings of Jesus all foods are clean (Mark 7:15, 19), and Paul's judgment was the same, although he granted that one may refrain from eating certain foods if such action should cause offense (Rom. 14:2-3; 1 Cor. 8:7-13; 10:23-33; see also Peter's vision at Joppa, Acts 10:9-16, and Col. 2:16, 20-23). The writer asserts that all that is created by God is good. According to Genesis, God himself saw that all things created were good (1:4, 10, 12, 18, 21, 25, 31), and both vegetation and animal life are given as food (1:29; 9:3). Therefore for this writer nothing is to be rejected if it is received **with thanksgiving** (4:3, 4; cf. Titus 1:15). Verse 5 reads literally, "for it is consecrated through God's word and prayer." **The word of God** appears to refer to the passages in Genesis which declare all things good, and **prayer** is the prayer of thanksgiving over food, which gives honor to God as giver (Rom. 14:6; 1 Cor. 10:31).

2. *Duties of Ministry (4:6-10)*

6—If you put these instructions before the brethren is unclear as to referent, but it is likely to refer to all instructions prior and after (cf. 1:18; 4:11; 6:2; Titus 2:15; 3:8)—all that is entrusted to Timothy (1 Tim. 6:20). **You will be a good minister** *(diakonos)* does not refer to a particular office within the ministry, such as deacon, but has the more general sense of "servant" (NEB). Although Timothy is being addressed, the message is for the leaders of the community.

7a—On **godless and silly myths,** see commentary at 1:4; Titus 1:14; and the Introduction, Part 5. A literal translation would be: "avoid the profane, old wives' myths." Cf. NEB ("godless myths, fit only for old women") which, offensive though it may be, is quite accurate in translation.

7b-8—The author uses imagery of the athlete (cf. 2 Tim. 2:5; 4:7-8), as does Paul at 1 Cor. 9:25. Timothy is to train himself in **godliness** (or "piety," *eusebeia*), a term appearing frequently along with "faith" as the proper religious attitude and manner of life (cf. 2:2; 6:3) or as an equivalent of true religion itself (cf. 3:16; 2 Tim. 3:5). Here the former nuance is intended. Piety "in reference to all things" *(pros panta)* is "beneficial" *(ōphelimos),* "since it possesses promise of the life which is now and which is about to come." The writer does not teach that "piety" brings eternal life as a reward, but that it possesses the promise of eternal life. God has made eternal life available through "our Savior Christ Jesus" (2 Tim. 1:10), and true "piety," like faith, takes hold of God's promise.

9—On this formula see the commentary at 1:15. The "faithful saying" is that given in 4:8. The NEB is edited to imply that it refers to what follows (4:10), but the fact that 4:10 is introduced by *gar* (**for**), making a transition, favors linking 4:9 with what precedes in 4:8.[23]

10—**For to this end**—that is, training in godliness, which possesses the promise of eternal life—**we toil and strive.** The basis for the toiling and striving is given: **because we have our hope set on the living God.** Since God is the **living God** (see commentary at 3:15), "piety" is the appropriate response; at the same time, the **living God** is able to confirm his promises, thereby giving a basis for hope. The last clause (literally, "who is Savior of all persons, especially believers") causes problems for translation, exegesis, and theology. First of all, does it imply a universal salvation? If so, why are believers spoken of separately ("especially believers")? Various proposals have been made: (1) that stress is to be upon the term **all**—over against the Gnostic idea of an elite group capable of salvation — but that the writer claims only believers in fact will be saved;[24] (2) that the writer means that God is potentially

Savior of all (cf. 2:4) or in some sense (as Creator and pre-server) is Savior of all, but that only believers will be granted eternal salvation in the end; [25] (3) that there is in fact en-visioned here a universal salvation of all people, but believers are singled out as those who have certainty of it on earth; [26] and (4) that the phrase "especially believers" is a scribal addi-tion.[27] With the exception of the last assertion (which is very speculative, since all known Greek texts contain the phrase), any of the other three interpretations is possible. But certain items should be stressed: (1) the clause speaks of God in a confessional sense, so the clause is not first of all a statement on soteriology or the destiny of the human race; (2) the term **especially** *(malista)* is inclusive (cf. 5:8, 17; Gal. 6:10; Phil. 4:22), not exclusive, which speaks against making a distinction between potential ("all persons") and actual recipients ("be-lievers") of God's salvation; and (3) the Greek genitive has an adjectival nuance so that the clause can be rendered: " [the living God], who is all persons' Savior, especially be-lievers' [Savior]," although this is awkward in English. There-fore the writer is saying that hope has been placed in **the living God,** who is **Savior** for **all** persons, among whom in particular there are believers living in faith and piety who know him as Savior already. That God is Savior of all persons remains for him a general truth (cf. 2:3-6), even though all persons may not recognize God as such. Believers know God as Savior already, so he is **especially** their Savior. This means that the writer holds in tension the universality of grace for all humankind—a grace which knows no limits (cf. Rom. 5:18-19; 11:25-32; 1 Cor. 15:22-28; 2 Cor. 5:19; Phil. 2:10-11; Eph. 1:9-10; Col. 1:19-20; 1 John 2:2) on the one hand, and the particularity of faith which accepts this grace for onself on the other. The ultimate salvation of the whole human race is not ruled out, but the focus is finally on the community of believers as those who belong to the redeemed.

3. Practice of Ministry (4:11–5:2)

11-12—Timothy is portrayed as a young man. According to Acts 16:1, Paul recruited Timothy after the Jerusalem conference (ca. A.D. 49). At that time Timothy could have been relatively young, born perhaps as recently as ca. A.D. 30, although an earlier date of birth would be equally possible. If the Pastorals were actually written by Paul, Timothy could still have been relatively young (30-35 years old) at the time of their composition, but hardly a "youth." It is more likely that the Pastorals are post-Pauline (see Introduction, Parts 1 and 2), and that the writer is "talking past" Timothy to the congregational leadership, for whom there is no prerequisite concerning age, except that adulthood would naturally be expected. Some presbyter-bishops could be relatively young (see Introduction, Part 4, A). Ignatius wrote, "It is not right to presume on the youthfulness of your bishop" (*Letter to the Magnesians* 3.1). In order to win respect, the leader is to set an example in speech, conduct, love, faith, and purity.

13—**Till I come** recalls 3:14 (see commentary there). Three things are required: **public reading of scripture** (RSV; the Greek says simply "reading," which the KJV preserves, but the term is not likely to mean private reading, for just as the next two items refer to public activities, so "reading" would be **public reading**, giving support to the RSV rendering; moreover, elsewhere the term refers to reading of the Old Testament at worship, e.g., at Acts 13:15; 2 Cor. 3:14), "exhortation" (NEB correctly; RSV renders the term as **preaching**), and **teaching.** Worship will contain all three elements, as well as prayer (2:8). Conspicuously lacking in the Pastorals is any reference to the Eucharist. The leadership of the congregation is to be well acquainted with Scripture (cf. 2 Tim. 2:15-17) and apostolic teaching (cf. Titus 1:9), and also able to teach and preach effectively (1 Tim. 3:2; 5:17; Titus 1:9).

14—Still speaking ostensibly to Timothy, but actually addressing the congregational leaders, the writer reminds them that they have received a **gift** *(charisma)* which was given—rendering the Greek literally—(1) "through prophetic utterances" (2) "with [or "accompanied with"] the laying on of hands of the presbytery" (RSV translates the last term, **council of elders**). If the verse speaks of the ordination of those who are presently congregational leaders involved in public reading, exhortation, and teaching (i.e., the bishop and the presbyters), not to Timothy's "ordination," then the discrepancy with 2 Tim. 1:6, where Paul is spoken of as the one who had laid hands on Timothy, is overcome. These congregational leaders belong already to the second or third generation, since some are apparently relatively young (cf. 4:12). They would therefore have been ordained by leaders before them. There can be little doubt—given the functions of the presbyters—that learning was a prerequisite for ordination (cf. 2 Tim. 3:14-17), although that is not mentioned here. The emphasis rather is that leaders are endowed at the time of ordination with a *charisma* of the Spirit (2 Tim. 1:6) as prophetic utterances and the laying on of hands take place in unison. The laying on of hands was performed by the presbyters, and the utterances may also have been made by them; or perhaps the utterances were made by charismatic prophets in the community, or even by members of the community who would not necessarily have been spoken of as "prophets," but who spoke spontaneously as the Spirit gave utterance.[28] It is not certain that there were prophets in the communities addressed by the Pastorals (the only reference to a prophet in the Pastorals is at Titus 1:12, but that person is a pagan poet at Crete). The term "prophecy" appears twice (1 Tim. 1:18; 4:14), and in each case it is best to take it as a charismatic utterance by members of the community, perhaps including certain presbyters at 4:14.

The laying on of hands by the presbyters is modeled on the rite of ordination in Judaism. At Num. 27:18-23 Moses invests Joshua, in whom the Spirit of the Lord dwells, with authority through the laying on of hands. At Deut. 34:9, however, Joshua is said to have received the "spirit of wisdom" as a consequence of the laying on of hands by Moses. At any rate, in both instances Moses commissions Joshua as his successor through this ceremonial act. In Judaism (the earliest literary evidence comes from about A.D. 80,[29] prior to the writing of the Pastorals) rabbinic ordination included the laying on of hands, by which authority was transmitted from a rabbi to the one being ordained, and it was thought that such a ceremony linked the ordained in an unbroken chain of succession to Moses. At 1 Tim. 4:14 the writer ostensibly refers to the ordination of Timothy, but in fact it is the bishop and presbyters in the community who are to recall their own ordinations as the moment at which they received a *charisma,* and who are therefore to exercise a ministry with authority in "true succession" from the apostles, especially Paul.

15-16—A congregational leader must be devoted to the tasks assigned, and then progress will become evident. **You will save both yourself and your hearers.** God alone is Savior and saves, but God's saving work takes place through the ministry of the Word, by which people are called to believe and to lead the Christian life (2:3-7; 2 Tim. 1:9-10).

5:1-2—These verses can be taken with the foregoing instructions on the practice of ministry; 5:3 begins a new section on order and duties in the congregation. **Rebuke** translates a Greek word which implies "striking out at a person." The leader is not to rebuke **an older man** (RSV, correctly; KJV and NEB have "elder," which can be confused with "presbyter," but here the context implies "older man"), but is to **exhort** such a person to realize his Christian responsibility (cf. 4:13; 6:2). The congregation is portrayed as an extended family. Older men and women are to be treated as parents; younger persons as brothers and sisters.

Order and Duties in the Congregation (5:3—6:2a)

1. Instructions Concerning Widows (5:3-16)

3-8—Only **real widows** are to be honored. Who are these persons? Clearly not every widowed woman qualifies. At 5:9 only certain women are eligible to be **enrolled** within a designated group of **widows** (the existence of a designated group of **widows** is also attested in Ignatius, *Letter to the Smyrnaeans* 13.1; *Letter to Polycarp* 4.1; and *Letter of Polycarp* 4.3). Their main function is intercessory prayer (5:4; *Letter of Polycarp* 4.3). The prerequisites for the widows who can be enrolled and honored are that they be at least 60 years old (5:9; cf. 5:11, 14), of sound reputation (5:10), lacking support from relatives (5:4-5, 8, 16), and of course willing to engage in the ministry of widows, particularly intercession. The syntax of 5:4 is as awkward in Greek as it is in English (RSV, NEB). Those who are to learn their **duty** are clearly not the widows, but the **children** and **grandchildren** of widows. A true widow is one who **is left all alone** and **has set her hope on God**. The words translated **is self-indulgent** (5:6) can have the stronger force of voluptuous and luxurious living (cf. James 5:5 where the same Greek terminology is used). At 5:8 the author speaks again of the **relatives** of a widow and their responsibility for her (as at 5:4). To fail to care for one's **family** (in this case, one's mother or grandmother) is to deny **the faith** (cf. the commandment of Exod. 20:12 and its application in Matt. 15:5-6).

9-16—The verb **to enroll** *(katalegō)* is a technical term used in Hellenistic culture for the "enlisting" of soldiers, senators, or members of a religious body. **Sixty years of age** appears arbitrary. The requirement implies that there were other widows in the community, and some principle of selection (however arbitrary) had to be imposed. At that age a woman would be less likely to **desire to marry** (5:11) or have opportunity to do so. But the **younger widows** should marry and **bear children**

(5:14), thereby sparing the church the expense which would result (cf. 5:16). From 5:11-12 it appears that there had been instances in which younger widows had been enrolled, but that they had grown **wanton against Christ,** had married, and had therefore **violated their first pledge.** The **first pledge** is not likely their first marriage vow, but a pledge of primary loyalty to Christ at the time of their being enrolled among the widows [30] (cf. Polycarp, *Letter to the Philippians* 4.3, "the widows should be discreet in their faith pledged to the Lord"). The requirement that the candidate for enrollment have been **the wife of one husband** corresponds to the requirements for the bishop (3:2) and deacons (3:12), i.e., she is not to have been divorced and remarried (see commentary at 3:2). Her good deeds must be well known to the community (5:10; cf. 3:7 regarding a similar criterion for the bishop), and these are specified—having reared children, having been hospitable (cf. 3:2, 4), having **washed the feet of the saints,** having **relieved the afflicted,** and having been devoted to any other good work. Although these are listed as prerequisites, it is likely that the ministry of the widows consisted precisely of these very activities, along with intercessions (5:5). Their ministry would have included home visitations (cf. 5:13) among the afflicted, bringing their needs to the attention of the community, and prayer. Offering hospitality would be another function. Foot washing (5:10) was a sign and gesture of hospitality, along with the offer of food and lodging, which is attested in the Old Testament, Jewish, and Graeco-Roman literature.[31] It is probable that the foot washing referred to here was conducted to welcome **saints** (Christians) arriving from other communities, and that this was followed by the offer of food and lodging. Hospitality is to characterize the community addressed by the Pastorals (3:2; Titus 1:8), just as in the case of other New Testament congregations (cf. Rom. 12:13; Heb. 13:2; 1 Peter 4:9).

2. Duties toward, Disciplining, and Selecting Presbyters (5:17-25)

17—Presbyters (**elders** in RSV and NEB) "preside" *(proïstēmi,* "to preside" or "to be at the head of"; RSV has **rule**) over the congregation. The verb is not limited to liturgical functions (cf. 1 Thess. 5:12) but includes leadership on a broad scale within the community. (On the office of the presbyter, see the Introduction, Part 4, A.) Presbyters who **preside well** are worthy of **double honor.** The Greek for the latter term can suggest "double pay," and the fact that 5:18 speaks of payment indicates that this is intended. It can be concluded from 5:17-18 that presbyters received financial support from the congregation, but certain ones received more than others. Who will these be? Included **especially** are those who labor **in preaching and teaching** (literally, "in [the] word and teaching"). Beyond this circle there may of course be additional persons, as local circumstances require. It is probable that the writer appeals to the congregation to provide full compensation (a "living wage") for its presbyters, for the similar wording of the instruction to "honor widows" (5:3) implies full support (cf. 5:16), and 5:18 implies the same in the case of presbyters as well. Already in Paul's letters (1 Cor. 9:4-14; 2 Cor. 11:9; Gal. 6:6; Phil. 4:15-18) there are indications that full-time service was to be recognized as deserving full support.

18—A scriptural "proof" is offered for the position taken. **For the scripture says** (a formula used by Paul in Rom. 4:3; 9:17; 10:11; Gal. 4:30) is followed by two sayings. The first is from Deut. 25:4, which Paul quotes at 1 Cor. 9:9. The second (**the laborer deserves his wages**) is found at Luke 10:7 (cf. also Matt. 10:10, which is similar). The writer clearly considers Deuteronomy as Scripture. Does it follow that he considers Luke to be Scripture too? Some commentators, who think of the Pastorals as deutero-Pauline and written after the writing of Luke's gospel, answer the question affirmatively.[32] Others, who maintain Pauline authorship of the Pastorals and therefore claim that they were written prior to Luke's gospel, have suggested that the author quotes from a collection of sayings of Jesus which Luke employed in his gospel and which Paul also used and considered Scripture.[33] But there is another option which is to be preferred. That is that the term **Scripture** applies only to the first saying from Deut. 25:4. The second saying is taken neither from Luke 10:7 nor a source employed by Luke, but from common tradition. The author does not concern himself with whether it is a quotation from Scripture (the Old Testament) or from Jesus, but simply appends it as a common proverbial saying which carries its own logical weight. Its existence in Luke can be taken as evidence of its currency in Christian tradition, as can the similar saying in Matt. 10:10. One need not think of a common literary source for the three instances of the proverbial saying.

19—The duty of the congregation toward its presbyters is to go beyond financial support. No **charge** or "accusation" against a presbyter is to be accepted unless it is supported by two or three witnesses. This rule has a basis in Jewish law (Deut. 19:15), which is also the rule in the communities of Matthew (18:16) and Paul (2 Cor. 13:1). In these latter texts the rule applies to charges against any person, while the writer of the Pastorals applies it to accusations against presbyters in particular. He does not want presbyters to be subject to charges on the basis of hearsay or possible personal antagonism by an individual, regardless of how important such a person may be. At least two must support charges as **witnesses** to actual misconduct.

20-21—It is unclear whether the phrase **those who persist in sin** (RSV; the Greek has simply "those who sin") refers to Christians in general or only to presbyters. Since the context concerns duties toward and the disciplining of presbyters, however, the latter is more likely. Verse 19 requires the presence of at least two witnesses in bringing charges; verse 20 reads, literally, "reprove [or "convict"] those who sin before all"; and then verse 21 indicates that no favoritism or partiality is to be allowed. Presbyters are to have no special treatment; the only due regard for them is to be met by proper and just procedures (the presence of at least two witnesses). The solemnity and seriousness of all this is underscored by the use of a phrase which has parallels at two other places at which special emphasis is made (2 Tim. 2:14; 4:1); it can be translated here, "I solemnly charge you in the presence of God. . . ."

22—It is not clear whether **the laying on of hands** refers to ordination, as at 4:14, or to the restoration of penitents after discipline. The NEB renders the verse, "Do not be over-hasty in laying on of hands in ordination," but it also has a footnote providing an alternative, "in restoring an offender by the laying on of hands." The Greek has neither interpretive, qualifying phrase. In this regard the RSV reflects the ambiguity of the Greek, as does the JB and NIV (TEV adds "for the Lord's service," implying ordination). Commentators are divided. Several think that ordination is being spoken of,[34] while others think that the restoration of penitents is the writer's concern.[35] One commentator leaves the question open,[36] and still another concludes that the writer is speaking of the restoration of offending presbyters.[37] While a conclusion cannot be certain, it is likely that the author has ordination in mind, since (1) elsewhere in the Pastorals the laying on of hands refers to ordination (4:14; 2 Tim. 1:6), but never to restoring penitents; and (2) the restoration of penitents through the laying on of hands is attested otherwise only in sources from the third century and later (Cyprian, *Letters* 74.12; Eusebius, *Ecclesiastical History* 7.2; *Didascalia* 2.41; *Apostolic Constitutions* 2.18.7); never does it have that meaning in the New Testament (unless here). Ordination is therefore reserved only for those who have become well attested in the community (cf. 3:2-7; Titus 1:6-9); the neophyte cannot be considered (cf. 3:6). To ordain a person who is not trustworthy (cf. 2 Tim. 2:2) and who may subsequently be charged with wrongdoing (5:19-21) would be irre-

sponsible. More than that, it would be equivalent of partici-
pating **in another man's sins.** The writer thinks of presbyterial
culpability in the matter of selection and ordination of fellow
presbyters. He adds, **keep yourself pure.** He therefore not only
provides qualifications for bishops and presbyters (3:1-7; Titus
1:5-9), but goes beyond that to affirm that the very selection
of presbyters is itself a spiritual and moral matter having consequences for those who make the selection themselves (cf.
4:14 and commentary on that verse).

23—Although the writer has said **keep yourself pure,** this
does not mean that one should practice asceticism. The Stoic
philosopher Epictetus (ca. A.D. 55-135) taught that one should
"drink water only" (*Discourses* 3.13.21), using the same Greek
verb as here *(hydropotein),* as a matter of discipline. Likewise,
certain heretical teachers taught asceticism in the communities
to which the Pastorals were addressed (cf. 4:3-5). But the
author will have nothing to do with that. His aim is moderation, not asceticism. He condemns drunkenness (3:3, 8; Titus
2:2), but he recognizes that wine can have positive medicinal
benefits. The writer stands in the center of Jewish-Christian
tradition, in which drunkenness is condemned (Isa. 5:11; 28:7;
56:11-12; Hab. 2:5; Hos. 4:11; 7:5; Prov. 20:1; Luke 21:34;
Eph. 5:18; 1 Peter 4:3), but moderation is accepted as a matter of course (Judges 9:13; Ps. 104:15; Sir. 31:28-29; cf. John
2:1-11), and the medicinal benefit of wine used in moderation
is known (2 Sam. 16:2; Prov. 31:6). The writer does not seem
to be confronted with the problem which Paul faced, in which
he wrote that a Christian should not drink wine if it causes
the "weaker brother" to fall (Rom. 14:21). For this writer the
concern is to stress a middle course between asceticism and
excess. Since **wine** has some positive benefits for **stomach**
troubles (caused perhaps by drinking impure water) and other
ailments, it is to be used in moderation (cf. 4:4).

24-25—Still concerned about the selection and ordination of
presbyters, the writer indicates that unworthy candidates fall

into two basic categories: those whose **sins** are **conspicuous,** and those whose sins are latent but will show up **later.** The point made shows why one should not be hasty in ordaining candidates (5:22). On the other hand, there are worthy candidates. They fall into two categories as well: either their good deeds are obvious already, or such persons show promise of good deeds, which **cannot remain hidden** for long.

3. *Duties of the Christian Slave (6:1-2a)*

The institution of slavery predates the New Testament era by centuries, and it was common in the Graeco-Roman world. According to one estimate, about 20% of the population of the Roman Empire consisted of slaves.[38] The New Testament writers accept the institution as a matter of course, and it is clear that many Christians of that time were slaves themselves. The mistreatment of slaves is repudiated (Eph. 6:9; Col. 4:1; *Didache* 4.10; *Epistle of Barnabas* 19.7), and Paul tells slaves to take the opportunity to gain freedom if it is offered (1 Cor. 7:21), affirms that in Christ there is no distinction between slave and free (Gal. 3:28; cf. 1 Cor. 12:13), and attempts a reconciliation between the slave Onesimus and his master Philemon, appealing to the latter to accept his slave as a brother (Philemon 16) and hinting that he ought to grant him freedom (Philemon 21). More often in the New Testament, however, Christian slaves are called upon in "household codes" to accept their situation and serve their masters in subordination and with respect (Eph. 6:5-8; Col. 3:22-25; 1 Tim. 6:1-2; Titus 2:9-10; 1 Peter 2:18-25). The writer of the Pastorals recognizes that masters of slaves may be non-Christians or Christians (**believing masters,** 6:2), which indicates that there were Christian slave owners (cf. Eph. 6:9; Col. 4:1). When slaves do not respect their masters, **the name of God and the teaching** are blasphemed (or **defamed,** RSV), he says. Why this is so is not said, but the most likely reason is that the Christian is to have respect for all persons (Titus 3:2); to treat anyone with contempt brings disrepute upon the Christian faith and the church. A special problem arises when the master is a Christian. The temptation is to appeal to the fact that in Christ both master and slave are **brethren,** and therefore the conventional proprieties of the master-slave relationship can be dispensed with. But the author calls for a second look on the matter: since the master is a Christian, **serve all the better,** since it is a fellow Christian who benefits from such service.

It can be regretted that the writer does not speak to the **believing masters,** calling upon them to treat their slaves with respect or even to free them. In this regard he appears to identify with the slave owners and their class over against those who are slaves. Nevertheless, this cannot be pressed. It may simply be that among the Christians addressed there were more slaves than masters, and so he spoke to them. It may also be the case that no cases of abuse were known. The writer does go on to say that the wealthy are to be "rich in good deeds, liberal and generous" (6:18), which would include fair and even generous treatment of any slaves they might have.

True and False Teaching (6:2b-21a)

1. False Teaching and Its Consequences (6:2b-5)

The command to **teach and urge these duties** belongs to the section following it. The writer speaks of the one who teaches false doctrine but does not present what is taught and then refute it; instead he devotes his energies to speak of such a person's character and tactics. The heretical teacher does not adhere to **the sound words of our Lord Jesus Christ and the teaching which accords with godliness** (6:3). It is possible that the **words of our Lord Jesus Christ** are words of Jesus preserved in the gospel tradition, whether oral or written. On the other hand, the verse can be read in another way. In this case the writer accuses the false teachers of not adhering to the **sound words** (or "sound doctrines," *hygiainousin logois*) of (in

95

the sense of "about") the Lord, i.e., Christian doctrine. That this interpretation is to be preferred is confirmed by the writer's use of the same term with that meaning at 2 Tim. 1:13, and his use of "word" *(logos)* in a doctrinal sense also at 1 Tim. 4:6 ("word of the faith"), 2 Tim. 2:15 ("the word of truth"), and Titus 1:9 ("the certain word as taught"). Cf. also 1 Tim. 1:10-11. Moreover, he says, the false teacher does not adhere to the **teaching which accords with godliness** either. **Godliness** or "piety" is the familiar *eusebeia* (see commentary at 2:2 for references).

The faults of the heretics are listed. Again the point is made that the heretical teacher is speculative and engages in controversy and verbal disputes (cf. 1:4; 4:7; 6:20; 2 Tim. 2:14; Titus 1:14; 3:9). The orthodox teacher and his community are to avoid such persons (cf. 6:20; Titus 3:9). The fruits of their quarrels are listed (6:4b). Moreover, they are accused of seeking profits by their proselytizing (cf. 6:5; Titus 1:11).

2. Two Ways (6:6-10)
The Way of Contentment (6:6-8).   While the heretical teachers imagine that **godliness is a means of gain** financially (6:5), for this writer **godliness with contentment** is **great gain.** The term **contentment** (KJV, RSV) represents the Greek *autarkeia,* which can mean "self-sufficiency" as well. That was its meaning among the Stoics, who considered it a virtue to be independent of outward circumstances. Since the writer has just dismissed **godliness** as a means of financial gain, this meaning of independence or self-sufficiency apart from one's financial condition may be implied: godliness with self-sufficiency is a great gain. Nevertheless, the translation **contentment** is well founded. The apostle Paul had written that he had learned to be content *(autarkēs)* in whatever state he was in (Phil. 4:11), and for this writer "godliness is a virtue in every way, as it holds promise for the present life and also for the life to come" (4:8). In contrast to the Stoic, the Chris-

tian is never totally self-sufficient or autonomous, but has his or her hope set on God who provides all that is necessary for life (6:17). Moreover, the next verse (6:7) makes the point of one's dependence on God. Translated literally it reads, "For we have brought nothing into the world, since we cannot take anything out." The syntax is awkward with the conjunction "since" (*hoti* in Greek), and so the RSV translators have taken the freedom to substitute "and" for it. Ancient copyists had difficulties too, and offered variations, although the evidence for "since" is strong. Following the best reading, the sense is this: there is nothing that we can take out of this world with us as a permanent possession at death; therefore, since this is true, it has not been granted us to bring anything into this world in the first place which we might claim as our own either in life or at the point of death; all is from God for this life only. The thought is not new with this author. Similar sayings are found in the Old Testament and Jewish tradition (Job 1:21; Eccles. 5:15; Wis. 7:6; Philo, *On the Special Laws* 1.294-295; and the Babylonian Talmud tractate *Yoma* 86b) as well as in Seneca (*Moral Epistles* 102.25). We should be content, says the writer, "if we have food and covering" (NEB). The RSV has **clothing** instead of "covering," but there is merit to the NEB rendering, since the Greek word (*skepasmata,* a plural) can include shelter as well as clothing. In any case, the writer reflects the attitude that as long as the minimal needs of human life are met, one should be content (cf. Prov. 30:8; Matt. 6:25-33; Luke 3:10-14; Phil. 4:11-12; Heb. 13:5).

The Way of Destruction (6:9-10).   In contrast to the way of contentment, there is the way of destruction, which the Christian is to avoid. Although the writer is aware that certain Christians are wealthy (6:17-19) and does not denounce them for being such, he affirms that the desire for wealth leads to **ruin and destruction.** There are two reasons why this is so. First, **the love of money is the root of all evils.** Second, however, it is by this craving that some have gone astray **from the faith.** The first statement (6:10a) is a common maxim which appears with slight variations in various Graeco-Roman writers.[39] The second, however, expresses the main concern of the author. By craving wealth certain persons have gone astray from **the faith** (the Christian religion; cf. 3:9; 2 Tim. 4:7). It is commonly taught that one cannot love both God and wealth (Matt. 6:24; Luke 16:13; Eph. 5:5; James 4:4; 1 John 2:15). Here, however, the writer goes beyond the more general truth to say that the consequences of desire for wealth have been apostasy for some former Christians. Not content with exhortation alone, the writer reminds his readers that the danger of which he speaks has had real, practical consequences.

3. *Exhortation to True Christianity (6:11-16)*

Although the section appears to be an address to Timothy **(But as for you, man of God),** this is another instance in which the author "talks past" Timothy to a broader audience (cf. commentary on 4:6, 11-12, 14). That audience may be either the congregation or the smaller circle of presbyters. It has been suggested that the section has been taken from an exhortation originally addressed to those who were being ordained, but which has now been incorporated into the letter.[40] The suggestion can neither be proved nor discredited. But in its present form, in any case, it has the marks of being addressed to the presbyters and bishop, for the admonition to preserve **the commandment unstained and free from reproach** (6:14) recalls the duty of these persons in particular (Titus 1:9; cf. 1 Tim. 6:20; 2 Tim. 1:13-14; 2:14-15; 3:14; 4:1-5), and also the address **man of God** appears at 2 Tim. 3:17 as a designation for the minister of the Word.

11—The term **man of God** is used in the Old Testament as a designation for Moses (Deut. 33:1; cf. superscription to Ps. 90), David (2 Chron. 8:14), and various prophets (1 Sam. 2:27; 9:6; 1 Kings 13:1; 17:18, 24; 2 Kings 4:7). Aside from its use in the Pastorals (here and at 2 Tim. 3:17), the term does not appear elsewhere in the New Testament. Its associations with the Old Testament prophets make it likely to refer to the presbyters, who have been appointed by prophetic utterances and endowed at ordination with *charisma* (see commentary on 4:14 and 1:18). This person is to **shun**—or "flee from" *(pheugein)* —the way to destruction and **aim at**—or "pursue" *(diōkein)*— Christian virtues. (The author uses the same *pheugein/diōkein* contrast at 2 Tim. 2:22). The list of virtues has similarities to Paul's list of fruits of the Spirit in Gal. 5:22. In fact, however, only two of the six listed here appear in Paul's list of nine, namely, **faith** and **love. Righteousness** *(dikaiosyne)* for this writer means moral uprightness, for which one strives (2 Tim. 2:22) and to which one is trained by study of Scripture (2 Tim. 3:16). Concerning **godliness,** see commentary at 2:2. **Faith** in this context, as in others (1:5, 14; 2 Tim. 1:5, 13), signifies true piety and genuineness of belief. On **love,** see commentary on 1:5. **Steadfastness** represents a Greek term *(hypomonē)* which can also be translated "fortitude" (NEB), "patience," or "endurance" (cf. 2 Tim. 3:10; Titus 2:2). The term translated **gentleness** *(praupathian)* is found only here in the New Testament and connotes a sense of consideration for others.

12—The imagery used is that of an athletic contest (the Greek terms *agōnizesthai* and *agōn* used here have that application), not a military campaign. Athletic imagery is used also at 4:8 within the context of a charge to those engaged in ministry (4:6—5:2). The same two Greek words are used in connection with Paul at 2 Tim. 4:7, where he is portrayed as having fought the good fight to the last day of his life. The admonition to **take hold of the eternal life to which you were called** assumes that **eternal life,** though future (1:16; Titus 1:2; 3:7), is a present possession of the person called to faith, which is also taught in the gospel of John (3:15-16, 36; 5:25, etc.). The **good confession before many witnesses** may refer to a confession of faith made at Baptism, ordination, or trial. Most commentators think it refers to Baptism,[41] but others think it refers to ordination.[42] A literal translation reads: "take hold of the eternal life, to which you were called; *and [kai]* you confessed the good confession in the presence of many witnesses." The *and* is important (although the RSV substitutes **when**); the NEB does well to translate, "and you confessed your faith nobly before many witnesses." The statement can therefore be taken to refer to ordination in the presence of other presbyters and the congregation (cf. 4:14; 2 Tim. 2:2). One can expect that a confession of faith would have been made at ordination; furthermore, the context, an exhortation to presbyters, supports such an interpretation.

13-14—The charge is to **keep the commandment unstained.** The **commandment** refers to the whole Christian religion (as at 2 Peter 2:21), not any specific commandment. The charge is therefore appropriate, especially for those engaged in preaching and teaching. Preservation of the faith in its purity is their duty until the **appearing** *(epiphaneia)* of the Lord. Here (and at 2 Tim. 4:1, 8; Titus 2:13) the term refers to the parousia (second coming) of Christ, while at 2 Tim. 1:10 it refers to his first "appearance" on earth. The phrase **in the presence of God . . . and of Christ** is used in solemn declarations (cf. 5:21; 2 Tim. 2:14; 4:1). The writer adds, concerning Christ, that **in his testimony before Pontius Pilate** he **made the good confession.** No specific allusions to any of the gospel accounts of the passion are made. The author draws upon common Christian tradition that Jesus witnessed to the truth (cf. John 18:36-37). His **good confession** concerning the truth is the model for those who make the **good confession** in the presence of witnesses at ordination (6:12), and who are now being charged to keep **the commandment** (Christian tradition) **unstained and free from reproach** until his coming again.

15-16—In the Greek text 6:15 opens with a relative pronoun "which" (RSV has **this**), referring to the "appearance" of Christ:

"which . . . the Sovereign will show at the proper time."
Against Paul, who expects the parousia imminently in most
references to it (1 Cor. 15:51-52; Phil. 4:5; 1 Thess. 4:15-18),
this writer thinks of the parousia as further into the future;
although it is still assured, the timing is known only to God.
The titles used in these verses (**Sovereign, King,** and **Lord**)
apply to God the Father (cf. 1 Tim. 1:17).

4. *Ministry to the Wealthy (6:17-19)*

The writer denounces seeking wealth (6:9-10) but recognizes that among Christians there are some who simply are
wealthy, and he does not negatively judge them and their
circumstances. Rather, given the fact that some are wealthy,
the question for Christians concerns the proper use of wealth
and the attitudes and conduct of the rich. They are not to be
haughty (RSV; the Greek means "to consider oneself superior"). They are to set their hopes **on God,** not riches (cf. Matt.
6:19-21, 24-33). As at 6:8, the writer stops short of asceticism:
God provides **richly** everything which we have **to enjoy.**
Beyond such fundamental attitudes there is a way of life
expected of the wealthy. They are to **do good** and **be rich
in good deeds.** The author's exhortation is subtle: **the rich
in this world** are to be truly rich, not in the sense of acqui-
sitions, but giving—**rich in good deeds.** And his subtlety can
be detected also in his statement that God furnishes **richly.**
All this is to say that if a person is **rich,** that is so because
God has **richly** provided; therefore the truly **rich** are to be
rich in good deeds, as God has been to his own people. The
rich are to be **liberal** (*eumetadotos,* a term appearing only
here in the New Testament, carrying the sense of being disposed to give away) and **generous** (*koinōnikos,* also appearing
only here in the New Testament, denoting a "sharing" manner
of life). Although one can bring nothing into this world or
take anything out of this world (6:7), those who act in the

proper way **lay up for themselves a good foundation for the future** (cf. Tob. 4:9; Matt. 6:20; Luke 12:33). This is followed by a purpose clause: in order that **they may take hold of the life which is life indeed.** At first reading this appears to teach a doctrine of merit. But it should not be pressed that far. In the context of exhortation and on the basis of having appropriated the Christian message, the rich are called upon to pass from a life of hopes set on uncertain riches to the life which is **life indeed** (RSV; literally, "truly life"), the life which has its hopes set on God and is generous and given to good deeds.

5. Call to Fidelity (6:20-21a)

The address is to Timothy, but again (cf. 4:6, 11-12, 14; 6:11) the author is "talking past" him to those engaged in teaching, preaching, and opposing heretical teachers. The Greek reads, "guard the deposit *(parathēkē)*. This Greek word is found only in the Pastorals (cf. 2 Tim. 1:12, 14) within the New Testament, and it refers to the Christian tradition, which has been received and is to be kept secure (cf. 1:18-19; 4:6; 6:14; 2 Tim. 1:13-14; 2:1-2; 3:14; 4:1-2; Titus 2:1; 3:8). Further, the leader is to **avoid godless chatter** and **contradictions** *(antitheseis)* of "so-called knowledge" *(gnōsis)*. The latter term refers to a type of incipient Gnosticism taught by the heretics (see Introduction, Part 5). The term *antitheseis* was taken by some earlier scholars to refer to the title of a book by Marcion bearing that name. That is unlikely, however, since that would place the Pastorals at a relatively late date (ca. A.D. 150). More likely, it refers to the rhetoric of the opponents (the term can also be translated "objections") and can refer to the manner of the Gnostic teachers who try to refute orthodox Christian teaching. It is plausible that Marcion gave literary expression to this genre. The readers are charged to **avoid** such disputes; they are not to enter into debates which get nowhere. The writer adds that those who profess *gnōsis* have **missed the mark as regards the faith,** i.e., true Christianity.

■ Closing Benediction (6:21b)

Grace be with you is used here and in two other places (2 Tim. 4:22; Col. 4:18); at Titus 3:15 the word *all* is added. The closing benedictions of the genuine letters of Paul are longer by comparison, but they usually contain these words within others (cf. Rom. 16:20; 2 Cor. 13:13; Gal. 6:18; Phil. 4:23; 1 Thess. 5:28; Philemon 25). Significantly the Greek pronoun for **you** is in the plural *(meth' hymōn)*, which the English (e.g., RSV) does not make clear (the NEB reads "with you all" to make it so). The writer may have simply modeled his benediction on the words of Paul, who uses the plural, but more likely the plural betrays the intention of the writer to speak to a broader audience, rather than to "Timothy" alone. That New Testament letters were intended for reading to congregations is attested at 1 Thess. 5:27. Some later manuscripts of 1 Timothy change the pronoun to the singular to clear up the "problem," but the plural is supported by the earlier and best witnesses.

II TIMOTHY

Arland J. Hultgren

OUTLINE OF 2 TIMOTHY

COMMENTARY

■ Opening (1:1-2)

As in the case of the other Pastoral Epistles, Second Timothy opens with the greeting formula as revised by Paul (see commentary on 1 Tim. 1:1-2) in which the writer is named first (**Paul**), then the addressee (**Timothy**), and finally there is a word of greeting (**grace, mercy, and peace**).

The letter is attributed to Paul, but like the other two Pastorals it must be judged pseudonymous (see Introduction, Part 1). Furthermore, while it is ostensibly addressed to Timothy, it, like the others, must be considered a letter addressed to a broader setting, a community (see Introduction, Part 2).

The opening is more restrained than that of 1 Timothy. Paul is designated as apostle **by** (RSV; literally, "through") **the will of God,** which is a phrase used in two of Paul's authentic letters (1 Cor. 1:1; 2 Cor. 1:1; cf. also Eph. 1:1; Col. 1:1). The phrase immediately following, **according to the promise of the life which is in Christ Jesus,** is found here only, although at 1 Tim. 4:8 the writer speaks of "godliness" as that which "holds promise for the present life and also for the life to come." Just how the phrase fits into the context is not clear. It appears that the writer is simply saying that Paul is an apostle by God's will, and his apostleship fulfills the divine promise of life in Christ, as the gospel is proclaimed. While at 1 Tim. 4:8 the writer speaks of promise as a possession of the believer, here he speaks of promises from God. This way of thinking is more "Pauline" (cf. Rom. 4:16; 15:8; 2 Cor. 1:20; Gal. 3:14, 29; 4:28).

Timothy is addressed as Paul's **beloved child.** This recalls the language of 1 Cor. 4:17 (cf. Phil. 2:22) in which Paul speaks of Timothy as "my beloved and faithful child," and the Pauline phrase is undoubtedly the basis for the terminology used here. Verse 2 contains a greeting identical to that at 1 Tim. 1:2. The greeting is not merely personal. The writer conveys a blessing from God and Christ: **grace** (God's undeserved favor), **mercy** (God's help for the helpless), and **peace** (God's power to establish well-being, conveying the sense of the Hebrew *shalom*). For more on these words, see commentary at 1 Tim. 1:2.

■ Thanksgiving (1:3-7)

The typical Pauline letter has a five-part structure: (1) opening, (2) thanksgiving, (3) body, (4) *paraenesis* (exhortation), and (5) closing (greetings and/or benediction).[1] Second Timothy corresponds to this five-part structure. The thanksgiving section begins at 1:3, but where it ends is not absolutely clear. It ends at either 1:5 or 1:7. For reasons stated below, it appears that 1:6-7 can be included, so that the thanksgiving section is 1:3-7.

The function of a thanksgiving section is essentially twofold in Pauline and other early Christian letters. First, the writer gives thanks for the faith and witness of the person(s) addressed. Second, the writer often gives some indication of the contents or theme of the letter. This can be seen especially at Rom. 1:16-17 within the larger thanksgiving section (1:8-17). Within 2 Timothy the writer gives thanks at 1:3 and the basis for it in 1:5. Then at 1:6-7 he reminds

Timothy of their initial bond of unity, which serves as a basis for the writer's exhortations to follow. Verses 1:6-7 are thematic, for throughout the letter Timothy is called upon to follow Paul's example and teaching and to be bold in doing his work as Paul's representative (1:8, 13; 2:1-2, 8-9, 14-15; 3:10-11, 14-15; 4:1-2). He is to remember God's gift, which was personally bestowed upon him by Paul (1:6).

3-4—In English the thanksgiving appears at the outset to be identical in wording to the Pauline "I thank God" (Rom. 1:8; 1 Cor. 1:4; Phil. 1:3; 1 Thess. 1:2; Philemon 4). Yet there is a distinction in Greek. Paul uses the verb *eucharistō* ("I thank"), while this writer uses *charin echō* ("I have/give thanks," or simply the English "I thank" can be used). The Pauline word is not used in the Pastorals. One may surmise that by the time of the Pastorals it had strong associations with the Eucharist, since it was used in that context (cf. Mark 14:23 and parallel passages; 1 Cor. 11:24). *Charin echō* was therefore used here, as at 1 Tim. 1:12 (see also Luke 17:9; 2 Cor. 9:15; Heb. 12:28).

The writer has Paul claim to serve God **with a clear conscience, as did my fathers.** The term **clear conscience** is used also at 1 Tim. 3:9; in both cases it means "without reservations," although here it also denotes the quality of one's service to God: Paul's conscience cannot accuse him of ever having not served God. **Fathers** (RSV) is not a good translation of the Greek *progonoi*. The term means "forebears" (progenitors) and can refer to parents and grandparents, both male and female, as 1 Tim. 5:4 illustrates, using the same term. The writer indicates continuity between the service rendered to God by Paul's forebears and the apostle himself. In his own writings Paul can speak of himself as having been blameless in his prior service to God (Phil. 3:4-6; cf. Gal. 1:13-14), but he also speaks of an abrupt change (Gal. 1:15-17), after which he evaluates the past differently (1 Cor. 15:9; Phil. 3:7-9). Here, as in 1 Tim. 1:13, the life of Paul is idealized, and the disruption is smoothed over.

The apostle remembers Timothy **constantly** in his prayers. The words are similar to those in certain Pauline thanksgiving sections (Rom. 1:9; Phil. 1:3-4; 1 Thess. 1:2-3; Philemon 4). Moreover, he desires to see Timothy in order that he **may be filled with joy.** Paul is portrayed later in this letter as being in prison at Rome (1:8, 16-17; 2:9; 4:6); he can see Timothy only if Timothy comes to him, which he requests (4:9, 21).

5—The **sincere faith** (or "unhypocritical faith," as the Greek can be rendered; cf. 1 Tim. 1:5) of Timothy is recalled, as well as that of his **grandmother** and **mother.** Here alone the names **Lois** and **Eunice** are given. At Acts 16:1 it is said that Timothy was "the son of a Jewish woman who was a believer; but his father was a Greek." While Eunice was thus a Jewish Christian, the father of Timothy was apparently not a Christian at all. The women would probably have become Christians originally through the preaching of Paul at Lystra (Acts 14:6-7, 20-21); there is no hint of evangelization there prior to Paul's arrival. The two women can probably be numbered among the original nucleus of disciples in Lystra mentioned at Acts 14:20. From 2 Tim. 1:5 (**faith that dwelt *first* in . . . Lois and . . . Eunice**), it appears that it is through the influence of these women that Timothy came to be a "disciple" (as he is called at Acts 16:1).

6-7—Timothy is called upon to "stir into flame the gift of God" (NEB) given through the laying on of Paul's hands. The English word **gift** represents the Greek *charisma,* which is found here and at 1 Tim. 4:14. (See commentary on 1 Tim. 4:14 also concerning the laying on of hands.) In the letters of Paul each Christian has a gift (1 Cor. 7:7); there is a variety of gifts but one Spirit which inspires them all (1 Cor. 12:4, 9). In the case of Ephesians the range of gifts already appears to be narrowed down to specific ministries (apostle, prophet, evangelist, pastor, and teacher) "to equip the saints for the work of ministry" (4:11-12). In the Pastorals this narrower focus is continued. While the Spirit is effective in the lives of all Christians since Baptism (Titus 3:5), there is no reference to "gifts" of the Spirit for all. The one **gift** spoken of is that which is imparted in ordination. This gift can be stirred into flame. The Greek verb is used only here in the New Testament. It appears in the Septuagint to speak of bringing a person back to life (2 Kings 8:1, 5) or reviving a person's spirit (Gen. 45:27; 1 Macc. 13:7). The gift bestowed at ordination (cf. 1 Tim. 4:14) is not named. What gift is this? It appears that while the Spirit is operative in the lives of all Christians, at ordination a "special portion" of the Spirit is given to the office bearer. This is confirmed at 1:14, at which the office bearer is exhorted to "guard" the good deposit (Christian teaching) "through the Holy Spirit which dwells in us." The Spirit dwells in the office bearer, and it is the power at work in him to propagate and defend the truth. While in Paul the Spirit imparts various gifts, in the Pastorals the Spirit itself is imparted as the **gift** for ministry. This view of a succession, by which the Spirit is transferred for ministry, is found in the Old Testament (Num. 11:25-26; Deut. 34:9; 2 Kings 2:9; cf. Exod. 35:31) and to some extent in the New (John 20:22; Acts 1:8). The Spirit equips God's servant for a task and can therefore be thought of as the gift itself. Furthermore, the life of the office bearer is to be characterized by the divine endowment (given by or with the Spirit) described as **a spirit** [not "Spirit"] **of power and love and self-control** (1:7). For all the insistence in the Pastorals that the presbyters and bishop must provide strong leadership, there is also the counterpoint of restraint and an emphasis on providing an example of Christian conduct.

■ Body of the Letter (1:8—3:17)

The Apostolic Witness (1:8-18)

1. Charge to Timothy (1:8-10)

8—A literal rendering would be, "Therefore do not be ashamed of the testimony concerning our Lord, nor of me his prisoner." The language is similar to that of Rom. 1:16 ("I am not ashamed of the gospel"). The "objective" character of the gospel and the Christian "testimony" are spoken of, respectively, in Romans and 2 Timothy. There is more at stake here than what the RSV translation (**testifying to our Lord**) suggests. There is a true testimony received by Paul and then transmitted to Timothy (cf. 1:13-14), who represents the orthodox leaders loyal to Paul; of this true "testimony" Timothy is not to be ashamed. Nor is he to be ashamed of Paul, the Lord's **prisoner** (*desmios,* a person in chains; the term is used also by Paul at Philemon 1 and 9; cf. also Eph. 3:1; 4:1). Only in 2 Timothy of the three Pastorals is Paul portrayed as imprisoned (at 1 Tim. 3:14-15 and Titus 3:12 Paul is free). Moreover, he has been tried once (4:16) and rescued from the death sentence (4:17), but he still expects that his imprisonment will end only through his martyrdom (4:6-8, 18). He has been abandoned by certain trusted friends (4:10, 14, 16). At 1:8 Paul asks for Timothy's continued loyalty. Moreover, he asks him (literally) to "suffer together with" him "for the gospel by the power of God." The thought stands solidly within the Pauline tradition. Paul speaks of his suffering as an apostle (referred to at 1 Cor. 4:9-13; 2 Cor. 4:7-12; 6:3-10; 12:8-10; Phil. 1:19-21) as a sign of being true to his calling (2 Cor. 6:8; 12:12) and as a means by which Christ may be proclaimed. The suffering of the witness shows that "the transcendent power belongs to God and not to us" (2 Cor. 4:7). Here at 1:8 the power of God is to be at work in the life of Timothy—and therefore in the lives of those persons entrusted with the ministry of the Word—while suffering for the gospel.

9-10—These verses extend in thought beyond the context and appear therefore to be based on a creedal formula, which can be detected when the clauses are arranged into three stanzas:

who [i.e., God] saved us and called us with a holy calling
    not according to our works, but according to his own
    purpose and grace,
which was given to us in Christ Jesus before time began
    but has now been manifested through the appearing of our
    Savior Christ Jesus,
who abolished death
    and brought life and imperishability to light through the
    gospel.

Each of the clauses makes an affirmation concerning the word before it: God—who saved us; grace—which was given; and Christ Jesus—who abolished death.

The main verbs in each of the clauses is a past tense (aorist in Greek), so that God's redemptive work in Christ is declared finished. The use of the past (aorist) tense is common in New Testament hymns and creedal formulas (cf. 1 Tim. 3:6; Rom. 1:3-4; 1 Cor. 15:3-7; Phil. 2:5-11; Luke 1:46-55). Elsewhere the writer can speak of salvation as future (2:10; 4:18; 1 Tim. 2:15; 4:16), but here it has already been given to believers (cf. Titus 3:5). Salvation is linked with God's election (**called us with a holy calling**) and grace. The salvation to come is a present possession of the Christian. It is not an achievement of one's own works, but is a gift of grace (as in Paul: Rom. 5:10; 6:23; cf. Eph. 2:8). This grace "was given" in Christ "before time began"; [2] i.e., before the creation of the world, the Son existed as bearer of divine grace. But now that same grace has been manifested in the **appearing** (*epiphaneia* in Greek, from which the English "epiphany" is derived) **of our Savior** in his historical ministry, death, and resurrection. The total Christ event, culminating in his resurrection from the dead, has broken the power of death (cf. similar language in 1 Cor. 15:26) and has illuminated life and imperishability. This passage contains the clearest statement of an atonement doctrine in the Pastorals. The doctrine is of an "objective" type, but it stresses the resurrection more than the cross as the means by which eternal salvation has been won. The salvation won by the victorious Christ is given as present and therefore as future possession of those called. Both **life** and "imperishability" (RSV, **immortality**) are eschatological gifts. By abolishing death, Christ reveals that life is ultimately God's intention for humankind. So "life and imperishability" are linked in thought. It is not, as sometimes proposed, that "life" is for this world and "imperishability" for the world to come. The word "imperishability" is a virtual synonym for **immortality** (a term used in reference to God at 1 Tim. 6:16). But "imperishability" is a literal rendering of the Greek, and it is better. Christ has not brought **immortality** to light, as though it has already existed, even if only in the dark. Rather, Christ has brought "imperishability" to light as a consequence of his abolishing death. Prior to that action, perishability leading to death was the known mode of human existence. To recognize the gift character of Christ's work is important. His work has been revelatory (as **brought . . . to light** indicates), and so he is the true "author" of the gospel. It is in this sense that the writer can say that Christ brought life and imperishability to light **through the gospel.** The gospel, preached in the church, comes ultimately from Christ.

2. The Witness of Paul as Pattern (1:11-14)

It is **for this gospel** (summarized in the creedal formula of 1:9-10) that Paul had been **appointed a preacher and apostle and teacher.** Of these terms, Paul uses only the term **apostle** concerning himself in his own letters (Rom. 1:1; Gal. 1:1; frequently elsewhere). The triad is used of him also at 1 Tim. 2:7. Because of such appointment, Paul suffered (see references in commentary at 1:8). But such suffering does not cause discouragement or shame, since the one whom Paul believes is also the one whom he knows. His trust is placed in God, who is ever trustworthy. Paul has confidence that God himself is able to guard **what has been entrusted to me.** This does not mean that the apostle has confidence that God will spare his

114

own life, but that he has confidence in Christian teaching and proclamation as that which God protects, and for which he therefore need not be **ashamed;** he need not be ashamed, because this Christian teaching will be vindicated at the last day. The thought is similar to that expressed in Mark 8:38. Jesus says, "For whoever is ashamed of me and of my words in this adulterous and sinful generation, of him will the Son of man also be ashamed, when he comes in the glory of his Father with the holy angels." In this saying Jesus affirms that the person who is ashamed of him and his teaching will be judged accordingly on the last day. The writer of 2 Tim. 1:12 affirms the obverse in terms of Paul: he is not ashamed. How people react to the Christian tradition entrusted to them in the present determines their standing at the final judgment. For that which is entrusted is guarded by God. It will not pass away; it stands firm (2:19).

The writer uses the term *parathēkē* (**what has been entrusted,** RSV) in 1:12 and 1:14, as well as in 1 Tim. 6:20. In each case the verb **guard** *(phylassein)* is used, and this noun is its object. God guards it (1:12), and Timothy is exhorted to guard it too (1:14; 1 Tim. 6:20). The term is sometimes translated "deposit," and that is quite literal, but in the Pastorals, the only place where it occurs in the New Testament, it is "the spiritual heritage entrusted to the orthodox Christian." [3] At 1:14 the writer calls upon Timothy to guard (literally) "the good deposit through the Holy Spirit which dwells in us." The Spirit is seldom mentioned elsewhere in the Pastorals (1 Tim. 3:16; 4:1; Titus 3:5). Here the Spirit is spoken of as dwelling within believers (cf. Titus 3:5). Moreover, it **is a power which aids** the task of guarding "the spiritual heritage." See commentary at 1:6 on the Spirit itself as "gift" *(charisma),* bestowed at ordination for a task. The Spirit itself empowers the minister to be a guardian of **the truth.**

The syntax of 1:13 is difficult. The phrase **in the faith and love which are in Christ Jesus** is much like that in 1 Tim.

1:14 (see commentary there). It is descriptive of the Christian life-style (faith and love are linked as primary Christian virtues also at 1 Tim. 2:15; 4:12; 6:11; 2 Tim. 2:22; 3:10; Titus 2:2). The phrase is adverbial, modifying the main verb. The verse can be translated as follows: "Preserve in the faith and love which are in Christ Jesus that which you have heard from me as a model of sound words." Pauline Christianity is the model for the preacher and teacher in the church. Such a person is to abide in authentic Christian faith and love (as did Paul, 3:10), and that will result in holding fast to Pauline Christianity. The two go together. The heterodox fall away from the Pauline model precisely because they are lovers of self, money, and pleasure—given to various vices (3:2-5).

3. Abandoned by Many, but Refreshed by One (1:15-18)

15—The statement **all who are in Asia Minor turned away from me** refers to Christians in Asia Minor, including Ephesus. The statement begs questions. Does it mean that Paul, portrayed in Roman imprisonment, has had no tangible support from—in fact has been disowned by—Asian Christians? Or does it mean that certain Asian Christians had been in Rome, had deserted Paul, and have now returned to Asia Minor? The latter appears more likely. At 4:16 it is said "at my first defense no one took my part; all deserted me" (which would include not only those who went to Asia, but also Demas, who went to Thessalonica; cf. 4:10). Among the Asians who had deserted were Alexander (4:14), who is presumed to be in Ephesus (4:15), and those mentioned in the present verse, **Phygelus and Hermogenes.** These latter two persons are not referred to elsewhere in the New Testament.

16-18—**Onesiphorus** is the exception. He is an Ephesian (1:18; 4:19) who had come to Rome, searched for Paul, found him, and frequently **refreshed** (RSV, or "revived") him. He **was not ashamed of** Paul's **chains** (cf. 1:8). It appears that at the time of the Pastorals this person has died. This can be concluded tentatively on the basis of 1:18, which refers to his service in Ephesus as over and past. It becomes clearer from 1:16 and 4:19 in which only the **household** of Onesiphorus is mentioned, as though this household is composed of his survivors. Assuming pseudonymity for the letters, it is likely that the Onesiphorus tradition is known at Ephesus. That would be the story of a faithful person who had rendered much service at Ephesus and who traveled to Rome, made a valiant search for Paul, and after finding him visited him often. But prior to the writing of the Pastorals, Onesiphorus had died, leaving the legacy of fidelity to Paul and also a Christian household. The writer of the Pastorals asks for **mercy** from the Lord upon this household. "Mercy" in this context has the sense of compassion or favor; it is not particularly a petition for forgiveness, since the household is Christian (4:19), but for divine blessing in this life (a usage for the term **mercy** at 1 Tim. 1:2; 2 Tim. 1:2 as well). At 1:18, however, there is a shift in meaning; now **mercy** is forgiveness on **that Day** (of judgment; cf. 1:12). Another shift in meaning is evident between 1:16 and 1:18 as well. The term **Lord** in the phrase **may the Lord** refers to Christ in both 1:16 and 1:18; but in the phrase **from the Lord** in 1:18 it refers to God the Father.[4] The hope expressed (in a play on words) is that Onesiphorus—who had **found** Paul (1:17)—be granted to **find** mercy from God on **that Day.** A few commentators have claimed that 1:18 offers precedent and sanction within the New Testament for prayers for the dead,[5] but the sentence is hardly an intercession. The verb expresses wish, and the sentence expresses no more than hope for the divine vindication of Onesiphorus. That vindication is of course assured already, for he was a Christian, but the piety expressed here recognizes that the day of judgment is in the future, and that the divine mercy will act on behalf of Christians who have died. May Onesiphorus be counted among them! The expression is a beautiful, loving sentiment, not an intercession.

Exhortation to Timothy (2:1-26)

1. Charge to Be Strong and to Endure (2:1-7)

1-2—Again Timothy is called "my child" (although KJV, RSV, NEB, and other versions read **my son**), which is Paul's designation for Timothy at 1 Cor. 4:17 and Phil. 2:22, and which appears elsewhere in the Pastorals (1 Tim. 1:2, 18; 2 Tim. 1:2). The command **be strong in the grace that is in Christ Jesus** has no parallel in the New Testament. The verb **be strong** *(endynamoun)* appears also in 1 Tim. 1:12; 2 Tim. 4:17, and in both cases it speaks of the strengthening which Christ provides. Here the exhortation is that Timothy be strong in the strength which **grace** provides. **Grace** is itself a power in the Pastorals (1 Tim. 1:14; 2 Tim. 1:9; Titus 2:11).

Timothy is exhorted to be strong and to **entrust** (the verb is a form of *paratithēmi,* which is related to the noun *parathēkē,* "deposit," in 1:14) **what you have heard from me.** The phrase **before many witnesses** represents a Greek phrase which can also be translated (on the basis of syntax) as "through many witnesses" (implying that the latter were mediators of Pauline tradition to Timothy, as the NAB does). In this particular context, however, the former sense is to be preferred.[6] (The NAB rendering also founders on the fact that in the purview of the Pastorals, Timothy is Paul's spiritual child; no mediating witnesses are needed between Paul and Timothy.) The picture is that of an ordination, at which Paul had not only laid his hands on Timothy (1:6), but also exhorted him in the presence of witnesses, among whom the presbyters are to be numbered (1 Tim. 4:14). The term **witnesses** is used here in a legal sense, as at 1 Tim. 5:19; 6:12—i.e., they are witnesses to the ordination event—rather than in the sense that they were persons who gave testimony at the event of ordination. Pauline tradition alone is "the witness" (1:8) which is given. Timothy is to entrust the same to **faithful men** who will be able **to teach others also.** The object of the exhortation being given is that the recipients of the letter in the post-Pauline era will attend carefully to the matter of choosing qualified candidates for ministry (cf. 1 Tim. 5:22); the latter must be able to teach (cf. 1 Tim. 3:2; 5:17; 6:3; 2 Tim. 2:24; Titus 1:9).

3-7—The writer exhorts Timothy to take his share of suffering as a **good soldier** of Christ. The designation of associates as "fellow soldiers" is found in Paul's own letters (Phil. 2:25; Philemon 2). Three images follow in 2:4-6 to round out the picture of what is required of Timothy. These are the images of soldier, athlete, and farmer. They are images of fidelity (of the **soldier,** 2:4) and discipline (of the **athlete,** 2:5). But what is the meaning of the third image (of the **farmer,** 2:6)? A literal translation is: "It is necessary for the hard-working farmer to share in the fruits first." By itself the verse recalls passages elsewhere which speak of the right of the preacher and teacher to compensation (1 Cor. 9:7-12; Gal. 6:6; Luke 10:7; 1 Tim. 5:18). The verse may represent a common maxim for that purpose. But placed in the context here the maxim is made to serve another purpose, and that is to impress upon Timothy that duty is a prerequisite for any benefits: as the hard-working farmer shares first in the fruits of his labor only through labor, so Timothy is to be engaged in unceasing effort if he is to share in the fruits of the apostolic efforts. There is thus a triad of expectations portrayed through the images; fidelity to Christ, discipline, and hard work. The charge to **think over what I say** refers to the exhortation (2:3) and imagery (2:3-6). These are not to be taken lightly; they are to be pondered, leading to the **understanding** which **the Lord will grant.** This need not imply that some "deeper meanings" will result, but rather that Timothy will understand more fully what is required of one who is to take his share of suffering as an apostolic emissary. For comment on the latter theme, see commentary at 1:8.

2. Charge to Remember the Gospel and Its Apostle (2:8-13)

8a—After the charge to endure in faithfulness (2:1-7) there follows the charge to **remember Jesus Christ**. The verb could also be translated "keep in mind," so the command is similar to that of Phil. 2:5 ("Have this mind among yourselves"). The remembering is an "efficacious remembering" of the saving work of God in Christ, as **preached in** [Paul's] **gospel**, which is set forth in a creedal summary: **Jesus Christ, risen from the dead, descended from David.** The language and form resemble the pre-Pauline creedal formula of Rom. 1:3-4, although the latter is longer and has a different sequence of members (Davidic descent, exaltation). Here the same two assertions are made: (1) Christ has been raised (passive voice) by God from the dead and is therefore the Exalted One; and (2) he is of the "seed of David" (literal translation). That the Messiah was to be of Davidic descent is based on God's covenant with David (2 Sam. 7:16; Pss. 89:3-4; 132:11). The promise of God has been fulfilled in Jesus Christ, son of David, who has been raised to sit at God's right hand as his Messiah (cf. Matt. 22:41-45; Acts 2:22-36; Heb. 1:3-5).

8b-10—What the creedal summary proclaims has been **preached in** [Paul's] **gospel** (the words "my gospel" are a Pauline expression found in Rom. 2:16; cf. Gal. 1:6-9). A play on words follows, which can be seen in most translations, but especially in a rather literal one: "for [the gospel] I am suffering hardship even to the point of wearing fetters as a common criminal; but God's Word is not fettered!" The thought expressed is strikingly Pauline. In Phil. 1:12-14 Paul writes that the gospel has been advanced in spite of his imprisonment, and at 2 Cor. 4:12 he writes, "so death is at work in us, but life in you." Through Paul's suffering, imprisonment, and wasting away in the flesh (death at work in him), he brought life through the gospel to others. Cf. also Col. 1:24.

The writer appeals to sympathy for Paul, who suffered imprisonment and finally death itself. Paul endured everything

for the sake of the elect, that they may obtain salvation in Christ Jesus (2:10b). The term **elect** (as in Titus 1:1) refers to Christians. It is rooted in the Old Testament. Israel as a nation is spoken of there as God's elect people (Deut. 7:6-8; Isa. 43:20; 45:4; 65:9, 15; Pss. 105:43; 106:5), and that understanding also appears in the New Testament (Acts 13:17; Rom. 9:11; 11:28). But already in the Old Testament three concepts develop which are important for the New: (1) election is for the sake of the nations (Gen. 12:1-3; Isa. 42:6-7; 49:6); (2) the Servant of the Lord is God's specially "chosen one" (Isa. 42:1; 43:10); (3) God will call (or elect) persons from other nations to be his people as well (Ps. 65:1-4; Hos. 1:10; 2:23; cf. 1 Peter 2:9-10). Early Christians claimed that the end times of expectation had come, and Jesus was the Lord's chosen servant (Matt. 12:8; Luke 23:35; 1 Peter 2:4-6). Now, apart from ethnic associations, the elect are those from believing Israel and the nations who, through faith, are the children of Abraham and heirs of promise (Rom. 4:16-25; Gal. 3:7-9). The term **the elect** is applied to such persons (Rom. 8:33; Col. 3:12; 1 Peter 1:2). They are portrayed here in 2 Timothy as a pilgrim people who are on the way to salvation. This salvation is "in Christ Jesus with its eternal glory" (2:10b). It is a future inheritance, which is a distinctly different understanding from that of the heretics who hold that the "resurrection is past already" (2:18) and think that the glory of salvation is present. The elect, like Paul, are to endure and serve as people on the way to salvation.

11-13—The **sure** saying is printed in the RSV and NEB in the form of poetry consisting of four lines, and that is as it should be. Although some commentators think that these lines were written by the author,[7] most conclude that the writer quotes from a hymn known to him, except that the last few words **(for he cannot deny himself)** are frequently thought to be the writer's own comment appended to the hymn.[8] This view appears to be correct, since the words break with the pattern in the four lines which precede.

Commentators have not agreed concerning the origins of the hymn. Was it composed for singing at Baptisms or for encouraging Christians in persecution? An answer can be worked out along these lines. The Pastoral Epistles do not give evidence elsewhere of persecution going on against Christians from the state; 1 Tim. 2:1-2 in fact indicates a peaceful situation. But the writer of the Pastorals quotes from a traditional baptismal hymn which would most likely have been composed when persecution and consequent apostasy were taking place. Baptisms have a social context and this hymn would have been composed when that context was perilous. It is a hymn which has survived both good and bad times, just as many great hymns used today reflect circumstances different from our own, and it is presented here by the author of 2 Timothy in connection with the theme of enduring (cf. 2:12 in the hymn with 2:10).

The first line (2:11) speaks of dying with Christ and living with him. The language is similar to that of Rom. 6:8 ("But if we have died with Christ, we believe that we shall also live with him"). In both cases the death spoken of is symbolical death through Baptism (cf. Rom. 6:3-7). But the usage of **we shall also live with him,** which appears in both Romans and 2 Timothy, differs. In Rom 6:8 Paul is speaking of the present life of the Christian (walking "in newness of life," 6:4), but in 2 Tim. 2:11 the writer has the future, eternal life in view, as the parallelism of 2:12 requires. Furthermore, the writer has just spoken of salvation in Christ with its eternal glory (2:10). Verse 2:12 with its verb **endure** recalls the endurance of the apostle spoken of in 2:10, but more than that, here it refers to the endurance of all Christians in times of persecution (cf. Matt. 10:22; Rom. 8:17, 25; 12:12; James 1:12; 5:11). **If we endure, we shall also reign with him.** To **reign** with Christ means that believers will share his heavenly kingdom (cf. 4:1; Matt. 19:28).

In 2:12b a warning is given. Although the RSV has, **if we deny,** the text should be translated: "if we *shall* deny him, he also will deny us." The line points to a future possibility of apostasy by those being baptized. All other lines are simple conditions, but this one places denial as a remote and almost unthinkable action; the future is "to mark a mere contingency, improbable in itself and to be deprecated." [9] The verb for denial *(arneisthai)* appears elsewhere in the Pastorals (1 Tim. 5:8; 2 Tim. 2:13; 3:5; Titus 1:16; 2:12), but here alone, drawing from a baptismal hymn, does it apply to apostasy from Christ. The line recalls the words of the Gospels, "whoever denies me before men, I also will deny before my Father who is in heaven" (Matt. 10:33; Luke 12:9; cf. Mark 8:38). The verb is used to signify apostasy also at 2 Peter 2:1; 1 John 2:22-23; Jude 4; and Rev. 2:13; 3:8.

The fourth line (2:13a), if it were parallel to the others, would read, "if we are unfaithful, he will be unfaithful." But such a thought is unthinkable. Though the Christian be unfaithful, **he remains faithful.** The line seems to contradict the third. Therefore some commentators want to draw a distinction between apostasy (overt, deliberate, decisive denial of Christ) and unfaithfulness (not being all that the Christian should be). But the distinction will not stand. The verb "to be unfaithful" does not signify lack of perfect fidelity (a shade of gray), but (in black/white terms) lack of fidelity pure and simple. There is a polarity here which cannot be overcome on a dogmatic level. The hymn expresses liturgical and pastoral theology. For persons standing on a "mountaintop" of religious experience and making a bold confession at Baptism there is the word of warning about possible apostasy leading to final judgment, which has significance for the believing community only. But for the longer course of life, in which introspection sees nothing in the self but doubt, denial, and betrayal of

Christ, the good news is declared that Christ remains faithful. The Christian is to look to him, not to the self, for salvation; there can be no glorying in one's own strength, but only in the gracious fidelity of Christ. The line recalls the words of Paul in Rom. 3:3-4. The hymnist celebrates the triumph of grace, but the writer of the Pastorals appends the line (2:13b), "for he cannot deny himself." He uses the verb of denial from 2:12b to assert that Christ does not apostasize from himself and the covenant sealed with those who have **died with him** in Baptism.

The hymn fits into the context of a "sure saying." The connecting link is the verb **endure** in 2:10 and in the hymn (2:12a). The hymn is used to show that the endurance of Paul is expected of every Christian. The **sure** (or "faithful") **saying** is none other than a hymn known in the community and sung at Baptisms, perhaps at the Baptisms of the very persons who read the letter.

3. Instructions for Tending the Congregation (2:14-19)

14—Timothy is to go on reminding certain persons of "these things" (RSV, **this**). The persons to be reminded are the ministers of the Word ("faithful persons") referred to in 2:2. What they are to be reminded of would include all the teachings which have been given to this point in the letter, such as the doctrinal affirmations of 2:8 and 2:11-13, but also the assertions about Paul's apostleship, suffering, and teaching. He is to charge them "before God" (as the better Greek witnesses read; RSV has **before the Lord,** based on other texts). The solemn charge is found at two other places in the Pastorals (1 Tim. 5:21; 2 Tim. 4:1); in each case the writer is making special emphasis. Timothy is to solemnly charge these persons **to avoid disputing about words,** a concern expressed also in 1 Tim. 6:4. Heretical teachers forsake the clear confession and the life which issues from it and enter into speculations, controversies, and disputes, which lead hearers to ruin. Since the persons to be reminded and charged are distinguished from the **hearers,** it is clear that the instructions here and following are for preachers and teachers (cf. 2:2, 24).

15-16—Do your best (RSV) or "try hard" (NEB)—the verb has an urgency about it and can mean "to hasten" or "to be eager" —**to present yourself to God as one approved.** As elsewhere, the writer "talks past" Timothy to anyone engaged in the ministry of the Word in the church. Such a person is to be a **workman** (RSV; the Greek word is the term used for a common laborer). Such a workman is "to cut a straight path for the word of truth" (as the Greek can be rendered: RSV is rather bland here), which word is therefore allowed to have its way among the hearers, uncluttered with sophistries. **Godless chatter** leads to **ungodliness,** which is to be renounced (Titus 2:12). Bad theology leads to bad attitudes and conduct.

17-18—The word of the heretics, the writer warns, will spread like gangrene. **Hymenaeus,** referred to in 1 Tim. 1:20, and **Philetus** are among the heretics to be avoided. Their teaching that **the resurrection is past already** (RSV, or more literally, "has already happened") sounds strange. (See Introduction, Part 5, for a summary of their teachings.) The heretical teachers promote a form of Gnostic teaching in which it is claimed that there is no need to look for a future resurrection; believers have already entered into a heavenly, immortal state, and will never die. Such a teaching may be based in part on a misuse of Paul's teachings in which it is said that believers have "put on Christ" (Gal. 3:27) who has been raised; that Christ is in them (2 Cor. 13:5); that they walk in newness of life (Rom. 6:3); and that whoever is in Christ is a new creation (2 Cor. 5:17). But of course Paul insisted that the resurrection of believers is future (1 Cor. 15:20-28; 1 Thess. 4:13-18). The writer of the Pastorals stands firmly in the Pauline tradition. Those who make such heretical claims are not only wrong, but their lives tend either toward asceticism or libertinism, and they **upset** (RSV, or "overturn") **the faith of some,** even entire families (cf. Titus 1:11). Verse 18 is one of the most specific in describing the teaching of the heretics. Most of the time the writer exhorts persons to avoid them and does little to describe what they teach. Another notable exception in this regard is 1 Tim. 4:3.

19—There is a **firm foundation** (RSV) bearing an inscription (**seal,** RSV) divinely established. Here the writer turns to architectural imagery to instruct by analogy. Interpreters have been divided, however, in discerning the meaning of the imagery. What is this **firm foundation?** Various meanings have been assigned: the church, Christ, or orthodox teaching. The clue to its meaning could very well be found in the fact that the foundation bears a **seal,** and that this consists of words of promise and admonition. The first (**The Lord knows those who are his**) is taken from Num. 16:5 (quoted from the LXX); the second (**Let everyone who names the name of the Lord depart from iniquity**) has no clear antecedent in the Old Testament, although phrases in it can be found in Isa. 26:13; Job 36:10; and Sir. 17:26. Such words are considered in the present context as oracles of God uttered through the community of believers, and so the **foundation** *(themelios)* is the witnessing community, the church, founded upon apostolic teaching. At Eph. 2:20 the apostles and prophets themselves are spoken of as the "foundation" of the church. Here in the Pastorals there is a slight shift: the **foundation** is the apostolic church. This corresponds to the imagery of 1 Tim. 3:15 at which another Greek word is used for foundation *(hedraiōma)*, but the concept is the same: the church upholds the truth (see commentary at 1 Tim. 3:15). The omniscient **Lord knows** who true believers are, and anyone who **names the name of the Lord** must shun the heretical teachers and all their ways and abide in true faith and its consequent conduct. They are to "call upon the Lord with a pure heart" (2:22), coupled with a "good conscience and sincere faith" (1 Tim. 1:5).

4. *The Aim of the Lord's Servant (2:20-26)*

20-21—The imagery of a building, suggested already in 2:19, is continued. But it is the imagery of a rich person's house, which contains various kinds of utensils for diverse purposes —**gold and silver** for **noble use** (Greek, "honor"), and **wood and earthenware** for **ignoble** use (Greek, "dishonor"). The **great house** being spoken of thus contains two basic categories of utensils. It is clear that these verses do not speak of a "variety of gifts" in the Pauline sense, but of a distinction between good and bad. The **great house** will then correspond to the large circle of persons professing to be Christians, orthodox and heretical alike. The person who **purifies himself from what is ignoble** is one who disavows fellowship with the heretical movement; **then he will be a vessel for noble use, consecrated and useful to the master**—who in this context is Christ—and **ready for any good work.** (The passage recalls Paul's statements in 1 Cor. 3:11-16, although Paul speaks of a final testing of how the Christian "builds" life—with gold, silver, and jewels, or with wood, hay, and straw; fire will test one's works.) The **vessels of gold and silver** correspond to persons in the ministry of the Word (cf. 2 Cor. 4:7) who believe the truth and conduct themselves accordingly. As vessels are **ready** at hand in a **great house** for the service of the **master,** so these persons are ready and responsive to the bidding of Christ and ready for **good work** in ministry.

22—**Youthful passions** are to be avoided. Again the writer "talks past" Timothy (who would hardly be a youth, even if the letter would have been written by Paul to him in the decade of the 60s; see commentary on 1 Tim. 4:12) to exhort those in the ministry of the word. Such **passions** need not be of a sexual nature, although that is not to be excluded, but may be impulses leading to a life contrary to the pursuit of **righteousness, faith, love, and peace** in the company of **those who call upon the Lord from a pure heart** (cf. commentary on 1 Tim. 1:5). Such passions are therefore schismatic and self-centered impulses. The community of **those who call upon the Lord from a pure heart** is itself a check on privatistic, subjectivistic ways of thinking and acting. Here the writer comes close to a concept of the priesthood of all believers over against a possible arrogant and high-handed clericalism. In the Pauline tradition the congregation itself is to test everything (1 Thess. 5:21; cf. also 1 John 4:1), and the writer stands in that tradition here.

23-26—The minister of the Word is to avoid **stupid, senseless controversies** (cf. 1 Tim. 6:4; Titus 3:9), since they give birth to **quarrels.** The term translated **senseless** is better translated "uninstructed." There will always be disagreements within the church, but danger arises when, due to ignorance, persons place peripheral matters of belief at the center, so that the apostolic witness is clouded over. The **Lord's servant must not be quarrelsome** in such situations but take a different approach. (The term **Lord's servant** appears only here in the New Testament. It is of interest that it is the only term used in this letter for persons engaged in ministry; the titles of bishop, presbyter, and deacon do not appear, but are found only in 1 Timothy and Titus.) That approach is to win over and correct opponents by exemplary, gentle conduct and sound teaching. "The end of Christian teaching is not to win an argument but to win a person." [10] Through such efforts "God may perhaps grant them repentance unto the knowledge of truth" (literal translation). And along with that they will **escape** (RSV, but the Greek reads, "come to their senses again") **out of the snare** (or trap) **of the devil, after being captured by him** (the devil, not God) **to do his** (the devil's) **will.** The **snare** of the devil is also spoken of in 1 Tim. 3:7; 6:9. The devil captures persons as with a trap (the common Greek verb for capturing animals and birds in a trap is used). But, through the ministry of the Word, God is able to work repentance. God works through the "means of grace."

Characteristics of Apostasy (3:1-9)

1—In keeping with Christian tradition, **times of stress** will arise **in the last days.** The **last days** for the Christian communities of the New Testament era are the times preceding the second coming of Christ. (The term **last days** appears also at Acts 2:17, where Joel 3:1 is quoted, and at 2 Peter 3:3; at 1 Tim. 4:1 the equivalent "later times" is used.) Things will go from bad to worse before the end comes. In this letter Paul is pictured as one who at an earlier time predicts what will transpire in the times of the recipients of the letter. The community should thus understand itself as living in the "end times," but at their beginning. The characterization of vices and corrupt religion during the end times corresponds to present tendencies. Yet there is no assertion in the Pastorals that the end is expected soon. The letter appears to be a "last will and testament" in which Paul is ready to depart from this life (4:6-8), and he provides then not only a call to fidelity but also a forecast of what is to come.

2-4—A list of 18 vices is given which characterize certain persons in the **last days.** The list is rather typical of vice lists (cf. Rom. 1:29-31; Col. 3:5), recalling also the list of 1 Tim. 1:9-10. Such vices are in fact quite "timeless"; they are hardly peculiar to the last days. But the point is not that these vices— known since the world began—are signs of the last days. Rather, in the last days they will characterize the lives of many even who profess to be religious, both orthodox and heretical. As the writer continues, however, it becomes clear that he is speaking particularly of false teachers (3:6, 8-9).

5—Now a 19th vice is listed, which brings the entire list to a close. It is specific, and gets at the root problem. The false teachers hold to **the form of religion but deny the power of it.** The Greek could be translated "the appearance of piety" or "the outward form of religion." Such persons appear outwardly to be religious, perhaps even orthodox. The vices listed are for the most part attitudinal and have to do with personal relationships. The problem is that persons **deny the power** of true religion. True communion with God and discipleship to Christ issue in a transforming power affecting one's thinking and acting (cf. Rom. 12:1-2; Phil. 2:1-5). But these persons have not been so transformed and are to be avoided.

6-9—The writer now gets to some of the actions of the false teachers. They (literally translated) "worm their way into houses." So they work by stealth, not openly. They mislead "little women" (Greek; RSV translates **weak women**) who are "overwhelmed by their sins" and are "led about by various desires, always learning and never able to arrive at knowledge of the truth." The writer lives at a time when women do not enjoy emancipation in the modern sense nor the benefits of education. Earlier the apostle Paul had declared that in Christ there is no distinction between male and female (Gal. 3:28; cf. 1 Cor. 11:11). This affirmation possibly led women to anticipate more than what the leaders of the church were willing to grant in the postapostolic era. The false teachers are thus able to capitalize on a Pauline teaching within a post-Pauline situation, in which Paul's teaching had not been realized in fact. Now they are able to conduct a special mission among women, claiming to offer emancipation and a religious philosophy which sounds quite Pauline. But from the point of view of orthodoxy, these false teachers are manipulators who take advantage of women and lead them astray into a religious philosophy which does not ring true in its doctrinal and moral teachings. The thirst for novelty in matters of philosophy and religion was commonplace (cf. Acts 17:21). The community to which 2 Timothy was addressed did not have a legacy and heritage of long standing; it was still in its infancy, and the definition and identity of Christian faith were still in flux.

The false teachers are compared to **Jannes and Jambres** who **opposed Moses.** The reference is to the magicians called forth by Pharaoh in Egypt to perform miracles similar to those of

Moses and Aaron, prior to the Exodus, to discredit them (Exod. 7:11, 22). Their names are not given in the book of Exodus, but are supplied in later Jewish, Christian, and even pagan traditions.[11] In fact there are attestations to a (now nonexistent) "Book of Jannes and Jambres." [12] The readers of the Pastorals would have known the story of these men, which went far beyond the story in Exodus. According to various sources, their opposition to Moses and Israel extended to opposing their crossing the sea, trying to lead Israel astray in the wilderness, and instigating the apostasy in the making of the golden calf.[13] The false teachers are likened to these men; they are opponents of **the truth,** the true doctrinal and moral teachings of the Christian faith. In 3:9 the writer expresses confidence that they will not succeed in their efforts. They represent the troubles of the **last days** (3:1), but such troubles will be overcome.

The Pauline Model (3:10-17)

10-13—The writer addresses the reader in second person singular in the Greek, as though addressing Timothy personally. Yet the writer is addressing any minister of the Word. At 3:15 it is said that Timothy has been acquainted with the sacred writings "from infancy" (Greek; RSV has **from childhood;** NEB has "from early childhood"; and NAB has "from your infancy"). Does this actually speak to the historical Timothy? As the son of a Jewish mother (Acts 16:1; cf. 2 Tim. 1:5), it is possible that he would have been acquainted with the Scriptures since infancy. Yet it must be recalled that one of the qualifications for presbyter and bishop is that the person must not be a recent convert (1 Tim. 3:6). The author can therefore be speaking past the figure of Timothy to any minister of the Word, presupposing that such a person has been raised in a Christian family.

Paul is the model to follow. The contrast to the false teachers (3:1-9) is bold and radical. The virtues listed in 3:10 are common Christian virtues. It is not likely that Paul would have listed these high virtues about himself. Indeed the Greek words translated **conduct** and **aim in life** do not appear in Paul's letters. Paul had written of his having endured persecutions and hardships (1 Cor. 4:12; 15:32; 2 Cor. 1:8; 4:9; 11:23-33; 12:10; Gal. 5:11), and he had asked others to join in imitating him (Phil. 3:17). Here the writer of the Pastorals makes use of such elements to make Paul the model for the true minister of the Word.

Commentators have had difficulty with 3:11. The geographical designation (**Antioch, Iconium, Lystra**) does not exhaust the places at which Paul experienced persecution and suffering. Persecution in these cities is narrated in Acts 13:50; 14:1-7, 19. But these precede Paul's first acquaintance with Timothy (16:1). How could Timothy have **observed** these? Acts records subsequent persecutions with which Timothy would more likely be familiar—for example, at Philippi (16:19-24, 37), Thessalonica (17:5-9), Beroea (17:13), and Corinth (18:12). Moreover, Paul himself alludes to what must have been persecutions and imprisonment in Ephesus as well (1 Cor. 15:32; 2 Cor. 1:8).

But the term translated **you have observed** need not denote observation in the sense of personal witness. It means only that one has "followed" a certain matter "with the mind." [14] Furthermore, the reference to persecution does not speak of persecutions at the three cities. A literal translation is: "my persecutions, my sufferings; what kind of things happened to me in Antioch, Iconium, and Lystra; what kind of persecutions I endured. . . ." The writer sets up a series which should not be collapsed so that one thinks that only persecutions in these three cities is being referred to. Rather, there were persecutions, and those things which happened in the three cities should be recalled in particular to illustrate concretely what persecution meant. The "rule of three" is perhaps operative here, and one need not go on to cite every other city in which persecution happened. In any case, these were the first three places of persecution, and others followed. It appears that the author of the Pastorals is familiar with Acts, and he expects that his readers are as well. The same sequence (**Antioch, Iconium, and Lystra**) appears in both books. The point is that in recalling Paul's persecutions one will naturally begin with those mentioned in Acts 13. Verse 3:11 can then be considered a cross-reference to Acts, not a complete recitation of all of Paul's persecutions.

The Lord **rescued** Paul from his persecutions (3:11b). This recalls the apostle's language (the same verb is used in 2 Cor. 1:10), and it is used again at 4:17. But it is not promised that the Lord will rescue others in similar circumstances. It is only said that **all who desire to live a godly life in Christ Jesus will be persecuted.** This general maxim recalls the sayings of Jesus in Matt. 5:10-11 (cf. also Acts 14:22; 1 Peter 3:14). Such persecutions are to be expected in the last days (3:1). But evil ones and **imposters** (RSV; NEB has "charlatans") "will make progress" (NEB)—the irony is intended—to the **worse** (condition), "deceiving and being deceived." The writer reflects the common view, especially prominent in apocalyptic literature, that in the last days the saints will suffer and the wicked will prosper until divine intervention vindicates the righteous.

14-15—The author now addresses Timothy directly, and therefore the minister of the Word. The minister is to continue in what has been **learned** and **believed.** There is a "deposit" (or content, 1 Tim. 6:20; 2 Tim. 1:12, 14) which is to be learned and represented in the work of ministry. That deposit is the faith of the Christian church, which is also to be appropriated by the minister as personal belief. This doctrinal content is chiefly the Pauline teaching, which is mediated by others. In the phrase **knowing from whom,** the **whom** is plural in Greek; therefore it speaks of persons from whom the minister has learned. These are teachers who have been faithful in representing Paul. The writer speaks then to persons who stand at least two generations from Paul. They have been raised in

Christian homes, as 3:15 attests. They have been acquainted
with the Scriptures "from infancy" (see commentary at 3:10).
The **sacred writings** (RSV, NEB) refer to the books of the Old
Testament; that is the term (in Greek) used for such by Philo
(*Life of Moses* 2.292) and Josephus (*Antiquities* 10.210). The
Scriptures are able "to make you wise" (**instruct you,** RSV)
"unto salvation through faith in Christ Jesus." This need not
mean that for the author the books of the Old Testament are
sufficient witnesses to Christ by themselves. Obviously there
must also be explicit teaching about him, particularly his passion, death, and resurrection. Yet the author reflects a common
view of ancient Christianity. The Scriptures of Israel make
the divine will and promises known. Paul, for example, writes
that the gospel concerning God's Son was promised before-
hand by God in the Holy Scriptures (Rom. 1:2). So, for this
writer, the study of Scripture is able to make one wise, leading
to salvation through faith in Christ. Coming to faith does not
follow automatically from the study of the Scriptures. The
offense of the cross cannot be dispensed with. Nevertheless,
the Scriptures witness to a saving God (this writer speaks of
God as "Savior," 1 Tim. 1:1; 2:3; 4:10, etc.), and the sending of
"Christ our Savior" is his supreme saving work (1 Tim. 1:15).

   16-17—Verse 16 is known for its difficulties in translation.
The Greek allows for several possibilities from the standpoint
of grammar and vocabulary: (1) **all scripture is inspired by God**
(RSV); (2) "every scripture [passage] is inspired by God";
(3) "all scripture inspired by God is . . ."; and (4) "every scripture [passage] inspired by God is . . ." (RSV footnote).

   The term translated **scripture** *(graphē)* can mean simply a
"writing" (sacred or secular). If that is its meaning here, either
the third or fourth translation would be possible. The writer,
in that case, distinguishes between "inspired" and "nonin-
spired" literature. Yet it is not likely that that is the meaning
intended.[15] The term is used in Hellenistic Judaism and in the
New Testament with reference to the Old Testament so fre-

quently that one can expect the same here. Paul himself uses this term for the Old Testament (Rom. 4:3; 1 Cor. 15:3-4; Gal. 3:8, 22), and that would be most likely the meaning in a work attributed to him.

The alternatives to be chosen are either the first, favored by some commentators,[16] or the second, favored by others.[17] Actually the distinction is immaterial between these two,[18] for the result is the same whether one speaks of the particulars of Scripture or the totality as being inspired. Translation requires a choice between the two, however, and perhaps the RSV is best (similarly, NAB and NIV), since the context (cf. 3:15, the "sacred writings") speaks of the Scriptures in their entirety and in their purpose collectively (teaching, reproof, correction, and training). It is not likely that "every passage of Scripture" can be thought of as **profitable** for all those functions and purposes.

Commentators are agreed that the term **scripture** applies to the Old Testament, but some have raised the question whether certain New Testament writings (particularly the letters of Paul) would also be included. The question has been answered affirmatively in recent years.[19] It is sometimes pointed out that Paul's letters are spoken of as Scripture already in the New Testament itself (2 Peter 3:15-16), and this could be another instance of the same. Yet this view concerning the Pastorals falters on two major grounds. First, as already indicated, the term translated "scripture" is the term used by Paul himself as a reference to the Old Testament, and it seems that this writer, in imitating Paul, would intend the same. Second, the thought expressed is that Timothy has been acquainted with the **sacred writings** (or "scriptures") since infancy. The Pastoral Epistles give the appearance of having been written by Paul. To preserve that appearance, the reference would have to be to the Old Testament. If Paul's letters are understood to be included under the term "scripture," the result would be the undermining of the appearance intended.

Paul would not have included his own writings under the term, nor would he have said that Timothy had been acquainted with them since infancy. As the son of a Jewish woman (Acts 16:1), Timothy could well have been acquainted with the Old Testament since an early age (according to the Mishnah tractate *Pirke Aboth* 5.24, one is ready for Scripture study at the age of five). But he could not have been acquainted with Paul's writings "from infancy," since they were written when Timothy was an adult already.

The passage is sometimes taken as a doctrinal statement concerning the inspiration of Scripture. The verse does indeed speak of the Old Testament writings as inspired by God, but it does not speak of any one theory of inspiration. Judaism had two basic conceptions. Some teachers taught verbal inspiration (every word was dictated by God, and so the biblical writers merely recorded the words), while others thought of divine inspiration as mediated through human consciousness with the result that the biblical writers wrote their own words, which is the view reflected in 2 Peter 1:21 ("men moved by the Holy Spirit spoke from God"). In the case of 2 Tim. 3:16, the phrase **inspired by God** represents a single Greek word *(theopneustos)* which means "God-breathed." It is said then, that the Old Testament books have their origins in God's creative work (cf. Gen. 2:7) and bear God's authority. But the term does not have the narrow meaning of divine dictation of every single word ("verbal inspiration").

The emphasis of the writer, in any case, is not so much on a doctrine of inspiration, but rather on the use of Scripture. The heretical teachers apparently make a selective use of Scripture and emphasize those portions—myths, genealogies, and human traditions (1 Tim. 1:4; Titus 1:14)—"which promote speculations rather than the divine training that is in faith" (1 Tim. 1:4). But this writer asserts that **all scripture** is to be employed —the "whole counsel of God" (Acts 20:27)—for it is all inspired and it is, in its entirety, **profitable for teaching, for reproof,** for correction, and for training in righteousness. Scripture is both **inspired by God** *and* **profitable** for its intended purposes (the conjunction "and" appears in the Greek text). The train of thought is to assert the function and authority of the Scriptures for the purposes listed, rather than to spell out a theory of inspiration for its own sake.

The purposes listed include both doctrine (**teaching, reproof;** NEB, "teaching the truth and refuting error") and moral guidance (**for correction, and for training in righteousness**). As elsewhere in the Pastorals (1 Tim. 6:3; 2 Tim. 2:14-18; Titus 1:9-16), it is held that doctrine and morality are inseparable. The false teachers teach false doctrine and encourage and practice immorality (3:1-7; Titus 1:10-16). A tradition of orthodoxy and sound morality is in the process of formation. It has its detractors. But the writer of these epistles seeks to establish a synthesis of teaching and practice which is true to apostolic teaching and to Christ (1 Tim. 6:3). That may be his greatest legacy. It is evident that Pauline tradition was being abused by both libertines (1 Tim. 3:6; 4:7-8; 6:3-5, 14; 2 Tim. 2:16-18, 22; Titus 2:4-6, 12) and ascetics (1 Tim. 4:3; 5:14, 23; Titus 1:14; 2:10; 3:9) alike. But this writer appeals to a strain of Pauline tradition which insists on the inseparability of faith and works and thereby paves the way for the preservation and reading of the apostle's letters in the church. "The aim of our charge is love that issues from a pure heart and a good conscience and sincere faith" (1 Tim. 1:5).

■ Exhortation: Preach the Word (4:1-8)

1—There has been exhortation earlier in the letter (1:8; 2:1, 8, 14, 23; 3:1, 14), but now comes the most solemn of all. The opening Greek word can be translated, "I solemnly charge you" (Phillips translation; TEV, "I solemnly call upon you"). The term is used on two other occasions (1 Tim. 5:21; 2 Tim.

2:14), and in each instance, including this one, there follows the phrase **in the presence of God;** here the writer adds **and of Christ Jesus** (as in 1 Tim. 5:21). At his coming, Christ will judge both those who are alive and those who have died (the KJV has the archaic, "the quick and the dead," which the traditional version of the Apostles' Creed used; cf. also Acts 10:42). The judgment will take place at his **appearing,** a term used by the writer for both the first coming of Christ (2 Tim. 1:10; 4:8) and, as here, for his second coming (1 Tim. 6:14; Titus 2:13). The second coming is the time at which Christ's "reign" (RSV, **kingdom**) will be established. At 4:18 this is called Christ's "heavenly kingdom." Christ is already enthroned in glory (1 Tim. 3:16), but he will appear to execute the divine judgment and the saints will enter into his eternal glory, life, and reign (2:10-12).

2—**Preach the word.** The **word** is the true testimony concerning Jesus Christ (cf. commentary on 1 Tim. 6:3). The verb translated **preach** can be translated "proclaim" in the sense of a herald's announcement of good news. The model is Paul, who was appointed a "preacher" (or "herald," 1 Tim. 2:7; 2 Tim. 1:11). Such preaching is to go on **in season and out of season,** whether people are predisposed to hear the word or not. Besides preaching the word, the preacher will have to **convince** (actually "refute" is a better translation), **rebuke** (thereby bringing a message of judgment), and **exhort** (bringing encouragement in thought and action). Law and gospel, judgment and grace, convicting and exhorting—these are similar ways of speaking of the content and function of preaching.

3-4—The prediction of 4:3—of a time when people will not endure **sound teaching**—would be understood by the readers as the present time. People will **accumulate** teachers who will satisfy their desires and curiosities. Elsewhere in the Pastorals the frequent problem is that heretical teachers work their way into the community (3:6; Titus 1:11). But here and at 1 Tim. 4:1 it is clear that persons within the community can also be eager to have them come, and even to go after them. They will have nothing to do with **sound teaching** (cf. 1 Tim. 1:10; 6:3; 2 Tim. 1:13; Titus 1:9; 2:1) and **the truth** (1 Tim. 2:4; 3:15; 2 Tim. 2:18; 3:7-8; Titus 1:1)—twin expressions of orthodox teaching, which leads to virtue as well. Their desire will be to listen to the **myths** of the heretics (1 Tim. 1:4; 4:7; Titus 1:14; see commentary at 1 Tim. 1:4).

5—But the true minister of the Word must remain "calm and sane" (NEB), **endure suffering** (like Paul, 1:12; 2:9; here it is not physical suffering from persecution, but the onslaughts of the heretics), **do the work of an evangelist,** and **fulfil** one's **ministry.** The word **evangelist** appears at Eph. 4:11 as a title for a particular office along with other offices. Here it is applied to the minister of the Word. Such a person is a proclaimer of the gospel, and that is the Pauline gospel (2:8).

6-8—Paul is portrayed as about to be **sacrificed.** The language recalls Phil. 2:17. Although cultic language is used, that does not mean that Paul's death is thought of as atoning. Paul is seen to be in his death a willing, silent victim (as was Jesus, Acts 8:32; cf. Isa. 53:7), a martyr, "becoming like him in his death" (Phil. 3:10; cf. Rom. 8:36; 2 Cor. 4:11-12). His death is **the time of my departure,** which for Paul was his departure to "be with Christ" (Phil. 1:23). Death is not a mere "passing on" to an afterlife, but a transition to eternal fellowship with Christ (2:11). With the use of athletic imagery again in 4:7 (as at 2:5; 1 Tim. 6:12; cf. also 1 Cor. 9:24-27 regarding Paul's ministry), Paul is described as one who has completed his ministry of apostleship to which he had been appointed (1:11), and who has kept the faith entrusted to him (1:12). What awaits him is the **crown of righteousness,** which will be given to him and other Christians **on that Day,** the day of judgment (1:18). The image of a **crown** for the righteous at the day of judgment is rooted in Judaism (cf. Wis. 5:15-16). Paul speaks of an "imperishable crown" ("wreath" in RSV) awaiting believers (1 Cor. 9:25), and others speak of a "crown" awaiting the saints (James 1:12; 1 Peter 5:4; Rev. 2:10; 3:11). The **crown of righteousness** is a metaphor for final justification. Does the author have in mind a crown given because of the apostle's righteousness, or does he speak of righteousness as a gift bestowed freely as a gift by God? The context supports the former, and **righteousness** is generally a virtue in the Pastorals (1 Tim. 6:11; 2 Tim. 2:22; 3:16). But even for this writer, God's salvation is based on his own mercy and "not because of deeds done by us in righteousness" (Titus 3:5). Rather than setting forth a doctrine of justification by works, the writer should be seen here as speaking of Christian hope in a God who vindicates the saints.

The crown will be bestowed also on **all who have loved his appearing.** The clause may refer to the **appearing** of Jesus Christ in his earthly ministry, death, and resurrection (1:10), pointing to the past. But the NEB translation is probably to be preferred: "all who have set their hearts on his coming appearance." Then the clause refers to the parousia (cf. 1 Tim. 6:14; 2 Tim. 4:1; Titus 2:13), as the context suggests, again speaking of Christian hope.

■ Closing (4:9-22)

Instructions and a Warning (4:9-15)

9—Paul has been portrayed to this point as being in prison at Rome (1:16-17), deserted by former Ephesian companions (1:15), and expecting martyrdom (4:6). Timothy, apparently portrayed as being at Ephesus (cf. 1 Tim. 1:3; 2 Tim. 1:18; 4:19), is summoned to join Paul at Rome **soon,** at least before winter (4:21) when travel becomes difficult or impossible. No reason is given why Timothy should come. He is to bring certain articles belonging to Paul (4:13), but that would not be a sufficient reason for the trek. Assuming pseudonymous authorship, the summons to Timothy must be considered a device to assert the intimacy of Paul and Timothy. Further, one is to assume that Timothy made the journey and was with Paul in the last days of his life. Timothy is therefore the successor of the apostle and the one who transmits the Pauline tradition with veracity. Finally, this device of the summons also "explains" why Timothy had left Ephesus "long ago" and had (conveniently) "left his letters behind."

10-12—Eight persons are named in 4:10-15 as companions, deserters, emissaries, or opponents of Paul. **Demas,** referred to in Philemon 24 as a "fellow worker" (cf. also Col. 4:14), has now **deserted** Paul. **Crescens,** still a co-worker, has gone to Galatia. Some texts read "Gaul," but **Galatia** is better attested. Since **Galatia** was sometimes used as a name for Gaul by some ancient writers (e.g., Josephus, *Antiquities* 17.344), Eusebius (*Ecclesiastical History* 3.4) and some modern interpreters have concluded that that is the meaning of the word here.[20] Yet it is more likely that the Galatia of Asia Minor is meant. The Pastorals have originated in Asia Minor, and a certain Crescens, probably the same person, resides in Asia Minor during the first quarter of the second century (the era of the Pastorals); on one occasion he carries a letter from there (Smyrna) to Philippi (Polycarp, *Letter to the Philippians* 14:1).

In the Epistle to Titus, **Titus** is portrayed as on Crete (1:5), but is summoned to Nicopolis (3:12). Here, however, he is said to have gone to **Dalmatia** (modern Yugoslavia), presumably from Rome. **Luke alone** is said to be with Paul in Rome (but at 4:21 four others are named, and reference is made to "all the brethren"). Luke had been with Paul at the time of an earlier imprisonment (Philemon 24; cf. Col. 4:14). **Mark,** an earlier co-worker and companion in imprisonment (Philemon 24; cf. Col. 4:14), is to accompany Timothy to Rome. According to Acts 15:37-39, Mark had fallen into disfavor with Paul. But Philemon 24 attests a reconciliation, as does this verse. Whether Mark is assumed to be in Ephesus or is to be summoned by Timothy along the way to Rome is not clear, although the latter appears more probable in meaning. In any case he, Timothy, and Luke are to be final witnesses at Paul's death; he is also to come because he is **very useful** to the apostle. According to 1 Peter 5:13, written about the same time as the Pastorals, Mark is at Rome. **Tychicus** (whom Luke calls an "Asian," Acts 20:24) has been **sent to Ephesus,** which is the place at which Timothy is supposed to be. At Titus 3:12 he is a possible emissary of Paul to Crete. (In Col. 4:7 and Eph. 6:21 Tychicus is spoken of as one of Paul's co-workers and the bearer of those two letters.) Perhaps Tychicus is supposed to be the bearer of 2 Timothy, but the reference to him does not say as much; in fact, it appears to preclude it.

13—Timothy is requested to bring Paul's **cloak** left **at Troas with Carpus,** a person otherwise unknown. Troas was located northwest of Ephesus and would in fact be on the way, via either land or sea routes, from Ephesus to Rome. According to Acts 20:6, Paul had spent seven days at Troas during his final missionary journey to Asia Minor. In addition to the cloak, Timothy is to bring "the books, especially the parchments" (RSV has **the books, and above all the parchments).** At this time **books** could be in the form of scrolls or, like modern books, codices with pages; and the term could refer either to those made of papyrus or parchment, which was made from the skins of animals. The word "and" (which the RSV includes) does not appear in the most reliable textual witnesses, so it is not likely that two kinds of possessions (e.g., written books "and" unused writing materials, "parchments") are being requested. Timothy is to pick up "the books" (papyrus and parchment), "especially the parchments." The latter are the more valuable of the various books, not only because parchment was more costly but also because it was used for writings of greater intrinsic value. What did these "books" contain, "especially the parchments"? Could these be copies of the Old Testament, Paul's correspondence, or something else? Although commentators have made conjectures, the question cannot be answered with certainty. Our own conjecture is that here we have an oblique reference to the "Pauline corpus" of letters, which had been collected by this time and was in use at Ephesus (see Introduction, Part 2). Paul is portrayed, then, as gathering up his correspondence into a corpus prior to his martyrdom in Rome, which corpus was then disseminated.

14-15—Alexander is mentioned in 1 Tim. 1:20 as one who has blasphemed and has been delivered to Satan. He was an opponent of Paul's message, and these verses suggest that he was active at Ephesus, so Timothy is to **beware of him.** The writer "talks past" Timothy to the congregation's leadership. (This Alexander may be identified with the Alexander active in Ephesus at Acts 13:33, or the name could be a cipher for a movement or party which perpetuated the historical figure's views and ways; we cannot know his identity for certain.)

Paul's Vindication (4:16-18)

16—The verse, with its reference to Paul's **first defense,** raises questions of chronology. It does not imply that Paul had two trials, i.e., that Paul was freed after a first trial, was given liberty to travel, and was then imprisoned a second time (see Introduction, Part 1). The Pastorals know of only one imprisonment, and here the **first defense** is expected to be followed by another, uninterrupted by any period of freedom. At the first defense, **all deserted me.** On the face of it, that would mean that even Luke (4:11) and the others mentioned in 4:12 and 4:21 deserted Paul, unless the writer intends that these persons arrived subsequently. The verse functions to portray Paul as a deserted, lonely person (cf. 1:15) near martyrdom. He experienced desertion as did Jesus before him (Mark 14:50). Yet, like a true martyr (Acts 7:60), he asks that those who deserted him be forgiven (4:16b). Then he declares that

143

Paul was not deserted by **the Lord,** who had given him **strength** for his ministry (1 Tim. 1:12). The thought recalls Paul's statements in 2 Cor. 12:9-10; Phil. 4:13. He was strengthened for a purpose: **to proclaim the message fully, that all the Gentiles might hear it.** The purpose clause attests to Paul's final witness to leading Gentiles, the Roman authorities, to whom Paul had to bear witness (cf. Acts 23:11). The reference to rescue **from the lion's mouth** can be literal in meaning, since the historical Paul did not so meet his death, or it could be the common metaphor for mortal peril in general (Pss. 7:2; 17:12; 22:21). In any case, **the Lord will rescue me from every evil.** Here it is spiritual, not physical, peril which is meant, for he will be saved **for his heavenly kingdom.** Martyrdom is expected (4:6-8), and at the time the Pastorals were written it had been accomplished, but Paul belongs to the company of those who are to receive the "crown of righteousness" (4:8).

Greetings (4:19-21)

19—Greetings are sent to **Prisca** (Priscilla in Acts) **and Aquila,** as well as to the **household of Onesiphorus** at Ephesus. According to Luke, Prisca and Aquila were among the Jews, including Jewish Christians, who were expelled from Rome by Claudius (Acts 18:2; ca. A.D. 49). They met Paul in Corinth and resettled at Ephesus (Acts 18:18-19, 26; cf. 1 Cor. 16:19). If Romans 16 was addressed to Rome, one has to conclude that they returned there (16:3), and then (on the basis of this verse) resettled in Ephesus a second time. Many commentators think, however, that Romans 16 was addressed to Ephesus. In any case, the couple is associated with Ephesus, and this verse assumes their presence there. Onesiphorus of Ephesus (1:18) is said to have visited Paul during his Roman imprisonment (1:16-18), but he may have died prior to the time the Pastorals were written (see commentary on 1:16-18), so greetings are sent to his surviving household—persons who are loyal to Pauline Christianity.

20-21—Information is given about two Christians formerly of Ephesus. **Erastus,** sent earlier by Paul with Timothy from Ephesus to Macedonia (Acts 19:22), is **at Corinth. Trophimus,** also from Ephesus (Acts 21:29), is said to be **at Miletus** (about 50 km. or 35 miles south of Ephesus). The command in 4:21a to **come before winter,** when navigation was suspended,[21] intrudes. See the commentary on 4:9 as to the significance of Paul's bid. Then follow greetings of persons portrayed as being with Paul in Rome (see commentary on 4:11). **Eubulus** is not mentioned elsewhere in the New Testament; a certain person by that name is a presbyter at Corinth in apocryphal *3 Corinthians* 1:1, but whether this is the same person is not certain. **Pudens** and **Claudia** are otherwise not mentioned in Christian sources. **Linus** may be the person whom Irenaeus (*Against Heresies* 3.3.3) and Eusebius (*Ecclesiastical History* 3.2; 3.4; 5.6) speak of as an early bishop of Rome (the tradition Eusebius knows is that he became bishop after the martyrdom of Peter and Paul; Irenaeus, however, says that these apostles "handed over" the episcopate to him). According to Eusebius (3.13), Linus served as bishop for 12 years (ca. A.D. 64-76). Linus would have been a (perhaps younger) contemporary of Paul, but the fact that Paul does not mention him in his letter to the Romans or otherwise shows that he rose to leadership either late in Paul's life or after it. By the time the Pastorals were written, Linus would have already completed his service as bishop. By having him send greetings, the writer adds a touch from the past, drawing upon the tradition of a link between Paul and Linus reflected in Irenaeus and Eusebius and giving the letter an appearance of authenticity.

Benediction (4:22)

The benediction consists of two sentences, while in the other Pastorals there is only one. The first recalls the presence of the Lord with Paul (4:17). Now that presence is wished for Timothy in order that he might be strengthened for his calling. The second is identical to that at 1 Tim. 6:21. Again the plural "you" (in Greek) is used, which indicates that this letter is to be read to the community, as Paul's letters were intended (1 Thess. 5:27). Although the letter is addressed to Timothy, it is in fact intended for the community, particularly its leadership.

TITUS

Arland J. Hultgren

OUTLINE OF TITUS

I. Opening (1:1-4)
II. Body (1:5—3:11)
   A. Qualifications of a Bishop (1:5-9)
   B. Characteristics of False Teachers (1:10-16)
   C. Instructions for a Christian Ethos (2:1-10)
      1. The Conduct of Older Men and Women (2:1-3)
      2. The Conduct of Young Women, Young Men, and Teachers (2:4-8)
      3. The Conduct of Slaves (2:9-10)
   D. Life Under Grace (2:11—3:11)
      1. The Transforming Power of Grace (2:11-15)
      2. Life Under Grace in the World (3:1-2)
      3. Life Prior to Grace (3:3)
      4. Baptismal Regeneration in Christ (3:4-8a)
      5. Faith and Works (3:8b-11)
III. Closing (3:12-15)
   A. Instructions (3:12-14)
   B. Greetings and Benediction (3:15)

COMMENTARY

■ Opening (1:1-4)

The opening is longer and more formal than in the other
two Pastoral Epistles. Some commentators have concluded that
Titus must therefore have stood first in the sequence of the
Pastorals, i.e., that this relatively long section served as an
introduction to all three. On this point, and for more on the
question of sequence, see the Introduction, Part 2, B. The
explanation favored here is that the greater length can be
attributed to another factor. What makes this opening longer
is that it contains notice of Paul's appointment as a **servant**
and **apostle** and his being **entrusted** as a preacher of the gospel
(1:3). In the case of the other two letters similar affirmations
appear not in the opening but in the body of the letters. In
1 Timothy the matters of being appointed and entrusted are
found in 1:11-14, and in 2 Timothy they are found in 1:8-14
(especially 1:11-12). Thus the same affirmations are made in all
three, but in Titus, the shortest of the three letters, these things
are stated at the outset, allowing the writer to go on to other
matters, starting with the qualifications of a bishop (1:5-9).

Aside from its length, the form of the greeting coincides
with that found in the other letters (see commentary on 1
Tim. 1:1-2) in which the writer (**Paul**) is named first, then
the addressee (**Titus**), and finally the word of greeting is

given (1:4b). Like the other Pastorals, in spite of its being attributed to Paul, this letter must be considered pseudonymous (see Introduction, Parts 1 and 2). Likewise, as in the case of the others, this letter is addressed to a community or communities, rather than an individual. The writer "talks past" Titus to a community and especially its leaders. See commentary on 3:15.

1a—Paul is called a **servant of God.** The phrase is not found in Paul's letters, although Paul calls himself a "servant of Christ" (Rom. 1:1; Gal. 1:10; Phil. 1:1). The title **apostle of Jesus Christ** differs in sequence from Paul's "apostle of Christ Jesus" (1 Cor. 1:1; 2 Cor. 1:1), but not theologically; the Pauline form is also found at 1 Tim. 1:1 and 2 Tim. 1:1. On the title **apostle,** see commentary on 1 Tim. 1:1.

1b-3—The Greek is difficult to translate, and English translations vary. Paul is an apostle "for the sake of" (NAB, literally; RSV has **to further**) the (1) **faith of God's elect** and (2) their **knowledge of the truth which accords with godliness.** The RSV (using **to further**) implies a missionary apostleship, but that is probably not intended in this instance. Rather, Paul is portrayed as the guardian of true, sound faith (cf. 1:13; 2:2), the faith of God's **elect,** which is a term for Christians (see commentary at 2 Tim. 2:10). He is an apostle "for the sake of . . . knowledge of the truth" (a phrase used also at 1 Tim. 2:4; 2 Tim. 3:7) among the elect over against error. Such knowledge coheres with **godliness,** one of the chief virtues of the Pastorals (see commentary on 1 Tim. 2:2), having to do with right belief and right conduct. For this writer, true faith and right conduct are twin attributes of the Christian life. The heretical teachers, on the other hand, "profess to know God, but they deny him by their deeds" (1:16; cf. also 1 Tim. 6:3-5; 2 Tim. 3:5).

Verse 2 interjects **in hope of eternal life,** and it is not clear grammatically what the phrase connects with. The context suggests that it is an explication of Christian **faith** and **truth,** which the apostle teaches (cf. 3:7; 1 Tim. 1:16; 6:12).

The **hope of eternal life** is not **hope** in the sense of wishing, but as assurance based on what God **promised ages ago.** The words **ages ago** represent a Greek phrase used also at 2 Tim. 1:9. In that case it points back beyond history to God's "purpose" and "grace" abiding with the preexistent Christ. Some commentators conclude that in the present instance the phrase refers to past historical time, i.e., the Old Testament era.[1] Others say its meaning is identical to that in 2 Tim. 1:9 ("before time began" or "before times eternal").[2] Then we might say that a preexistent promise was given in the pre-existent Christ. The latter appears more sound.[3] (The RSV, NEB, NAB, and JB preserve the ambiguity; but TEV and NIV have, "before the beginning of time," and the KJV has "before the world began"). The **hope of eternal life** is rooted in the once hidden eternal purposes of God (cf. Rom. 16:25); it is not promised in the Old Testament. "But" (**and** in RSV) God has (translating literally) "manifested at the right time his word in proclamation." The **hope of eternal life** is not known by human speculation. It is known through the "proclamation" of God's Word, God's revealed message to humankind, which **preaching** represents. Paul himself was entrusted with this "proclamation" by divine command (cf. 1 Tim. 1:11). The term **word** (*logos* in Greek) is not to be identified with the concept of Christ as the "Word" in John 1:14, even though the writer speaks of God's manifesting his Word which is associated with the Christ event. The "Word of God" (cf. 1 Tim. 4:5; 2 Tim. 2:9; Titus 2:5) for this writer is God's saving message in the gospel which is proclaimed through Paul and those true to it (2 Tim. 4:2); it is the "word of truth" (2 Tim. 2:15), the "sure word as taught" (Titus 1:9). In 1:3 the term **Savior** is applied to God the Father, but at 1:4 it will be applied to Christ. See Introduction, Part 3, B, for a discussion of this.

4—Titus is portrayed as being on Crete at 1:5, and later in the letter he is asked to meet Paul at Nicopolis (3:12). There is no indication of where Paul is supposed to be located, except that the Roman imprisonment setting of 2 Timothy (1:8, 16-17; 4:6, 16) has to be excluded, since Paul is free to travel. Although not mentioned in Acts, Titus is mentioned by Paul in his authentic letters. He was a Gentile Christian (Gal. 2:3) who accompanied Paul and Barnabas (apparently from Antioch of Syria) to the Jerusalem conference of A.D. 48 or 49 (Gal. 2:1). He is associated with Paul particularly in his mission to Macedonia (2 Cor. 7:5-6) and Corinth (2 Cor. 7:7, 13-15; 8:16-24). Paul speaks of him as one who cares earnestly for the latter congregation, but also as one who is "famous among all the churches for his preaching of the gospel" (2 Cor. 8:18) and as one who had been "appointed by the churches to travel" with the apostle (8:19). Paul had written to Corinth a letter of strong rebuke (2 Cor. 2:2-4; 7:7), and it was Titus who brought news to Paul of the positive effects of that letter (7:7) and probably of the effects of his own efforts at mediation. Paul then sent Titus (presumably from Ephesus) to Corinth again to receive a collection for "relief of the saints" in Jerusalem (2 Cor. 8:4-7, 20, 24).

Titus is called Paul's **true child in a common faith.** The term **true child** can also be translated "genuine" or even "legitimate child" (its meaning in other Greek sources [4]). So he is portrayed as Paul's authoritative successor in his teaching and ordering of the church, as was Timothy (1 Tim. 1:2). Concerning **faith** in the Pastorals, see Introduction, Part 1, and commentary on 1 Tim. 1:1-2. **Grace and peace** is the twin greeting given in Paul's genuine letters (Rom. 1:7; 1 Cor. 1:3, etc.), and it differs from "grace, mercy, and peace" in the other Pastorals (1 Tim. 1:2; 2 Tim. 1:2). While the author applies the term **Savior** to God the Father at 1:3 (also at 1 Tim. 1:1; 2:3; 4:10; Titus 2:10; 3:4), here he applies the term to **Christ** (as at 2:13; 3:6; 2 Tim. 1:10). Christ is the manifest Savior who delivers us from death and brings "life and immortality to light" (2 Tim. 1:9-10; cf. Titus 3:5-7), according to the purpose of "God our Savior" (3:4).

■ The Body (1:5—3:11)

On the typical form of a Pauline letter, after its opening, see the commentary at 1 Tim. 1:3. While 2 Timothy contains a thanksgiving section (1:3-7), which is typical of Paul, that is not the case with the other two Pastorals. The writer moves directly into the body (1:5–3:11) at this point.

Qualifications of a Bishop (1:5-9)

5—Paul has reportedly **left** Titus on the island of **Crete.** There is no reference in Paul's genuine letters to a visit of Paul to Crete. In Acts, Paul passes along Crete but does not step foot on it during his journey to Rome (27:7-21). The letter presupposes a setting therefore for which no other information exists, nor can it be reconciled with known chronology (see Introduction, Part 1). There is no indication that the church in Crete was founded by Paul. According to Acts 2:11, Cretans were present in Jerusalem at the first Pentecost. The church at Crete could therefore have been founded relatively early by a nucleus of early believers apart from Paul. It was Paul's practice not to build on foundations laid by others (Rom. 15:20), so it is not likely that Paul carried on a mission to Crete after the events narrated in Acts or after the writing of his letters. It is possible, of course, that Titus carried on a mission to Crete, for he was a traveling missionary (2 Cor. 8:18). This letter could rely on that known and remembered history for its own supposed occasion. But we cannot be certain one way or the other. In any case, Titus is portrayed as having been left at Crete for a purpose. The RSV reads, to **amend what was defective, and appoint elders in every town.** The impression left is that **defective** and the lack

153

of **elders** are equivalent. But the words translated **amend what was defective** can be translated literally, "set right what remains" (to be done). That concern is not limited to matters of polity, for the letter also speaks of doctrinal matters (1:9—2:2; 3:9). Two concerns, doctrine and order, are spoken of, not order alone: Titus is to set what remains to be done in order before his departure (3:12), and he is to **appoint** presbyters **in every town.**

That Titus is to **appoint** presbyters raises questions. Do the communities have any choice concerning the appointments? The outlook of the Pastorals suggests that persons entrusted with leadership roles must meet certain qualifications, have a good standing in the community (1 Tim. 3:2, 5, 7; 5:22; 2 Tim. 2:2, 24-25), and have what can be called a theological education (2 Tim. 3:14-17). Furthermore, "prophetic utterances" from within the community attend the laying on of hands at ordination (1 Tim. 1:18; 4:14; 2 Tim. 1:6). Therefore one need not assume that Titus is to have autocratic authority. The term can mean that persons are to be appointed after community deliberation. Yet there can be no doubt that a main concern expressed is for a "linkage" between Paul, Titus (Paul's emissary), and those persons in charge of the communities. (At Acts 14:23, on the other hand, there is an instance at which Paul and Barnabas "elect" presbyters for certain communities in Asia Minor without community consensus as an explicit prerequisite.)

Near the end of the letter (3:12) Titus is summoned to meet Paul at Nicopolis before winter. In light of that, it can hardly be thought that Titus is now to begin the work assigned in 1:5. The verse speaks of work to have begun in the past, when Paul **left** Titus to attend to things still "left to be done," which should now be under way. Yet the work of confronting heretics and teaching is to continue with Titus as long as he is there (1:13; 2:1-6, 15; 3:1, 8), plus completing the work of appointing presbyters **in every town** (or "city by city").

6-9—On the meaning of **elders** (or presbyters) and **bishop,** see Introduction, Part 4. At 1:7 the singular "the bishop" is used in the Greek text (not brought out in RSV and NEB, which read **a bishop**). The term **bishop** applies to the leading presbyter of a congregation (and later for a district); that is the most satisfying solution to the question why 1:5 speaks of presbyters and 1:7 continues, using the term "the bishop." Since the bishop arises out of the presbytery, it is necessary that each person selected as a presbyter have qualifications for being a bishop, for he might become one. The list of qualifications is similar to that given in 1 Tim. 3:1-7, although more items are listed here. Again, as before, the list consists mainly of moral virtues, although in 1:9 there is a concern for his fidelity to **sound doctrine** and an ability to **give instruction** in it, as well as to oppose heretical teachers. While it is possible, as some commentators have suggested, that the writer has drawn upon a standard written list of virtues for the bishop in writing both 1 Tim. 3:1-7 and Titus 1:6-9, there are variations among the two, and these are sufficient to support the view that the writer speaks of qualifications typically considered necessary. Neither list is exhaustive, therefore, and a fixed source need not be posited. The term **blameless** at 1:6, 7 appears among the deacon's qualifications in 1 Tim. 3:10. On **the husband of one wife,** see commentary on 1 Tim. 3:2. That the bishop's children are to be **believers** is an additional qualification without parallel in 1 Tim. 3:1-7, but that they are to be of good conduct, under the bishop's control as head of the household, is similar to 1 Tim. 3:4-5. The bishop is called **God's steward,** which recalls the Pauline designation of himself and his co-workers as "stewards of the mysteries of God" (1 Cor. 4:1), i.e., ministers of the gospel, which reveals God's heretofore held "mystery" or "secret" (Rom. 16:25-26). The writer lists vices which should not characterize a bishop (1:7), and then the virtues which he should have (1:8), while in 1 Timothy 3 the virtues are listed first, and then the vices. Of the five vices, two are found in 1 Tim. 3:3 (**drunkard** and **violent**); one is listed in 1 Tim. 3:8 concerning deacons (**greedy for gain**), although **lovers of money** is listed in 1 Tim. 3:3 as a vice bishops should avoid. Two additional vices (**arrogant** and **quick-tempered**) are without parallel in the Pastorals and the Pauline corpus in general; they appear to replace the positive "gentle" and negative "quarrelsome" appearing in 1 Tim. 3:3. Of the six virtues which follow in 1:8, two (**hospitable** and **master of himself**) appear in 1 Tim. 3:2 (although RSV translates the latter as "sensible"). Four other virtues (**lover of goodness, upright, holy, and self-controlled**) appear only in this list regarding the bishop. The first and last are found only here in the entire New Testament as virtues. Verse 9 rounds off the list, concluding with a particularly Christian concern (most of the virtues in 1:7-8 can be considered common qualities required of any leader even in the "secular" sphere). While 1 Tim. 3:2 says that the bishop must be an "apt teacher," here the bishop is required to be firmly committed to the **sure word as taught** (i.e., the Pauline doctrine; cf. 1 Tim. 4:6; 2 Tim. 1:13) in order to instruct and to oppose heretics (cf. 2:1). The concern of 1 Tim. 3:6, that a bishop not be a recent convert, is not mentioned, which is surprising in a situation which calls for new appointments. It may be that necessity precludes that. Nor is the concern of 1 Tim. 3:7, that the bishop be well thought of by outsiders, mentioned in this place. The impression left is that the instructions of 1 Timothy are applicable to a more settled, organized community, while those in Titus are applicable to a younger mission field.

Characteristics of False Teachers (1:10-16)

10-11—After mentioning those who contradict **sound doctrine,** the writer leaves off listing qualifications of the bishop and shifts attention to the opposition. That they are **insubordinate** implies that they are not from outside, but that they are heretics within the community. The same is implied in 1:11 (that **they are upsetting whole families**) and 1:13b (that they ought to be brought back to soundness in faith). It is **especially the circumcision party** that is to be confronted. The term (Greek, "those of the circumcision") is found at Rom. 4:12, referring to Jews, and at Acts 10:45; 11:2; Gal. 2:12; and Col. 4:11, referring to Jewish Christians. The latter is the meaning here. The opponents are involved in speculations based on "Jewish myths," human traditions (1:14-15; see commentary there), and the law (3:9). Yet the question has to be left open whether these persons are recent converts from Judaism who have introduced former Jewish ways into Christian thought and practice, or whether they may be of Gentile origin. What is more clear is that they represent a form of Jewish-Christian Gnosticism (see Introduction, Part 5, for discussion of the false teachers and their teachings).

12-13a—The epithet about Cretans (**Cretans are always liars, evil beasts, lazy gluttons**) is attributed by Clement of Alexandria (*Stromata* 1.59.2) to Epimedes, a Cretan poet (sixth century B.C.). He was considered to have unusual powers of forecasting the future, so the term **prophet** was applied to him. Actually many such sayings about Cretans are extant.[5] The stereotyped national character attributed to the Cretans, an ethnic slur, is said by the writer to be **testimony** that **is true.** Both the epithet and the endorsement raise a critical question. The letter is to be read publicly in the community (see commentary at 3:15). If the letter was indeed addressed to the church at Crete and was to be read there, it must be said that the writer lacks both manners and tact. Furthermore, if the epithet is to be accepted as true, Cretans would actually be precluded from appointment as presbyters; yet it is from among the Cretans themselves that presbyters are to be selected (1:5)! Perhaps these verses (1:12-13) point to the "unreal" character of the letter, i.e., that the letter was not actually addressed to the church at Crete, and that "Crete" is only a cipher for the Pauline field outside Ephesus. We cannot resolve the issue. What is more certain is that the writer has taken the opportunity, recalling an epithet, to attack the opponents further, not only by "name calling" (frequent enough in the Pastorals), but also by asserting that heretics, for all their religiosity, tend not to be truly transformed (cf. 1:16; 2 Tim. 3:5) but carry old habits with them, such as being perpetual liars.

13b-14—Rebuking the opponents is not for the sake of driving them away. A purpose clause is used, "in order that" (simply **that** in RSV) **they may be sound in the faith.** On "faith" in the Pastorals, see commentary on 1 Tim. 1:2 (and Introduction, Part 1). On **Jewish myths** (1:14), see commentary on 1 Tim. 1:4 (and Introduction, Part 5). The term **commands of men** (or "human commandments") refers to legal prescriptions of Jewish or Jewish-Christian tradition which are not, according to this and other writers of the New Testament, binding on the Christian. At Mark 7:5-13 a distinction is made between the clear commandment of God (7:8, 9) and human traditions (or commandments, 7:5, 7, 8) in Jewish tradition; cf. also Col. 2:22. The writer shares the outlook of Jesus and Paul (Rom. 7:12) that the law is "good" (1 Tim. 1:8). But the law is also clear in what it teaches (cf. Rom. 13:8-9; Gal. 5:14), and the problem with adding human traditions to it is that such additions can lead a person away from the true intention of the law and also lead to excusing oneself from doing God's will (cf. Matt. 23:23-24; Mark 7:8; Luke 11:42); thereby one will finally **reject the truth.**

15-16—The phrase **to the pure** speaks of those who are "pure in heart" (1 Tim. 1:5; 2 Tim. 2:22), which Christians are through baptismal regeneration (3:5). To such persons, **all things are pure** (cf. Luke 11:41). The teaching goes against the cultic and dietary laws of uncleanness, considered by the writer as "human commandments." Such laws are found in Jewish tradition (Lev. 10:10; 11:1-47; cf. Mark 7:1-5) and, as the present passage indicates, in the precepts of the heretical Christians, who insist on laws of cleanliness. The teaching given here (that **all things are pure**) is rooted in the ministry of Jesus (Mark 7:14-23) and the teaching of Paul (Rom. 14:14-21; cf. also Acts 11:9). The heretics teach abstinence from certain foods in particular (1 Tim. 4:3), but for this writer, "everything created by God is good, and nothing is to be rejected if it is received with thanksgiving" (1 Tim. 4:3-4). For the opponents, who are **corrupt and unbelieving, nothing is pure.** This is undoubtedly hyperbole, setting up a contrast between **all** for believers and **nothing** for unbelievers. The erroneous judgment of the heretics on these matters is rooted in the corruption of their **minds and consciences.** This corruption is their commitment to a Jewish-Christian Gnosticism. They claim to **know God** (Gnostic movements claim superior knowledge of God as the means of salvation), but what they claim to know is false, not true to what is known through the "sure word as taught" (1:9). Their **deeds** (immoral conduct and deception, 1:10-11) demonstrate that **they deny** God. Being **disobedient** to sound teaching and its representatives, they are incapable of any **good deed.**

Instructions for a Christian Ethos (2:1-10)

1. The Conduct of Older Men and Women (2:1-3)

1—Titus is exhorted to teach **what befits** (RSV, or is "in keeping with," NEB) **sound doctrine. Sound doctrine** itself is to be taught (1:9; cf. 2 Tim. 2:3), but here it is recognized that Christian teaching must always be developed in light of new situations, and a Christian outlook must grow out of what has been received. Cf. Matt. 13:52. In the verses which follow there is instruction for developing a Christian ethos in the community in line with what has been received.

2-3—Many of the virtues expected of the various groups mentioned in 2:2-10 correspond with ideals for each group in Graeco-Roman culture (such as Stoic teaching, in which one should practice virtue in accord with one's station in life); each of the five groups is to live in accord with what is proper to itself. Early Christian teaching, including Paul (cf. Phil. 4:8-9), did not despise the higher moral teaching of Graeco-Roman tradition—for the Christian life is not lived away from the world, but within it (cf. 1 Tim. 3:7)—but accepted that which coheres with Christ and the earliest witnesses to him. This section therefore shows **what befits** (or can be derived from) **sound doctrine** (2:1). Similar lists of duties can be found in Eph. 5:22—6:9; Col. 3:18—4:1; and 1 Peter 2:18—3:9.

Three of the six expectations of the **older men** can be found in sections prescribing the virtues of bishops (**temperate, serious, sensible,** 1 Tim. 3:2, 8). The next three form a triadic cluster of virtues; the word **sound** applies not only to **faith** but to the other words as well, meaning: "sound in faith, sound in love, sound in steadfastness." To be **sound in faith** is to believe what is true (1 Tim. 6:3; 2 Tim. 1:13; 4:3; Titus 1:9, 13; 2:1). But the older men are also to be **sound** in **love** and **steadfastness** (or "endurance," persisting in both true faith and right conduct). These virtues are listed elsewhere as typifying the Christian life (1 Tim. 1:5; 4:12; 6:11; 2 Tim. 1:13; 3:10).

Instructions concerning women in the community are given in 1 Tim. 2:9-15; 3:11; and 5:9-10. Here the **older women** are singled out for special instructions. The words **to be reverent in behavior** represent a Greek phrase, found only here in the New Testament, which can be rendered more literally, "to be in conduct as befitting priests." The verse is not evidence for the existences of priestesses in the community, for there is no special priesthood envisioned in the Pastorals—nor elsewhere in the New Testament; the church itself is a priestly people (1 Peter 2:5), offering themselves as living sacrifices to God (Rom. 12:1). The older women are not to be **slanderers** (prohibited elsewhere for women, 1 Tim. 3:11; 5:13, and men, 2 Tim. 3:3), nor are they to be **slaves to drink** (cf. 1 Tim. 3:8). What has been given to this point concerning older women are qualities which should actually characterize all Christians, but what follows is a special role. The older women are to **teach what is good.** This does not contradict the prohibition against teaching in 1 Tim. 2:12, for what and whom they are to teach follow in the next two verses. By word and example the older women are to teach young women about their role in the community.

2. The Conduct of Young Women, Young Men, and Teachers (2:4-8)

4-5—The older women are to teach **the young women** in domestic virtues; therefore 2:4-5 serves a double function. It continues the duties of the older women (2:3) but speaks also of virtues for young women. To **love their husbands and children** typifies the virtues of women seen elsewhere in the Pastorals (1 Tim. 2:15; 5:10, 14) as well as in Jewish tradition (Gen. 3:16; 4 Macc. 15:4-5) and Hellenistic culture.[6] The word translated **sensible** appears also at 2:2 concerning older men and at 1 Tim. 3:2 concerning a bishop. The word translated **chaste** (RSV, NEB) can also mean "holy" or "pure," but in this context (as in 4 Macc. 18:7; 2 Cor. 11:2) "chaste" is meant. Attending to duties in the home (**domestic**) is particularly important for the Christian wife (contrast the consequences of not so doing in 1 Tim. 5:13; 2 Tim. 3:6). Being **submissive to their husbands** is a common theme in early Christian teaching (1 Cor. 11:3; Eph. 5:22; Col. 3:18; 1 Peter 3:1). Here it may have special bearing on a situation in which the heretical teachers have promised a level of emancipation that is disruptive to family and community life and therefore to true piety as well (see 2 Tim. 3:6 and commentary there). This view is made more certain by the motivation for it: **that the word of God may not be discredited.** God's Word is the saving

message in the gospel proclaimed by Paul and those who
are faithful to that gospel (see commentary on 1:3). Any
conduct, by men or women, which causes reproach from
either within or without the community brings the Christian
message itself into question and renders it incredible. True
Christian teaching results in virtuous living (1 Tim. 1:5).

6-8—As being "sensible" is a virtue for the older men (2:2)
and young women (2:5), so young men are to "be sensible concerning all things." The RSV translation is based on a decision
about punctuation which is not followed here nor by most
commentators. A better translation is: "Exhort the younger
men likewise to be sensible concerning all things, showing
yourself as a model of good deeds." As Timothy is called upon
to be a model for others (1 Tim. 4:12), so Titus is, and consequently the community leaders. Teaching is to be done with
integrity and **gravity** (the latter can be translated also as "in a
respectful manner"; cf. its usage at 1 Tim. 2:2; 3:4). The **sound
speech that cannot be censured** refers to the content of the
teaching. The second half of the verse (2:8b) has a purpose
clause in Greek (not made clear in the RSV), "in order that"
(instead of **so that,** which RSV has) the **opponent may be put
to shame, having nothing evil to say of us.** What is taught
should be **sound,** in accord with Pauline tradition. The heretical teachers may indeed have a different doctrinal position,
but they should not be given opportunity to fault the moral
teaching of the leaders or the behavior of members of the
community.

3. The Conduct of Slaves (2:9-10)

As elsewhere in the New Testament, the institution of slavery is assumed (see the discussion of slavery in commentary on
1 Tim. 6:1-2). It is clear that **slaves** were members of the Christian community being addressed here. Such persons are to be
submissive **in every respect.** This latter phrase can be linked
grammatically with either **be submissive** or **give satisfaction.**

While the RSV links it with the latter, virtually all commentators and the NEB link it with the former. That is probably to be preferred, given the absolutistic tone of the passage. Christian freedom is not freedom from life in this world and its order. On the contrary, slaves are to **give satisfaction** and not **be refractory** (literally, "talk back"). They are not **to pilfer** (misappropriate goods for their own satisfaction), but show **fidelity** to their masters. The motivation for such conduct is Christian witness, not fear of punishment. By their conduct slaves will **adorn the doctrine of God our Savior.** The heretical teachers may have urged slaves to rebel according to the freedom declared in their message (2 Tim. 2:18), but for this writer nothing less than exemplary conduct is the fruit of the Christian faith, regardless of social position. On the phrase **God our Savior,** see the Introduction, Part 3, B.

Life Under Grace (2:11—3:11)

1. The Transforming Power of Grace (2:11-15)

11—This section provides the theological underpinnings of what has gone before and what will follow. It can be considered the fulcrum of the letter. Correct doctrine and right living are rooted in the prevenient grace of God, which has been manifested in the Christ event, rather than in speculative philosophy or religion, which leads to indulging in myths, human traditions, and base conduct. The **grace of God** is the divine favor which **has appeared** in the coming of Christ in time past. The words recall the statement of 2 Tim. 1:9-10, which also speaks of "grace" in Christ, which has been "manifested through the 'appearing' of our Savior Christ Jesus." In the present verse Jesus Christ is not named as the one through whom the divine grace is given, but that is meant. The verse can be translated literally, "for God's grace has appeared, bringing salvation to all persons." [7] The appearance of God's grace is in the Christ event, and it is effective **to all** persons.

163

The latter phrase is important. The heretical opponents would not affirm that salvation is offered to all, but only to those "enlightened ones" who follow their speculations and manner of life. But for this writer salvation is offered through the proclamation of the gospel (1:3; 1 Tim. 4:10; 2 Tim. 1:10), and God wills the salvation of all (1 Tim. 2:4).

12—The grace which has appeared in Christ has an educating effect, not in a speculative way, but in the sense of moral training. It leads the Christian to renounce certain things (**irreligion and worldly passions**) and to affirm others (sobriety, uprightness, and godliness). **Irreligion** (or "impiety," "godless ways," NEB) is the fruit of heretical teachings (2 Tim. 2:16). **Worldly passions,** a term used only here in the New Testament, are desires arising out of a life not yet transformed by the gospel (see 3:3). The positive virtues listed are three of the writer's most highly valued qualities of Christian life (sobriety, 2:2, 5; 1 Tim. 3:2; uprightness, 1:8; 2 Tim. 2:22; 3:16; godliness, 1 Tim. 4:7; 6:3, 11).

13-14—The Christian life is one of **awaiting our blessed hope.** The heretical teachers, who hold that "the resurrection is past already" (2 Tim. 2:18), make no distinction between life in this world and in that to come. But the writer of the Pastorals speaks of living **sober, upright, and godly lives in this world** (2:12); the latter phrase can also be translated "in the present age" (a term appearing also at 1 Tim. 6:17; 2 Tim. 4:10), which is an age dominated by secular values (in Paul it is ruled by Satan, is evil, and is to pass away, 2 Cor. 4:4; Gal. 1:4; 1 Cor. 2:6; 7:31). Living "in the present age," the Christian awaits an age to come and aligns thought and conduct with it in this world, expecting its coming.

The content of the **blessed hope** is the parousia, the coming of Christ. The writer uses a circumlocution; the community awaits **the appearing of the glory of our great God and Savior Jesus Christ.** The concept of the appearance of **glory** is rooted in the Old Testament, particularly in connection with theophanies (e.g., the "glory" of the Lord on Mount Sinai, Exod. 24:15-18), actually signifying God's presence. Postexilic writers speak of apprehending the "glory of God," and thus God's glorious presence, as a future hope (Ps. 102:15-16; Isa. 24:23; 40:5). Paul (Rom. 5:2), the author of 1 Peter (4:13; 5:1), and the writer of the Pastorals share in speaking of the coming **glory** of Christ at his parousia. (KJV reads "the glorious appearing" rather than "the appearance of the glory"; although the KJV is not literal here, it captures the thought.) The one to appear is **our great God and Savior Jesus Christ.** The Greek can be translated "the great God *and* our Savior Jesus Christ," which would make a distinction between God and Christ, subordinating Christ to the Father. In favor of this, it can be said that rarely does the New Testament speak unequivocally of Christ as God (the only other places are John 20:28; Heb. 1:8). While some commentators conclude that the translation "God and our Savior Jesus" is correct,[8] as do the translators of the KJV and NAB, most opt for the former,[9] **our great God and Savior Jesus,** as do the translators of the RSV, NEB, JB, TEV, and NIV. The pattern of the Greek, placing the word for **our** after both **God and Savior,** favors this rendering (contrast 2 Thess. 1:12 and 2 Peter 1:1, which separate "our God" and "Savior," distinguishing God and Christ).[10] Also, of course, it is one appearing (that of Christ)—not two (God and Christ)—which is anticipated. Here we reach a high point of New Testament Christology. The attributes of "God" and "Savior" are applied to Jesus Christ. This does not mean that the writer is incapable of distinctions (see 1:4; 3:4-6; 1 Tim. 1:1; 2:5-6; 5:21; 2 Tim. 4:1), but at the parousia Christ will bear the divine glory and do the saving work of God. In that sense, he will be our **God and Savior.**

The next verse (2:14) also shows that Christ alone is referred to in 2:13. **Our great God and Savior** is the one who **gave himself for us.** That in Christ God has condescended to save lost humanity is the core and substance of the Christian gospel, apart from which there is no gospel at all. The thought expressed, which is filled with the purpose clause **to redeem us from all iniquity and to purify for himself a people,** recalls other passages using the language of "giving himself" and "redemption" (1 Tim. 2:6; Mark 10:45; Gal. 1:4). It uses but does not quote Old Testament formulations, such as Ps. 130:8 ("he will redeem Israel from all iniquities") and others which speak of God's purifying his people (Ezek. 37:23) and claiming them as a possession (Exod. 19:5-6; Deut. 4:20; 7:6; 14:2). The passage lacks the radicality of Paul, for whom believers have been redeemed from the objective, external powers of the present age (Gal. 1:4). Redemption here is forgiveness of sins, and its attendant consequences are purification and special ownership by God (cf. 1 Peter 2:9). The verse uses cultic language, and the church is seen to be the new Israel, God's people in the present age (the Pastorals do not take up the question of the significance of Israel's continuity in Judaism). As Israel was "zealous" for the law (Deut. 26:18; Rom. 10:2-3), so the church is to be **zealous for good deeds** (cf. 1 Peter 3:13).

15—Titus is admonished to **exhort** the faithful and to **reprove with all authority** those who might be attracted to heretical teachings. Cf. a similar admonition to Timothy at 1 Tim. 4:12. Again, as in other contexts in the Pastorals, the admonition is addressed to the authoritative teachers, but also to the congregation. (**Let no one disregard you** makes this clear.) The doctrinal and moral teaching of the apostle, mediated through select leaders who adhere to the teaching of the Pastorals, is the norm for Christian thought and life. Other teachers are to be avoided if the congregation is to be truly Christian.

2. *Life Under Grace in the World (3:1-2)*

1-2—The teaching on submission to governing authorities, addressed to the whole congregation, recalls the teaching of Paul (Rom. 13:1-7; cf. also 1 Peter 2:13-17). For a treatment of this teaching in the Pastorals, see the commentary at 1 Tim.

2:1-2, which shows that other options were possible. Although the rulers were pagans, Christians are taught to serve them, thereby promoting a good social order while the present age (2:12) endures; the gospel of Christ does not emancipate a person from life in the world, but sets the Christian free for service within it. Therefore the Christian is **ready for any honest work** (literally, "every good work"); cf. 3:8. The message of the heretical teachers promotes indolence and love of pleasure (2 Tim. 3:2-4), as elsewhere in the Pauline field (2 Thess. 3:6-12). Here, as also in Rom. 13:1-7 and 1 Peter 2:13-17, no limits to obedience are stated (although we can assume that some things, such as emperor worship, would be precluded); the church lives at a time of relative peace (cf. 1 Tim. 2:2), and limits to obedience are not contemplated.

Along with civic virtue and well-doing in general, there are some specifics of conduct mentioned in reference to life in society. The words rendered **to speak evil of no one** have to do with slander (as the NEB, "slander no one," makes clear). **Quarreling** is a vice to be avoided not only within the Christian community (1 Tim. 2:8; 2 Tim. 2:24) and with heretical teachers (Titus 3:9), but also in the public arena. Gentleness is expected of Christians (cf. 1 Tim. 6:11), and they should show **perfect courtesy** toward all persons, not just Christians (cf. commentary at 1 Tim. 2:1-2), a teaching which has antecedents in the teachings of Jesus (Matt. 5:47-48) and Paul (Gal. 6:10).

3. *Life Prior to Grace (3:3)*

Already in 2:11-12 there is a contrast between a life transformed by the grace of God, communicated through the revelatory Word, and that prior to grace. Here that contrast is painted in darkest colors. That from which "he saved us" (3:5) is a list of vices which do not appear elsewhere in the Pastorals. The vices given are not so much those which fall short of an objective standard of virtue, but are rather those of an existential kind, having to do with lack of understanding, perverted will, enslavement to passions and pleasures, and hatred. Here the writer goes deeper than usual in an analysis of the human condition. The section is closer in outlook to Paul's discussion in Rom. 1:21-31 than to vice lists elsewhere in the Pastorals (e.g., 2 Tim. 3:2-4). Likewise, the device of referring to a former life in contrast to the present is found in Paul (1 Cor. 6:11) and other places in the New Testament (Eph. 2:2; 5:8; Col. 3:7-8; cf. 1 Peter 4:3-4). The words **we ourselves** differ from "you" in the other instances, however. This is a literary device, not intended to be autobiographical (see Phil. 3:4-7 regarding Paul's speaking of himself prior to his call as an apostle), or descriptive of the readers (who may in the main be second or third generation Christians; cf. 2 Tim. 3:15). It is used to make a theological analysis of the general state of humankind prior to receiving the gospel and seen from the standpoint of the life transformed by it.

4. Baptismal Regeneration in Christ (3:4-8a)

The 26th edition of the "Nestle-Aland" Greek New Testament indents 3:4-7 into a poetic format. It has been suggested that the section is a hymn used at baptisms.[11] There is disagreement over how many lines of our text such a hymn would have contained. One commentator, for example, includes only 3:5b-7,[12] but this can hardly stand without 3:4-5a as introduction and counterpoint to what follows. Whether 3:4-7 as given is an exact quotation of a hymn cannot be determined, but that the section has a liturgical background, using phrases from a baptismal setting, is clear. Verse 8a (**The saying is sure**) refers to what has gone before (3:4-7) and supplies a close for the lines quoted. While elsewhere these words introduce material following it (1 Tim. 1:15; 3:1; 4:9; 2 Tim. 2:11), the context in this instance requires that it refer to what precedes. As in most other instances (see commentary at 1 Tim. 1:15), it is used in connection with soteriological teaching (given in 3:4-7).

4—Rather than speaking directly of Christ, the subject of the clause is **the goodness and loving kindness of God our Savior.** The word translated **goodness** is used by Paul at Rom. 2:4 in connection with God's patience (cf. also Rom. 11:22), but it becomes linked with grace in Eph. 2:7. Here it becomes associated with God's **mercy** (3:5) and **grace** (3:7). The term used for **loving kindness** (more literally, "love for humanity") is used in 2 Macc. 14:9 as an attribute of God. Both terms have a rather humanitarian ring to them (the latter, *philanthrōpia*, becomes the loan-word for the English "philanthropy"). Soteriology is thereby expressed in the language of common life. The words **the goodness and loving kindness of God our Savior** stand as a circumlocution for the Christ event, expressed by the verb **appeared.** The term **God our Savior** is God the Father (as at 1:3; 2:10; 1 Tim. 1:1; 2:3; 4:10). In the Christ event ("the appearing of our Savior Jesus Christ," 2 Tim. 1:10) God has acted in goodness and loving kindness (see 2:11 for a similar expression), and therefore God can be spoken of as **our Savior.**

5—The subject of **he saved us** is God the Father, as the "he" of 3:6 shows. The words following can be translated more literally than the RSV has: "not because of works done in righteousness which we did." Righteousness by works is excluded, as in Paul (Rom. 3:20; 9:11; cf. Eph. 2:8-9). The basis and initiative of salvation is purely God's **mercy** (cf. Eph. 2:4), a term which is equivalent to the Pauline "grace" (Rom. 3:24; 5:15), as seen in 3:7.

God's saving work is spoken of here in past tense (**he saved us**) and as operative in Baptism, **the washing of regeneration and renewal in the Holy Spirit.** That God saves through Baptism is also affirmed at 1 Peter 3:21. The word for **washing** *(loutron)* appears elsewhere in the New Testament only at Eph. 5:26, which speaks of Christ as having cleansed his church "by the washing of water with the word," which is even more clearly a usage of "washing" for Baptism. Moreover, at John 13:1-11 there are references to washing which symbolize Baptism (especially at 13:8, 10).[13] Ideas of **regeneration** and **renewal** were connected with baptism already in Judaism, which practiced the baptism of proselytes in the New Testament era.[14] The combined data make it clear that the verse refers to Baptism, not to a spiritual experience apart from the sacramental act. The term for **regeneration** is found elsewhere in the New Testament only at Matt. 19:28; there it means "the new (messianic) world" or "age." But the two concepts are not unrelated in Christian thought. Particularly in Paul one can see the connection. Through Baptism a person is incorporated into Christ, and that is into the crucified Christ, so that the baptized person shares in his death (Rom. 6:3-4). But as the crucified Christ was raised, so the Christian walks in "newness of life" and is a "new creation" (2 Cor. 5:17), belonging to the new (messianic) age or world. This alliance between "regeneration" and "new age" is brought out in the following phrase, **renewal in the Holy Spirit.** The gift of the Spirit is a sign of the messianic age (cf. Joel 2:28-29; Acts 2:14-21). Through Baptism a renewal in the Spirit takes place, so that the baptized person belongs to the new age, while living in the old (see commentary at 2:12). Earlier Paul had spoken of Christians as being baptized "by one Spirit" and "into one body" (1 Cor. 12:13). Baptism is seen to be an action by which the Spirit operates to transfer a person into the one body of Christ, the new humanity. Again, an alliance found in Paul between Baptism and the Spirit informs the thinking of the present passage. It is also found at John 3:5.

6—God has **poured out** his Spirit **upon us richly through Jesus Christ our Savior.** The verb is the same one used in Acts 2:17, 33 (from Joel 2:28, LXX) to signify the outpouring of the Spirit at Pentecost. The verse does not allude to continuing ecstatic or pentecostal outpourings in the community. The "completed past" tense (aorist in Greek) is used, signifying that the new (messianic) age of Christ has dawned upon the world, with its attendant gifts of the Spirit. The outpouring has come **through Christ,** who is the mediator of the Spirit (as elsewhere, Acts 2:33; John 15:26; 16:7).

7—The verse consists of a purpose clause. It completes the whole section 3:4-6, for the main verb ("he saved us," 3:5) governs the entire passage. The salvation of God consists of justification and a consequent inheritance. The phrase **justified by his grace** is almost identical to the words of Paul in Rom. 3:24. As in Paul the term **justified** has the meaning of having been set right in relationship to God. This is purely by **grace** apart from works (3:5; cf. 2 Tim. 1:9). The accent is on God as the one who saves (3:5) "in order that" being justified **by his grace** (not by our works) we might become **heirs in hope of eternal life.** The term **heirs** is again Pauline (Rom. 4:14; 8:17; Gal. 3:29), but the phrase **hope of eternal life** is idiomatic of this writer (cf. 1:2). Why the author does not simply say "heirs of eternal life" is puzzling. Yet that meaning is not far away. The Christian lives in hope (as assurance, not wish; cf. 1:2; 2:13) in the present age (2:12). The heretical teachers collapse the "already" and "not yet" distinction (2 Tim. 2:18), but the writer maintains the tension; we are **heirs in hope.** On the one hand, the Christian lives in the "already" of the new age, which **regeneration and renewal** in the Spirit bring, but **eternal life** is still a "not yet," future hope (cf. 1 Tim. 1:16; 6:12), as in Paul (Rom. 2:7; 5:21; 6:22-23; Gal. 6:8).

Questions can be raised concerning the entire passage (3:4-7). Is Baptism the means by which salvation is mediated? If so, is it the only means? In working out an answer it must be said that the passage is first of all hymnic, not a dogmatic statement. The accent is on God's saving power. God **saved us . . . in virtue of his mercy** (3:5). Believers are **justified by his grace** (3:7). But how is this justifying grace to be made known? It is made known through the proclamation of the good news of its manifestation in Christ (2 Tim. 1:9-11), and it is also communicated through Baptism (3:5). The hymn celebrates the regeneration and inheritance which Baptism bestows. Baptism is taken to illustrate and to declare, not to limit, the saving activity of God, who desires all persons to be saved (1 Tim. 2:4). We cannot expect a hymn or hymn fragment to provide a dogmatic system.

5. *Faith and Works (3:8b-11)*

8b—Titus (and so teachers in the community) is to **insist on these things,** which probably refers to all that has been said previously in the letter. And that is for a purpose, that believers **may be careful to apply themselves to good deeds.** The heirs of eternal life, awaiting final salvation, are to live out the new, transformed life in the world. The imperative of good conduct is based on the indicative of baptismal identity. The verb translated **apply** can be translated "be foremost in the practice of" [15] good deeds. NEB has "honorable occupations" instead of **good deeds** (RSV, which has a marginal note allowing an alternative, "enter honorable occupations"). Yet the words rendered usually mean "good deeds" in the Pastorals (1 Tim. 5:10, 25; 6:18; Titus 2:7, 14; 3:14), and that is probably the meaning here. Such deeds are **excellent** (Greek, "good") and **profitable** (or "useful") to others. As earlier (3:1-2; cf. 1 Tim. 2:1-2), the writer has an outlook which extends beyond the community to the larger society. Christians live in the world and are to practice good deeds within it, especially deeds of compassion (3:14), not limiting their generosity to the Christian community.

9—But Titus (and therefore the community teachers/leaders) is to avoid certain things which are **unprofitable** and **futile** and which particularly beset the community, out of which the heretical teachers themselves have come (see commentary at 1:10-11). These are **stupid controversies, genealogies, dissensions, and quarrels over the law** incited by the heretical teachers, who represent a Jewish-Christian Gnosticism. On their teachings, see Introduction, Part 5, and commentary on 1

Tim. 1:4, 6-10; 2 Tim. 2:18, 23-26. The writer typically does not refute the teachings of these persons, and he prohibits others from doing so, because to do so gains nothing. It is better to avoid them. At 1:9 he writes that a bishop should be able to "confute those who contradict" sound doctrine. But that refers more to admonition, as the following verse shows, rather than to substantive refutation in depth. The bishop should be able to discern what is heretical, name it as such, and confront it, but not spend time in refutation. More appropriately the bishop should provide sound teaching and exhort the community to good deeds.

10-11—The term rendered **factious** is the basis for our loan-word "heretical" (Greek, *hairetikon*), and the NEB translates accordingly ("a heretic"). Yet the RSV is better. The adjective appears only here in the New Testament, and although the Pastorals combat "heretical" teachers often, this term is not applied to them as it has been by us. The noun from which the adjective is derived is *hairesis* (from which "heresy" comes.) It does not usually mean "false teaching," as our word "heresy" connotes, but "sect" or "party" (Acts 5:17; 15:5; 24:5, 14; 26:5; 28:22) or a "faction" (1 Cor. 11:19; Gal. 5:20). The term comes to mean "heretical sect" in 2 Peter 2:1 and in the letters of Ignatius (*Letter to the Ephesians* 6.2; *Letters to the Trallians* 6.1), but the person spoken of in Titus 3:10 is a person within the community who is **factious**, causing division and perhaps insubordination. Such a person is to be warned twice (RSV has **once or twice,** but literally the phrase translates, "after one and a second warning"; so NEB, "once, and once again"), and if that does not lead to correction, it is necessary to "avoid" or perhaps "reject" such a person (RSV, **have nothing more to do with him,** is probably too mild; the verb has stronger connotations when it appears elsewhere, 1 Tim. 4:7; 5:11; 2 Tim. 2:33). The verse prescribes an informal form of church discipline (cf. Rom. 16:17; admonitions are to be given, but no step-by-step procedure for a process is given, as for example in Matt. 18:15-16). Exclusion of a **factious** person may be necessary, but that is to be decided through the personal, spiritual authority of the community leadership (cf. 1 Cor. 5:1-2 for an example of exclusion of a member for a blatant offense). Such a person is to be considered **perverted** (or better, "turned aside"—a term used only here in the New Testament) and **sinful.** He is **self-condemned** (a term only here in the New Testament). In other words, the act of exclusion is the community's recognition that the factious person has already turned aside and excluded himself.

■ Closing (3:12-15)

Instructions (3:12-14)

12—Titus has been portrayed as residing on the island of Crete (1:5) where he is to finish the work assigned for him by Paul and as set forth further in the letter. Yet he is now instructed to "make haste" (Greek; RSV, **do your best**) to come to Paul at **Nicopolis** before the onset of the succeeding **winter** (on the matter of travel prior to winter, see commentary on 2 Tim. 4:21). The departure from Crete, however, is not to take place until the arrival there of either **Artemas** or **Tychicus,** who are presumably to be thought of as being with Paul. Of Artemas we know nothing from the New Testament or other sources. Tychicus is identified at Acts 20:4 as an "Asian" and as one of those, including Timothy, who accompanied Paul on his final journey to Jerusalem. He is mentioned at Eph. 6:21 and Col. 4:7 as an emissary of Paul who bears the letters to Ephesus and Colossae, and at 2 Tim. 4:12 he is Paul's emissary to Ephesus. Now he is a possible candidate to follow up the work of Titus at Crete. Nicopolis is the name of several cities,[16] but it is commonly thought that this one is the Nicopolis of Epirus in Greece. Paul is portrayed as a free man in this letter, as also in 1 Timothy

(4:13), while in 2 Timothy he is portrayed as imprisoned (1:15-18; 4:6, 16-18).

13—It is unclear whether **Zenas the lawyer and Apollos** are supposed to be with Titus on Crete, or whether they are supposed to be the bearers of the letter from Paul to Titus. In any case, they are to be sent on, not necessarily to Paul, lacking nothing in the way of provisions. Zenas (presumably a secular "lawyer," not a religious "teacher of the law" as in 1 Tim. 1:7) is not mentioned elsewhere. Apollos may be the person of that name mentioned at Acts 18:24; 19:1 as an Alexandrian Christian of Jewish birth who came to Ephesus and later to Corinth. He was eloquent and "well versed in the Scriptures." Yet he was instructed further by Priscilla and Aquila. In 1 Corinthians he is mentioned several times (1:12; 3:4-6, 22; 4:6; 16:12). Apparently he followed up the work of Paul in Corinth (1 Cor. 3:6) and gained some personal following, but Paul continued to speak of him as his spiritual brother and urged him to visit Corinth again (1 Cor. 16:12). It is probable that this Apollos is the one alluded to in Titus 3:13, although one cannot be certain, since the name was common at the time.

14—**Our people,** an endearing expression used only here, are to **learn to apply themselves to** (or "be foremost in the practice of"; cf. the commentary at 3:8) **good deeds.** As in 2:12; 3:1-2, 8, the exhortation is to do good in the public sphere. Particularity is prescribed in the words which follow, translated literally, "for pressing needs, lest they be unfruitful." As in 3:10 there is a prescription for church discipline within the community, here there is a prescription for "social ministry" which reaches beyond the Christian community into the larger community setting.

Greetings and Benediction (3:15)

The **all who are with me** are unspecified in the letter except for Artemas and Tychicus (3:12). The phrase translated **those**

175

who love us in the faith is, more literally, "those who love us in faith" (the article "the" does not appear) or perhaps "with fidelity" (which the Greek term can mean; cf. 2:10). Yet it probably refers to persons "in faith" (cf. 1 Tim. 1:2; Titus 1:4), i.e., Christians.

As at 1 Tim. 6:21 and 2 Tim. 4:22, the closing benediction contains the plural form for **you** in Greek; here the word **all** is added (not in the other two letters). This letter, like the others, was intended for public reading, as even the letters of the apostle himself (cf. 1 Thess. 5:27).

SELECTED BIBLIOGRAPHY
FOR 1-2 TIMOTHY AND TITUS

Annotated Bibliography of Commentaries in English

C. K. Barrett, *The Pastoral Epistles* (Oxford: Oxford University, 1963). A brief commentary, but one of the best in recent years, drawing upon modern scholarship and making its own contribution. The introduction is one of the most extensive and helpful available, and the commentary is excellent, based on the NEB.

J. H. Bernard, *The Pastoral Epistles* (Cambridge: Cambridge University, 1899). Based on the Greek text, this commentary is one of the most valuable in matters of Greek language and syntax.

Martin Dibelius and Hans Conzelmann, *The Pastoral Epistles* (Hermeneia Commentary; Philadelphia: Fortress, 1972). This is translated from a respected German series of commentaries, based on the Greek text. It is indispensible for the specialist. It offers much background material (especially Graeco-Roman texts) and provides extensive bibliography. It is the leading critical commentary available on the Pastorals.

Burton Scott Easton, *The Pastoral Epistles* (New York: C. Scribner's Sons, 1947). The commentary is quite brief. The value of the book lies chiefly in its extensive word studies.

It treats the Pastorals in the sequence Easton thought they were written: 2 Timothy, Titus, 1 Timothy.

Robert Falconer, *The Pastoral Epistles* (Oxford: Oxford University, 1937). The commentary, based on the Greek text, offers illustrative material from Graeco-Roman literature to aid translation and interpretation. Of 164 pages, 72 are devoted to introductory questions. The commentary treats the Pastorals in this sequence: 2 Timothy, Titus, 1 Timothy, although the author thinks Titus was the first written.

Fred D. Gealy, *The First and Second Epistles to Timothy and the Epistle to Titus (Interpreter's Bible* 11; Nashville: Abingdon, 1955). This commentary remains one of the best to have been written in terms of actually interpreting the text. It is one of the most thorough in both its introductory essays and exegetical treatment. It also summarizes the views of other, previous scholars up to the time of its publication, but much has happened since.

Donald Guthrie, *The Pastoral Epistles* (Tyndale New Testament Commentaries; Grand Rapids: Eerdmans, 1957). Although formally based on the KJV, the author actually makes use of the Greek text and modern versions to go beyond it. The point of view is that the Pastorals were written by Paul, and the author provides one of the most extensive discussions in modern English commentaries to defend that point of view.

Anthony T. Hanson, *The Pastoral Epistles* (New Century Bible Commentary; Grand Rapids: Eerdmans, 1982). Based on the RSV, this commentary appears in a distinguished English-language series. It is excellent in many respects: introductory essays, bibliographical references (found within the exegesis), and commentary. It summarizes and contends with virtually all significant scholarship on the Pastorals up to the time of its writing in masterful fashion.

J. L. Houlden, *The Pastoral Epistles* (Pelican New Testament Commentaries; New York: Penguin, 1976). Written for the general reader, it nevertheless provides a fine introduction to scholarship on the Pastorals and crisp, but usually ample, commentary.

Robert J. Karris, *The Pastoral Epistles* (New Testament Message 17; Wilmington: M. Glazier, 1979). This commentary has been written in a popular style for a general audience. It is informative and insightful and seeks to apply the "message" to the modern context when appropriate and relevant.

J. N. D. Kelly, *A Commentary on the Pastoral Epistles* (Harper's New Testament Commentaries; New York: Harper & Row, 1963; reprinted, Thornapple Commentaries; Grand Rapids: Baker, 1981). This is one of the most extensive of recent commentaries written in English in terms of commentary on the text. The introduction is ample, but in its treatment of various topics it is often building the case for Pauline authorship rather than treating the topics in their own right. Nevertheless, this commentary will continue to be one of the most important for exegetical purposes.

Walter Lock, *A Critical and Exegetical Commentary on the Pastoral Epistles* (International Critical Commentary; Edinburgh: T. & T. Clark, 1924). Based on the Greek text, and making use of Greek extensively, this commentary is essential for specialized study. It provides extensive comment and illustrative material regarding the Greek text and some fine studies of words and topics.

E. F. Scott, *The Pastoral Epistles* (Moffatt New Testament Commentary; New York: Harper, 1936). Based on James Moffatt's translation of the New Testament, this commentary treats the text with care in regard to matters of translation. It is the first major commentary in English to regard the Pastorals as pseudonymous. It offers detailed commentary in a very readable fashion.

E. K. Simpson, *The Pastoral Epistles* (London: Tyndale, 1954). Based on the Greek text, this commentary (like those of Bernard and Lock) provides helps on matters of vocabulary and syntax. The author does not provide a translation of the Greek text, however, nor does he use a standard translation, so the reader is expected to be able to use Greek well.

Bibliography of Selected Commentaries in Foreign Languages Cited in This Commentary

Norbert Brox, *Die Pastoralbriefe* (Regensburger Neues Testament 7; Regensburg: Pustet, 1969).

Victor Hasler, *Die Briefe an Timotheus und Titus: Pastoralbriefe* (Zürcher Bibelkommentar NT 12; Zürich: Theologischer Verlag, 1978).

Gottfried Holtz, *Die Pastoralbriefe* (Theologischer Handkommentar zum Neuen Testament 13; Berlin: Evangelische Verlagsanstalt, 1965).

Joachim Jeremias, *Die Briefe an Timotheus und Titus* (Das Neue Testament Deutsch 9; 11th ed.; Göttingen: Vandenhoeck & Ruprecht, 1975).

C. Spicq, *Saint Paul: Les Épitres Pastorales* (Études Bibliques; 4th ed.; Paris: Gabalda, 1969).

NOTES

Introduction

1. Cf. H. J. Rose, *A Handbook of Greek Literature from Homer to the Age of Lucian* (New York: Dutton, 1960) 268; idem, "Pseudepigraphic Literature," *Oxford Classical Dictionary* (London: Oxford University, 1949) 743.

2. These figures differ slightly from those of P. N. Harrison, *The Problem of the Pastoral Epistles* (London: Oxford University, 1921) 20, 137-40; idem, *Paulines and Pastorals* (London: Villiers, 1964) 12. In his book of 1921 Harrison wrote that there are 902 words in the Pastorals, 306 of which do not appear in the other 10 Paulines, and 122 of these 306 appear in the Apostolic Fathers and Apologists. But in his book of 1964 he revised the figures. Because of a misprint in the concordance he had used earlier, he had included the verb *hybrizō* (p. 139) among the Pastorals, but it is found at 1 Thess. 2:2 and not in the Pastorals, so the result is 901 words in the Pastorals, of which 305 do not appear in the other 10 Paulines, and of which 121 (in the 305) appear in the Apostolic Fathers and Apologists. He summarized this data also in his article, "Important Hypotheses Reconsidered. III. The Authorship of the Pastoral Epistles," *ExpTim* 67 (1955) 77-81.

   Harrison worked on the basis of the Westcott-Hort text of the Greek New Testament (1881). Our own work on the basis of the now widely used 26th edition of the Greek text of E. Nestle and K. Aland (1979) yields slightly different statistics, but the same results bearing on authorship. The Nestle-Aland text of the Pastorals contains 901 words. Cf. the same conclusion by Robert Morgenthaler, *Statistik des neutestamentlichen Wortschatzes* (Zürich: Gotthelf, 1958) 30, 164. While Harrison claimed that there are 54 proper nouns, a review of the Nestle-Aland text and Morgenthaler's vocabulary list yields 52. Harrison does not provide a list of proper nouns, but apparently he took Jesus Christ and Pontius Pilate as four items (as in a concordance), but we have taken them as two. Once these 52 nouns are set aside, there are 849 (rather than 847) words in the total vocabulary, of which 306 (not 305)—or 36.04%—are not found in the other 10 letters attributed to Paul. The 306 words consist of those listed in Harrison, *The Problem*, 137-40, with the following revisions. The term *hybrizō* is to be dropped (as indicated above), and the verb *phimoō* is to be added. The latter word appears at 1 Tim. 5:18. It did not appear in Harrison's list because the Westcott-Hort text includes it also at 1 Cor. 9:9 (so it is not distinctive to the Pastorals in this text). But the Nestle-Aland text, based on a different text-critical judgment, has the word *kēmoō* at 1 Cor. 9:9, leaving *phimoō* distinctive to the Pastorals.

3. Cf. P. N. Harrison, *The Problem*, 36-37.
4. C. F. D. Moule, "The Problem of the Pastoral Epistles: A Reappraisal," *BJRL* 47 (1965) 430-52; A. Strobel, "Schreiben des Lukas?," *NTS* 15 (1969) 191-210; J. Quinn, "The Last Volume of Luke: The Relation of Luke-Acts to the Pastoral Epistles," *Perspectives on Luke-Acts*, ed. C. Talbert (Danville: Association of Baptist Professors of Religion, 1978) 62-75; S. G. Wilson, *Luke and the Pastoral Epistles* (London: SPCK, 1979); and A. Feuillet, "La doctrine des Épîtres Pastorales et leurs affinités avec l'oeuvre lucanienne," *RevThom* 78 (1978) 181-225.
5. Luke-Acts fills up over 21% of the New Testament (37,810 of its 177,422 words) and contains 43% of the total vocabulary (4,093 of the 9,355 words used in the vocabulary of the New Testament). See R. Morgenthaler, *Statistik*, 164.
6. That Ephesus was the location of a "Pauline school" is the conclusion of several scholars, such as Günther Bornkamm, *Paul* (New York: Harper & Row, 1971) 86; Eduard Lohse, *Colossians and Philemon* (Hermeneia Commentary; Philadelphia: Fortress, 1971) 177-83; and Nils A. Dahl, "Ephesians, Letter to the," *IDBSup*, 268.
7. J. Quinn, "The Last Volume of Luke," 63, and "Paul's Last Captivity," *Studia Biblica 1978*, ed. E. A. Livingstone (JSNTSS 3; Sheffield: Sheffield University, 1980) 291. This is also the sequence proposed by J. Jeremias in his commentary, 2.
8. B. S. Easton, *The Pastoral Epistles*, 17-20.
9. Ibid., 30-31.
10. Cf. E. P. Sanders, "Literary Dependence in Colossians," *JBL* 85 (1966) 28-45; E. Lohse, *Colossians and Philemon*, 177-83; and N. Dahl, "Ephesians," 268-69.
11. See commentaries of C. Spieq, C, and J. Jeremias, 4-5.
12. See commentaries of B. S. Easton, 31; C. K. Barrett, 2; M. Dibelius-H. Conzelmann, 2; and J. L. Houlden, 40.
13. F. G. Kenyon, *The Chester Beatty Biblical Papyri* (London: Walker, 1936) viii; and Bruce M. Metzger, *The Text of the New Testament:*

Notes

Its Transmission, Corruption, and Restoration (New York: Oxford University, 1964) 37-38.

14. Texts are cited in H. L. Strack and P. Billerbeck, *Kommentar zum Neuen Testament aus Talmud und Midrasch* (6 vols.; Munich: C. H. Beck, 1923-61) 4.467-70.
15. Cf. G. Lohfink, "Die Normativität der Amtsvorstellungen in den Pastoralbriefen," *TQ* 157 (1977) 93-106.
16. Cf. B. E. Thiering, "*Mebaqqer* and *Episkopos* in the Light of the Temple Scroll," *JBL* 100 (1981) 59-74.
17. *Treatise on the Power and Primacy of the Pope*, 60-73; this can be found in *The Book of Concord*, ed. T. G. Tappert (Philadelphia: Fortress, 1959) 330-32.
18. Virtually every commentary gives some treatment to the heretical teachings. Those offering extensive treatment are commentaries by F. Gealy (pp. 350-60), D. Guthrie (pp. 32-38), C. K. Barrett (pp. 12-18), and M. Dibelius-H. Conzelmann (pp. 65-67). Other recent studies include J. M. Ford, "Proto-Montanism in the Pastoral Epistles," *NTS* 17 (1971) 338-46; R. J. Karris, "The Background and Significance of the Polemic of the Pastoral Epistles," *JBL* 92 (1973) 549-64; and L. T. Johnson, "II Timothy and the Polemic Against False Teachers: A Reexamination," *JRelS* 6 (1978) and 7 (1979) 1-26. On Gnosticism, see E. H. Pagels, "Gnosticism," *IDBSup*, 364-68, and James M. Robinson, "Introduction," *The Nag Hammadi Library in English* (San Francisco: Harper & Row, 1977) 1-25. On the relationship of the Pastorals to Gnosticism, see R. McL. Wilson, *Gnosis and the New Testament* (Philadelphia: Fortress, 1968), particularly pp. 41-44.
19. Quoted from *The Nag Hammadi Library in English*, 53.
20. Cf. E. H. Pagels, *The Gnostic Paul: Gnostic Exegesis of the Pauline Letters* (Philadelphia: Fortress, 1975). On pp. 163, 166 (n. 41 and 42) Pagels indicates that the Pastorals were considered inauthentic by Gnostics, and she cites Tertullian and Clement of Alexandria as evidence.

The First Letter to Timothy

1. For a discussion of this pattern in detail, see William G. Doty, *Letters in Primitive Christianity* (Philadelphia: Fortress, 1973) 27-47 (especially the chart on p. 43). On letter writing generally in antiquity, see Nils A. Dahl, "Letter," *IDBSup*, 538-40.
2. Cf. Jerome D. Quinn, "Parenesis and the Pastoral Epistles," *De la Tôrah au Messie*, ed. M. Carrez *et al.* (Paris: Desclée, 1981) 495-501.
3. Cf. M. P. Miller, "Midrash," *IDBSup*, 593-97.
4. M. Dibelius-H. Conzelmann, *The Pastoral Epistles*, 23.
5. For more on this, see Arland J. Hultgren, "Paul's Pre-Christian Perse-

1-2 Timothy, Titus

cutions of the Church: Their Purpose, Locale, and Nature," *JBL* 95 (1976) 97-111.

6. Cf. the note on this phrase in C. F. D. Moule, *The Birth of the New Testament* (New York: Harper & Row, 1962) 222. A book-length study has been written by George W. Knight, *The Faithful Sayings in the Pastoral Epistles* (Grand Rapids: Baker, 1979). A fine survey of interpretation appears in the commentary by A. T. Hanson, 63-64.

7. W. Lock, *The Pastoral Epistles*, 19.

8. Cf. Hans Conzelmann, *1 Corinthians* (Hermeneia Commentary; Philadelphia: Fortress, 1975) 246; Reginald H. Fuller, "The Pastoral Epistles," *Ephesians, Colossians, 2 Thessalonians, The Pastoral Epistles* (Proclamation Commentaries; Philadelphia: Fortress, 1978); D. Georgi, "Corinthians, First Letter to the," *IDBSup*, 183; and R. Scroggs, "Woman in the NT," *IDBSup*, 966.

9. So W. Lock, *The Pastoral Epistles*, 33.

10. Examples are given in the commentaries by M. Dibelius-H. Conzelmann, 158-60 (Appendix 3), and B. S. Easton, 197-202. For further discussion and bibliography, see Hans Dieter Betz, *Galatians* (Hermeneia Commentary; Philadelphia: Fortress, 1979) 281-83.

11. Yet this (that polygamous persons are excluded) is the view of A. Schulze, "Ein Bischof sei eines Weibes Mann . . . Zur Exegesis von 1 Tim. 3, 2 und Tit. 1, 6," *KD* 4 (1958) 287-300.

12. In his commentary, C. Spicq, 78-79, says that the verse prohibits anyone who has remarried—either after divorce or the death of his wife. Cf. also the similar view in the commentary by N. Brox, 142-43, and in Bruce Vawter, "Divorce and the New Testament," *CBQ* 39 (1977) 528-42.

13. This is the view adopted in the commentaries by E. F. Scott, 31; C. K. Barrett, 58-59; J. L. Houlden, 78; and R. J. Karris, 75. Cf. also the NEB translation, "faithful to his one wife," as well as P. Trummer, "Einehe nach den Pastoralbriefen," *Bib* 51 (1970) 471-84; and R. L. Saucy, "The Husband of One Wife," *BSac* 131 (1974) 229-40.

14. Cf. A. Oepke, "*Anēr*," *TDNT*, 1.362-63, note 11. Cf. also the commentaries by B. S. Easton, 212-15; F. Gealy, 411; J. Jeremias, 24; and A. T. Hanson, 75, 78. M. Dibelius - H. Conzelmann, 52 allow that this may be the meaning but leave the question open.

15. Cf. commentaries of B. S. Easton, 132-134; J. Jeremias, 26; J. L. Houlden, 80; and A. T. Hanson, 80-81.

16. Cf. A. Oepke, "*Gynē*," *TDNT*, 1.788, and commentaries by W. Lock, 40; E. F. Scott, 36-37; C. Spicq, 100-101; C. K. Barrett, 61-62; J. N. D. Kelly, 83-84; and G. Holtz, 85.

17. The commentaries of F. Gealy, 417-18; M. Dibelius - H. Conzelmann, 58; and N. Brox, 154.

18. D. Guthrie, *The Pastoral Epistles*, 85.

19. Cf. R. M. Lewis, "The 'Women' of Timothy 3:11," *BSac* 136 (1979) 167-75.

Notes

20. J. Jeremias, *Die Briefe an Timotheus und Titus*, 27.
21. Eduard Schweizer, *Lordship and Discipleship* (SBT 28; Naperville: Allenson, 1960) 64-68; idem, "Two New Testament Creeds Compared," *Neotestamentica* (Zürich: Zwingli, 1963) 125-57; Jack T. Sanders, *The New Testament Christological Hymns* (SNTSMS 15; Cambridge: Cambridge University, 1971) 15-17; and commentaries by J. Jeremias, 27-28; J. N. D. Kelly, 92; N. Brox, 160; J. L. Houlden, 85; and A. T. Hanson, 85.
22. Commentaries by E. F. Scott, 42; B. S. Easton, 136.
23. Cf. C. K. Barrett, *The Pastoral Epistles*, 70.
24. Cf. commentaries by E. F. Scott, 50-51, and F. D. Gealy, 431.
25. Commentaries of W. Lock, 51-52; J. Jeremias, 33; D. Guthrie, 96; C. K. Barrett, 70; M. Dibelius - H. Conzelmann, 69; N. Brox, 178; and A. T. Hanson, 92.
26. Commentaries of C. Spicq, 145; J. N. D. Kelly, 102; G. Holtz, 107; and J. L. Houlden, 89.
27. B. S. Easton, *The Pastoral Epistles*, 146.
28. Cf. Jerome D. Quinn, "Ordination in the Pastoral Epistles," *Communio* 8 (1981) 358-69 (especially p. 364).
29. E. Lohse, *"Cheir," TDNT*, 9.429.
30. Cf. A. Oepke, *"Gynē," TDNT*, 1.788.
31. Cf. Gen. 18:4; 19.2; 24:32; 43:24; Judg. 19:21; 1 Sam. 25:41; 2 Sam. 11:8; *Sifre Deut.* 355; *Joseph and Asenath* 7.1; 13.12; 20.1-5; Homer, *Odyssey* 19.343; 19.503-507; Plato, *Symposium* 175a; 213b; Plutarch, *Pompey*, 73.7; cf. also Luke 7:44.
32. This view is held in the commentaries of B. S. Easton, 159, 161; and F. Gealy, 442-43.
33. Cf. commentaries by W. Lock, 62-63; C. Spicq, 177; and D. Guthrie, 105-106.
34. Commentaries by E. F. Scott, 67-68; J. Jeremias, 42-43; C. Spicq, 179; D. Guthrie, 107; J. N. D. Kelly, 127-28; C. K. Barrett, 81; and N. Brox, 201-203.
35. Commentaries by W. Lock, 63-64; B. S. Easton, 160; M. Dibelius - H. Conzelmann, 80; G. Holtz, 129; and A. T. Hanson, 103.
36. F. Gealy, in his commentary, 444-45.
37. J. L. Houlden, *The Pastoral Epistles*, 96.
38. W. G. Rollins, "Slavery in the NT," *IDBSup*, 830.
39. See commentaries of W. Lock, 69-70; and M. Dibelius - H. Conzelmann, 85-86, for texts.
40. Ernst Käsemann, "Das Formular einer neutestamentlichen Ordinationsparänese," *Neutestamentliche Studien für Rudolf Bultmann*, ed. W. Eltester (2nd ed.; Berlin: Töpelmann, 1957) 261-68.
41. Cf. commentaries of W. Lock, 71; B. S. Easton, 166; E. F. Scott, 77; C. Spicq, 196-97; F. Gealy, 453; J. N. D. Kelly, 142; D. Guthrie, 115; and J. L. Houlden, 100. A. T. Hanson, 111, suggests that the verse is a reminder—at ordination—of the confession made at Baptism.

1-2 Timothy, Titus

42. Cf. commentaries of J. Jeremias, 46; C. K. Barrett, 86-87; G. Holtz, 141; and N. Brox, 213-15.

The Second Letter to Timothy

1. Cf. W. G. Doty, *Letters in Primitive Christianity,* 27-47. See discussion at the outset of commentary on 1 Tim. 1:3—6:21a.
2. BAGD, 28.
3. BAGD, 616.
4. Cf. commentaries by W. Lock, 90; F. Gealy, 476-77; J. Jeremias, 52-53; C. Spicq, 735; J. N. D. Kelly, 170; N. Brox, 239; and A. T. Hanson, 127.
5. Cf. commentaries by W. Lock, 90; B. S. Easton, 48; C. Spicq, 735; and J. N. D. Kelly, 171.
6. BAGD, 180, "in the presence of many witnesses."
7. Cf. commentaries of J. Jeremias, 55; and J. L. Houlden, 119.
8. Cf. commentaries by C. Spicq, 348; C. K. Barrett, 104; J. N. D. Kelly, 179; and A. T. Hanson, 133.
9. J. H. Bernard, *The Pastoral Epistles,* 121.
10. F. Gealy, in his commentary, 496.
11. The Essene *Damascus Document* (5.17-19) speaks of "Jannes and his brother." In later documents—Jewish, Christian, and pagan—both names appear. The texts are cited by M. Dibelius - H. Conzelman, *The Pastoral Epistles,* 117.
12. Cf. H. Odeberg, "*Iannēs,*" *TDNT,* 3. 192-93.
13. Ibid.
14. BAGD, 619.
15. Contra E. F. Scott, *The Pastoral Epistles,* 127.
16. As in commentaries by W. Lock, 110; and J. L. Houlden, 128.
17. Commentaries by J. Jeremias, 62; G. Holtz, 188; F. Gealy, 506; D. Guthrie, 163; J. N. D. Kelly, 202; and A. T. Hanson, 152.
18. B. S. Easton, *The Pastoral Epistles,* 67.
19. So, in his commentary, F. Gealy, 505-507; and Charles M. Nielsen, "Scripture in the Pastoral Epistles," *Perspectives in Religious Studies* 7 (1980) 4-23.

   Nielsen writes that in the Pastorals "Scripture mainly means Paul's letters" (p. 21) and suggests that the writer derives even his Old Testament quotations from Paul's letters, rather than from the Old Testament directly. Moreover, he suggests that, like Marcion later, the Pastorals have a "nearly Marcionite view" (p. 4) in their actual disregard of the Old Testament and high estimation of Paul as *the* apostle.

   It is true that the writer of the Pastorals does not make much use of the Old Testament, but then it is not necessary that he do so, since the major concern of the writer is to establish Pauline tradition. It is

186

true also that many of the Old Testament quotations and allusions in the Pastorals can be found already in Paul's letters. But finally (1) this only shows how ardent a Paulinist the author was; and (2) it says nothing about his estimation of the Old Testament itself. Against the claim that the Pastorals reflect a "nearly Marcionite view," it can be said that, if this were correct, it is precisely the Old Testament quotations in Paul's letters that the writer should *not* have quoted, but in fact it is these quotations which are sometimes used as evidence of dependence on Paul. Therefore the position does not hold up.

There are places at which the author appears to make use of the Old Testament independently (rather than in dependence upon Paul). At 2 Tim. 2:19 he quotes from Num. 16:5 (LXX), which does not appear in Paul's letters. Moreover, there are instances at which phrases from the LXX are used which are not found in Paul (1 Tim. 4:4 recalls Gen. 1:31; 5:19 is founded on Deut. 19:15; and 6:7 recalls Job 1:21 and Eccles. 5:14).

20. Cf. commentaries by C. Spicq, 391-92; F. Gealy, 514; G. Holtz, 195; J. N. D. Kelly, 213; and N. Brox, 269. But this view is rejected in the commentaries by E. F. Scott, 136; D. Guthrie, 172; and J. L. Houlden, 139. M. Dibelius - H. Conzelmann, 122, tend toward "Galatia" as correct.

21. In his commentary, J. Jeremias, 67, says that navigation was suspended between November 11 and March 10.

The Letter to Titus

1. John Calvin, *Commentaries on the Epistles to Timothy, Titus, and Philemon* (Grand Rapids: Eerdmans, 1948) 284; and commentaries in modern times by W. Lock, 126; E. F. Scott, 150; F. Gealy, 528; G. Holtz, 205; and J. L. Houlden, 141.

2. This includes Augustine and Jerome, and commentaries in modern times by J. H. Bernard, 155; B. S. Easton, 80; C. Spicq, 593; E. K. Simpson, 95; J. N. D. Kelly, 227; J. Jeremias, 68; and A. T. Hanson, 170. N. Brox, 280, appears to favor this view, but he leaves the question open.

3. Cf. B. Reicke, *"Pro,"* TDNT, 6.687-88.

4. Cf. BAGD, 162-63.

5. See M. Dibelius - H. Conzelmann, *The Pastoral Epistles*, 136-37, who also supply references in Cicero and Aristotle.

6. Hellenistic texts are provided in M. Dibelius - H. Conzelmann, *The Pastoral Epistles*, 140.

7. So BAGD, 801.

8. Commentaries by E. F. Scott, 169; J. N. D. Kelly, 246-47; G. Holtz, 227-28; M. Dibelius - H. Conzelmann, 143; and J. Jeremias, 73. N.

Brox, 297, adopts this translation, but in his commentary on the text remains indecisive.

9. Commentaries by J. H. Bernard, 172-73; W. Lock, 145; B. S. Easton, 95; C. Spicq, 640; F. Gealy, 540; D. Guthrie, 200; C. K. Barrett, 138; J. L. Houlden, 150; and A. T. Hanson, 184-85.
10. See also C. F. D. Moule, *An Idiom-Book of New Testament Greek* (2nd ed.; Cambridge: Cambridge University, 1959) 109-110; BDF, 145 (#276); and E. Stauffer, *"Theos," TDNT*, 3.106.
11. Cf. commentaries by J. Jeremias, 74; B. S. Easton, 100; C. Spicq, 656; and A. T. Hanson, 192.
12. B. S. Easton, *The Pastoral Epistles*, 99.
13. Cf. Arland J. Hultgren, "The Johannine Footwashing (13:1-11) as Symbol of Eschatological Hospitality," *NTS* 28 (1982) 539-46.
14. Cf. A. Oepke, *"Baptō," TDNT*, 1.535-36.
15. J. H. Bernard, *The Pastoral Epistles*, 180.
16. Cf. M. Dibelius - H. Conzelmann, *The Pastoral Epistles*, 152-53.

ABOUT THE AUTHOR

Arland J. Hultgren is a graduate of the Lutheran School of Theology at Chicago. His Th.D. in New Testament is from Union Theological Seminary in New York. Since 1977 he has been a professor of New Testament at Luther Northwestern Theological Seminary. He is the author of *Jesus and His Adversaries* (Augsburg, 1979).

II THESSALONIANS

Roger Aus

OUTLINE OF 2 THESSALONIANS

    I. Address and Greeting (1:1-2)
   II. Thanksgiving, Revelation of Christ as Judge, and Prayer (1:3-12)
  III. Explanation of Why the Day of the Lord Has Not Yet (Started to) Come (2:1-12)
  IV. Resumption of the Thanksgiving, Prayer for Comfort (2:13-17)
   V. Prayer for the Author(s) and the Addressees (3:1-5)
  VI. Instructions Regarding the False Behavior of Some of the Recipients (3:6-15)
 VII. Final Prayer, Personal Remark, and Benediction (3:16-18)

INTRODUCTION

With the exception of Philemon, 2 Thessalonians, containing only three chapters, is the shortest of the Pauline letters. Yet, because of its subject matter, it is one of the most interesting, and has had a very extensive and influential history of interpretation.

Part of the interest centers on the "man of lawlessness" described in 2:3-10. Throughout the centuries scholars have sought to ascertain his identity. Martin Luther, for example, thought the "man of lawlessness," the "Antichrist," was the papacy of his own time. The temptation to make such an identification is due to Paul's veiled language, which is typical of Jewish and Jewish-Christian apocalyptic (revelatory) literature. Other examples in the New Testament are the Synoptic Apocalypse (Mark 13 and parallels) and the Revelation to John. Such writings tend to arise when there is persecution (cf. 2 Thess. 1:4-8; see also 2:15 and 3:5). They do not explicitly quote the Old Testament but only allude to it. Also, language originally applied in the Old Testament to the Lord *God* is often transferred to the Lord *Jesus* in apocalyptic writings. 2 Thessalonians, dealing with the "Day of the Lord" (2:2), shows many such transfers (see the commentary).

■ Occasion of the Letter

The major reason for the writing of the epistle was that some of the Thessalonians interpreted their severe persecutions as the "messianic woes." Persecution was already a major issue when 1 Thessalonians was written (1:6; 2:14; and 3:3-4). According to this second epistle, it has increased in intensity. This is not surprising, since confessing belief in Jesus as the messianic "king," their "Lord," would have gotten the Thessalonians into bitter conflict with the Gentiles. In the eastern half of the Mediterranean at that time the Gentiles insisted on there being only one king, the Roman emperor. There he let himself be called both "lord" and "king" (see Acts 17:7). Those who refused to acknowledge him as such were suspected of a lack of loyalty and were severely persecuted.

Since severe persecution was thought of as one aspect of the messianic birth pangs (also alluded to in 1 Thess. 5:3), some members of the addressed congregation, probably Jewish Christians or the Greek "God-fearers" who worshiped with the Jews at the synagogue, maintained that the Day of the Lord had (started to) come. A part of that Day, severe persecution, was already present; therefore they spoke of it as already having arrived (2:2). Similar expressions are to be found in Judaism, as this commentary will point out.

Paul must deal with three issues arising out of this false belief: persecution, the events preceding the end, and idlers in the church. First, as a good pastor he deals in Chapter 1 with the question most affecting his addressees—persecution. They are indeed being persecuted now, but he emphasizes that their afflictions nevertheless have a positive value. They provide the recipients with the opportunity of growth (1:3), and they make them worthy of God's future kingdom (1:5, 11). Paul gives an extensive look forward to the imminent return of Jesus in his might and glory to judge the earth (1:7b-10), which is intended to *comfort* those who are now powerless and crushed. The apparently vengeful tone is typical of works written during intense persecution, for example in the Old Testament psalms of lament. It expresses God's justice. If he is a righteous God, he will not let present evil go unpunished, even if repayment is to occur only at the final judgment. Compared to similar contemporary Jewish writings, however, Paul's description of the future judgment is relatively mild. It should not be forgotten that he, as a Jewish Christian (see the commentary for his probable knowledge of Hebrew), was a child of his religious culture and time.

Secondly, in 2:3-12 Paul describes what and who must come before the arrival of the Day of the Lord (Jesus), the "End." This includes the man of lawlessness, a figure separate from Satan, who is painted in apocalyptic colors, in part drawn from another apocalyptic writing, Daniel. The strong emphasis in this section on *God's* actions undergirds the proposal that he who now restrains the Day of the Lord (Jesus) is God himself. It is God's purpose that first the gospel must be allowed to spread throughout the world. Since this has not yet happened, the persecutions have not yet reached their peak, and the man of lawlessness has not yet been revealed, the Day of the Lord cannot have already (started to) come. However, because the mystery of this lawlessness is "already at work" (2:7), the delay caused by God's restraining power is not thought of as lasting for a long period.

Thirdly, some of the Thessalonians argued that if the Day of the Lord had already (started to) come, there was no sense in pursuing everyday occupations. They became idle, "busybodies," perhaps even trying to convince others of their opinion. Paul places his complete authority, as well as that of the Lord Jesus, behind a rebuttal of this opinion. Despite their error, however, these idlers should still be treated as fellow Christians.

■ Authorship and Time of Writing

For centuries the authorship of 2 Thessalonians was not questioned. It was understood that Paul, aided by Silvanus and Timothy (1:1), wrote the letter. Yet, ever since the early 19th century, a number of serious scholars have questioned this. The arguments they use include the following: the differing timetables of the final events in 1 and 2 Thessalonians are impossible for the same author; some of the same words and phrases are employed in a different sense in the two letters; 2 Thessalonians is cooler or more ponderous in tone and it moralizes; and the personal greeting in 3:17 is a later attempt by a pseudonymous writer (a Christian writing *in the name of* Paul) to appropriate apostolic authority for his own epistle. In general, those who dispute Pauline authorship have had difficulty proposing a concrete time or occasion for 2 Thessalonians. One scholar, however, has recently suggested the period between A.D. 70-110, when the destruction of Jerusalem by the Romans in A.D. 70 and later intense persecution by pagans led a Christian community to believe that it was enduring the messianic woes. Its members then maintained that the Day of the Lord had arrived.[1] This, in part, agrees with my understanding of the setting of the letter.[2]

The large majority of recent commentators on 2 Thessalonians in English and French, however, still advocate Pauline authorship. They maintain that it was written shortly after the first letter (approximately A.D. 50-51), from Corinth, on Paul's "second" missionary journey. Increased persecution and a forged letter (2:2) led to the conclusion that the end was to come very soon. This would account for the special material on the final events in 2 Thessalonians, found nowhere else in the Pauline corpus. They also point out the numerous indications of an oral style in the letter, which they consider atypical of a carefully thought out pseudonymous epistle. In order to avoid certain difficulties, some would even propose that 2

Thessalonians preceded 1 Thessalonians; yet this is very improbable in light of 1 Thess. 2:17—3:10, which does not seem to be aware of an earlier letter.

At the moment neither side has been able to convince the other regarding the question of authorship. There are simply too many variables in 2 Thessalonians for any great certainty. For the purpose of this commentary, however, I shall stand with the tradition and assume Pauline authorship.

■ Contemporary Relevance

Regardless of whether or not 2 Thessalonians is by Paul, the epistle helps us to see the positive aspects of persecution and affliction endured on behalf of one's Christian faith. Instead of being viewed only negatively, such crises can become opportunities for mission when, through our example, the gospel becomes credible to others. Crises can also lead to personal growth. As Paul states in 1 Cor. 10:13, God allows us to be tried, yet he is ultimately in control and will not allow us to be tested beyond our abilities.

The letter also warns us against apocalyptic fervor based on what *we* consider to be the final page of God's eschatological timetable. The end lies in God's hands alone, and up till now it has been revealed to no one (cf. Mark 13:32 and Acts 1:7). Those who in earlier centuries interpreted the "man of lawlessness" to be a definite historical person are now, like those they named, long dead. Yet God's restraining the second coming of the Messiah, the Lord Jesus, still provides us with the opportunity of proclaiming the good news of his love to us in Jesus Christ to all those who do not yet know him as their own Lord.

The author's treatment of the idlers is also instructive. They were probably using their new free time in order to gain others for their belief that the Day of the Lord had already (started to) come. Paul's response is sobering. He says that eschato-logical fervor does not justify individuals becoming purely "otherworldly," living off the labor of others. Reprimanding such people, however, should be done in a spirit of reconciliation.

Finally, this epistle shows us the immense value of intercessory prayer. Although at times our help for persecuted Christians and others has to be limited to this means alone, God is faithful and hears our prayer. If, in addition, letters of support from us are allowed to reach such afflicted persons, they receive great comfort and encouragement from them.

Without the short letter of 2 Thessalonians, the New Testament would indeed lose a valuable part of its total richness.

COMMENTARY

■ Address and Greeting (1:1-2)

1:1—The traditional Greek letter prescript was in the third person. Here, however, Paul addresses his readers in the warmer first person. This is also the case in other letters of Paul. He also adds *our* **Father** (see 1 Cor. 1:2) to the greeting. The possessive pronoun is not found in 1 Thess. 1:1, suggesting that there is no slavish copying here. In the very first verse of this letter Paul emphasizes Jesus' role as **Lord** which is his central title for Jesus (Phil. 2:11; Rom. 1:4; 10:9).

1:2—The phrase **from God the Father and the Lord Jesus Christ** is also not found in 1 Thess. 1:1. It basically repeats the previous verse, so it is redundant, like many other phrases in the letter. It is probably a traditional formula from the early church's worship setting, just as many pastors today begin their sermons with "Grace to you and. . . ."

■ Thanksgiving, Revelation of Christ as Judge, and Prayer (1:3-12)

1:3—The thanksgiving begun here is interrupted by an appeal in 2:1 and only concluded in 2:13-15. The thanksgiving of 1 Thess. 1:2 is repeated in 2:13 and 3:9 and leads up to 4:1,

199

so it is more complex and is not simply copied here in 2 Thessalonians.

We are bound to give thanks, repeated in 2:13, derives from Jewish liturgical language, as does the phrase **as is fitting** (see a similar phrase in Phil. 1:7). There are direct Hebrew parallels. This language is reflected in the church's eucharistic terminology: "It is meet, right and salutary to give thanks. . . ." Such language is not "cool" as claimed by some who deny Pauline authorship. Indeed, it is warmer than similar Greek phrases.[3]

There are good reasons for Paul's giving thanks. The recipients' faith is not only growing, it is **growing abundantly.** The love of *all* of them for each other is also increasing. This **love** is not only esteem or affection; it is also meant as concrete mutual aid in the persecutions and afflictions of v. 4.

1:4—The Greek of this verse begins with a dependent clause implying an actual result: *so that* **we ourselves boast of you.** . . . The general content of v. 3 is the reason for boasting, supplemented by new, definite reasons. In all the **persecutions** and **afflictions** (synonyms, as in Rom. 8:35 and Mark 4:17; see also 1 Thess. 3:7) which the addressees are *presently* enduring, they maintain **steadfastness / endurance** and their **faith.** In the Psalms of Solomon 18:5, from the first century B.C., the endurance of chastisements is thought of as aiding in bringing the Anointed One (the Messiah) on the day of mercy and blessing. The present tense of the verb **enduring** in 1:4 is purposely chosen. This is neither a minor nor a passing unpleasantness. It is a major, lasting condition, triggering the whole section vv. 5-10.

1:5-10—Paul is a true pastor. Without the present verses, the (false) message about the Day of the Lord, referred to in Chapter 2, would lead to despair, perhaps even to apostasy. He thus tries to balance the disappointment of Chapter 2 and the consternation at persecution by publicly acknowledging the great value the addressees' afflictions have.

The fact that the persecutions are mentioned so soon in the letter shows their great importance for him. Chapter 1 is thus not merely a polite introduction to the later "meat" of the letter. It deals with the main issue at the outset. I shall propose at 2:2 that some of the recipients thought of these persecutions as the "messianic woes," which were believed to precede the coming of the Messiah (see Mark 13:19, 24; Matt. 24:9, 21, 29). The eschatological section 1:5-10, like 1 Thess. 4:15-18, is intended as comfort (see also 2 Thess. 2:16-17 and 2 Cor. 1:3-7).

1:5—To express it in English terms, Paul loosely employs a dash or semicolon here, marking a shift in thought. The awkward construction in Greek suggests that the letter is written extemporaneously.

The preceding things (v. 4) are **evidence** or "proof" **of the righteous judgment of God.** A similar thought is expressed by Paul in Phil. 1:28, also in a context of persecution. The addressees' persecution is not thought of as a (positive) sign in itself, but their steadfast faith under such negative conditions is.

The righteous judgment points to the final judgment, as in vv. 7b-10. Rom. 2:5-6 has a very similar phrase. The addressees are not suffering *in order to* be accounted worthy of the kingdom of God. Rather, their suffering (the present is again emphasized; cf. NEB: "for which indeed you are suffering") *leads to or results in* their worthiness. The verb "to account worthy" occurs elsewhere in the New Testament only in Luke 20:35 and Acts 5:41. It is God who accounts or makes them worthy; the passive here implies divine action. It is the *future* kingdom of God, the world to come, of which they are made worthy, as in 1 Thess. 2:12.

"Being worthy" was a major motif in Judaism, especially connected to the Messiah's arrival and to the world to come. In the Babylonian Talmud (Sanhedrin 98b) Rabbi Joseph says regarding the Messiah: "Let him come, and may I be worthy of sitting in the shadow of his ass's dung." In Judaism the present suffering of the righteous was thought of as a testing; it also atones for or expiates whatever sins people have. Then in the world to come they will receive only reward. **1:6-7a**—These verses describe *how* part of the just judgment of God will proceed and are logically followed by vv. 7b-10, the *when* of that judgment. The conjunction **since** at the beginning of v. 6 introduces the entire section up to v. 11, and only loosely connects it to the preceding vv. 3-5 (the RSV correctly has a dash here). This is another sign of Paul's extemporaneous, unpolished style. If God is just (and he is!), he will **repay with affliction** the oppressors and **grant rest** to those oppressed. A similar cluster of terms of retribution is found in Obadiah 12-15, also a Day of the Lord passage.

The word **rest** in v. 7 has its exact Hebrew equivalent in the Jewish theology of suffering. Rest **with us** again emphasizes Paul's pastoral concern. Being united with his converts and then with the Lord is an important theme in Paul (see 1 Thess. 4:17-18; 5:10; and 2 Cor. 4:14).

1:7b—The section from here to the end of v. 10 has been thought by some to be a borrowed and reworked Jewish apocalypse or an inserted Christian hymn. Yet it most likely stems from Paul himself, as will be indicated below. Verses 7b and 8 modify the "repaying" of v. 6: they tell *when* (**when the Lord Jesus is revealed**) and *how* (**from heaven with his mighty angels in flaming fire**), and then repeat the function of retribution, specifying it.

A "revelation" is something which has been hidden until the time of unveiling (see the "revelation of our Lord Jesus Christ" in 1 Cor. 1:7-8, also in the opening thanksgiving of the letter, as well as Rom. 2:5). The Aramaic paraphrases, the targums, of Isa. 66:7 and 1 Chron. 3:24 also speak of the messianic king's being **revealed. From heaven** tells us where Jesus has been dwelling since his departure from this earth (see Ps. 110:1). In 1 Thessalonians Paul says the Lord (Jesus) will descend from heaven, from where he is to be awaited (4:16; 1:10).

The **angels** with whom Jesus is to come recall those who descended with God at his appearance to Moses on Mt. Sinai (Exodus 19–20; Deut. 33:2). In Mark 13:27 and 8:38, the Son of man sends the angels to gather his elect at his parousia or (second) coming (see also 4 Ezra 13:52, which probably refers to angels when it mentions "those who are with him," the servant of God, on his "day"). The reference to **mighty** angels is intended to give the persecuted addressees consolation. The latter may appear to be powerless now, but soon the Lord will share his power with them.

Jesus will be revealed in **flaming fire**. This phrase still belongs to v. 7, not as in KJV to the participle "taking vengeance" used of Jesus in v. 8. The phrase may be borrowed from God's appearance to Moses in the burning bush (Exod. 3:2) or, more probably, from Isa. 66:15, referring to the Lord's final appearance in Jerusalem at the gathering of all the nations. There is no allusion to the destructive role of fire here, as in the "fires of Gehenna (i.e., hell)" (contrast Matt. 13:41-42, 50 and 25:41).

1:8—The participial phrase describing Jesus, **inflicting vengeance upon those who do not know** and **who do not obey,** is a conflation of expressions from Isa. 66:15, Ps. LXX 78:6 and Isa. 66:4. This argues for a further dependence on Isa. 66:15, as suggested above. While some people today may be uncomfortable with this language of vengeance, it is an integral part of God's justice: evil may not be allowed to go unpunished. It is also typical of appearances of God for rescue or judgment in the Old Testament. In addition, the Levites used to sing on the steps of the temple in Jerusalem: "Yahweh, God to whom vengeance belongs, you God to whom vengeance belongs, show yourself!" (Ps. 94:1). In the Old Testament it is God alone who appears in flaming fire and inflicts vengeance. It is important to note that here this attribute and this function have been applied to Jesus. The Thessalonians themselves are not to repay present evil with their own evil actions (see 1 Thess. 5:15) but are to leave this up to God and Jesus (see 1 Thess. 4:6 and Rom. 12:17-19).

1:9—In Greek this verse is a relative clause: "who shall pay (the) penalty. . . ." Part of the penalty is **destruction,** which is also connected in 1 Thess. 5:3 with the Day of the Lord, as it is in 1 Cor. 5:5. Its **eternal** aspect is used as a comforting foil to the fate of the persecuted addressees, who will enjoy **the presence of the Lord** (Jesus) and **the glory of his might.** The latter phrases derive from identical refrains in Isa. 2:10, 19, and 21. Here, however, the "fear" or "dread" mentioned in Isaiah is purposely omitted.

The emphasis is on the Lord's splendor and majesty. **Glory** is often associated in Paul with sufferings and affliction, as in Rom. 8:17-18 and 2 Cor. 4:17. Jesus' **might** at his future coming (see also Mark 13:26, with power) contrasts with the persecutors' present dominance. Rev. 18:8 and 10 have the same thought.

1:10—Part of the reward of the Christians is that they will somehow participate in the "glorification" and "admiration" of Jesus at his coming. The two passive Greek verbs behind these English nouns are probably derived from the Greek text of Pss. 88:8 and 67:36a. In the Greek Old Testament these verbs can be synonyms and are best translated here, "to show himself glorious" and "to show himself wonderful/marvelous."

The participial phrase **in all who have believed** links the persecuted addressees to many others who have already shown steadfastness in their faith. The addressees are not alone.

The KJV correctly puts into parentheses "for our witness to you was believed." 1 Cor. 1:6 has a similar interruption, a sign of a loose style, typical of dictation.

After the preceding general remarks, the author again becomes pastoral by emphasizing **our testimony to *you*.** In the Greek, Jesus' coming **on that day** (the Day of the Lord; see

2:2) is at the very end of the sentence, where, as in Rom. 2:16, it adds powerful solemnity to the whole passage. The long sentence begun in v. 3 finally ends here, specifically closing vv. 7b-10. The opening section of Romans (1:1-7a) is similarly long.

Paul was neither the first nor the last to use the language of the Day of the Lord to describe an intermediary agent such as Jesus as effecting the final judgment. In Jewish writings the angel Michael (Assumption of Moses 10:1), the Son of man (1 Enoch 62), the Messiah (4 Ezra 13), and Melchizedek (11 Qumran Melchizedek) are similarly described, most of these also being in settings of persecution.

1:11—Verses 11-12 form a prayer designed to encourage the Thessalonians to continue in their good works even under persecution. A similar transition from thanksgiving to prayer for the addressees is found in Phil. 1:9. Here in 1:11 the tone becomes personal again: **for *you*, that he may account *you*, our God.** Paul's constant prayer recalls 1:3. *Our* God is reminiscent of vv. 1 and 8, and anticipates v. 12 (twice). James E. Frame points out that as there is common suffering and common relief, so there is a common fellowship in God.

The same emphasis on worthiness as found in v. 5 reappears here. The phrase **work of faith** is similar to one found in 1 Thess. 1:3 and at first seems, in Protestant ears, to be a contradiction in terms. Yet "(every) good work deriving from faith" is meant, as in "faith working through love" in Gal. 5:6.

The same strong emphasis is given to the expression **by his power** at the end of v. 11b as was given to "on that day" in v. 10b. As a foil to the present power of the persecutors (see vv. 7b, 9b, and 2:9), it is also intended to console their victims, the Thessalonians.

1:12—The aim of the activity mentioned in v. 11 is **that the name of our Lord Jesus may be glorified.** This phrase is borrowed from Isa. 66:5. The use of expressions from Isaiah 66 also in v. 8 shows that vv. 7b-10 depend on that chapter and most probably do not derive from another source. This borrowing from Isaiah is another application of Old Testament God language to Jesus. Some commentators would like to read here "according to the grace of our God and Lord, Jesus Christ," yet frequent usage of "Lord" without the definite article to mean Jesus refutes this (cf. 1:1, 2; 2:13; 3:4, 12). The thanksgiving begun in v. 3 is now interrupted by an appeal in 2:1, and is taken up again in 2:13.

The numerous allusions to Isaiah 66 in this chapter are probably due to the fact that texts from Isaiah 40–66 were commonly used as passages of comfort in the Judaism of that time and were read in the synagogues on Sabbaths which stressed consolation. Thus it was natural to allude to Isaiah 66 in this section, which stresses consolation in the midst of persecution. It was also natural to apply those Old Testament texts to Jesus, since the birth of a son mentioned in Isa. 66:7 was interpreted in Judaism as a reference to the messianic king.[4]

■ Explanation of Why the Day of the Lord Has Not Yet (Started to) Come (2:1-12)

2:1-2—After the main theme of present persecution, and before the issue of idlers (3:6-15), Paul deals with what is normally thought to be the major section of the letter. Jesus' **coming** (see 1 Thess. 2:19; 3:13; 4:15; 5:23), and the Christians' **assembling to meet him** (an eschatological term; see the motif in Isa. 66:18-21 and 1 Thess. 4:14, 17), will take place on the future Day of the Lord.

Yet someone in the congregation has convinced at least one group that the day has already arrived. This leads to the whole congregation's being **shaken in mind** (a term often found in theophany and Day of the Lord passages) and **excited.** The author is not sure how this happened. Was the prophetic spirit at work in an individual (see 1 Thess. 5:19-20)? Did someone compose a misleading letter in his name (see 3:17)? 2 Tim. 2:18 shows that so-called Gnostics could upset others' faith by maintaining that the resurrection was already past, probably meant in a "spiritual" sense. Certain other Christians thought they were already "reigning," again understood in a spiritual sense (1 Cor. 4:8). In the gospel of Luke, Jesus himself warns that some will "lead others astray" by maintaining, "The time is at hand!" (Luke 21:8). The rabbis, too, were very much interested in determining the exact advent of the Messiah. In the Babylonian Talmud (Sanhedrin 97b) Rabbi Jonathan says: "Blasted be the bones of those who calculate the end. For they would say, since the predetermined time has arrived, and yet he (the Messiah) has not come, he will never come." On the basis of their false calculation they thus maintained that the "End" had come, even though the Messiah was not yet present. Another relevant passage is found in the Jewish writing Pesikta Rabbati 36, where, after a description of the "birth pangs," God tells a frightened Israel: "The time of your redemption has come." This manner of expression is also found in the rabbinic commentary Numbers Rabbah 15/12 on Num. 8:6, which states regarding the exodus of the Israelites oppressed in Egypt: "the time fixed for the redemption has arrived." Also, in Peter, in a situation of intense persecution, the author writes, "the time has come for judgment to begin . . ." (4:17).

It is most probable that some members of the congregation considered the intense persecution they were presently enduring to be one major aspect of the messianic birth pangs or woes which would precede Jesus' coming (see Dan. 12:1; 1 Thess. 5:3; Mark 13:8, 13). Another of these woes was war (see Mark 13:7). In the Babylonian Talmud (Megillah 17b), for example, war is designated "the *beginning* of redemption," after which the son of David, the Messiah, will come. What some of the addressees maintained was not that Jesus himself had already returned, but rather that his Day had (started to)

come (not "is at hand," as in KJV).[5] Paul says no to this
thought. While the Thessalonians' persecution is indeed great
and even has a positive value to it (1:3-12), before the Lord
returns certain other things must also happen. These he eluci-
dates in 2:3-12.

2:3-4—"Deception" of the Thessalonians is a danger from
outside (v. 10), but also from groups within the congregation
(Rom. 16:18). In Greek, the conditional clause beginning with
unless in v. 3b extends to the end of v. 4 and awkwardly
breaks off without stating what the RSV supplies: **that day
will not come.** This is another example of spontaneous, oral
style, not a carefully planned writing, and thus suggests
Pauline authorship. The **rebellion** which is to come first is not
against secular power, but God. As Jesus is to be revealed in
1:7, so here a counter figure, the **man of lawlessness** or **son of
perdition** is revealed (see also vv. 6 and 8). Ps. 88:23 in Greek
forms part of the background of this expression (see the use
of Psalm LXX 88 also in 1:10). This figure **opposes** God (from
Isa. 66:6); he proudly **exalts himself** (from the Hebrew of
Dan. 11:36, a description of the contemptible ruler Antiochus
IV Epiphanes, who in 168 B.C. had an altar dedicated to
Olympian Zeus erected in the Jerusalem Temple). He **takes
his seat in the temple of God** in Jerusalem (see Isa. 66:6),
proclaiming himself to be God (from the Hebrew of Ezek.
28:2, where Hiram of Tyre calls himself "god").

2:5-8—Before Paul continues with his description of the
destruction of the man of lawlessness in v. 8, he parentheti-
cally inserts remarks on why this figure has not yet been
destroyed. An impatient, half-chiding **Do you not remember?**
introduces the assertion that he had told them this repeatedly
(the Greek imperfect), though perhaps not in exactly these
terms. When Paul states in 2 Cor. 1:13 that he only writes what
his addressees can read and understand, it would imply that
the content of 2:6-7 is already known to the Thessalonians,
though unfortunately no longer to us. 1 Thess. 5:1 says that the

·eschatological scenario" was a basic part of the apostle's early missionary instruction.

What the Thessalonians are supposed to know is expressed by the neuter participle of the Greek verb *katechein* in v. 6, **what is restraining** (not **him,** the man of lawlessness from v. 3, as filled in by the RSV, but more probably the Day of the Lord, that day, from vv. 2-3). This has been thought to be the Roman government or other factors (see below in v. 7). Yet more probably it is God's plan that first the gospel must be preached to the whole world (see on 3:1; Rom. 15:22; Mark 13:10; Matt. 24:14; 28:19; Luke 24:47; Acts 1:8; 3:21; 1 Cor. 15:24-25; 2 Peter 3:9; Justin Martyr, First Apology 45). This motif has its prototype in Jewish and Jewish-Christian interpretation of Isa. 66:18-21, which describes the mission to the Gentiles as part of the final events. An inverted parallel to the motif of universal conversion, namely universal apostasy, is found in the Babylonian Talmud (Sanhedrin 97a; see also Yoma 10a), where Rabbi Isaac says: "The son of David (the Messiah) will not come until the whole world is converted to the belief of the heretics." Here Christianity may be meant.

The time of the revelation of the man of lawlessness in 2 Thess. 2:6 (**in his time**) is determined by God, who in spite of everything is in control. Because **the mystery of lawlessness is already at work** (v. 7a), the end cannot be far off.

Verse 7b is one of the most problematical passages in the entire New Testament because the individual phrases are open to a wide variety of interpretations. One possible translation, favored by many in the early church, is: "Only he who is now restraining (masculine present participle of the same Greek verb as in v. 6a, *katechein*) will do so/let him do so until it is removed/disappears." [6] Here the restrainer would be the Roman emperor, who will do so until the Roman government ceases. Although Paul did enjoy the protection of the imperial government for his missionary work (he was a Roman citizen; cf. Acts 16:37-39; 22:25-28; 25:10), it is very improbable that he viewed Rome's power as soon ceasing. The opposite was rather the case.

Another interpretation has the restraining one as an angel, God, Christ, or the Spirit, and the subject of "is removed/disappears" as the lawless one. Yet v. 8 says the latter figure still has to be revealed and destroyed.

Another possibility is that he who restrains is Paul himself, who will preach the gospel until he disappears/dies. Yet the apostle to the Gentiles believed he would be among those still alive at Jesus' second coming (cf. 1 Thess. 1:10; 4:17; 1 Cor. 7:26, 29; 10:11; 15:51; Rom. 13:11; Phil. 3:20; 4:5).

Still another suggestion takes the neuter participle of v. 6 as a negative "seizing force" and the masculine participle of the same verb in v. 7b as a false prophet incorporating this force. False prophecy regarding the Day of the Lord had thus "seized" the Thessalonians. Yet it is difficult to see how the false prophet's disappearance should be related to the lawless one's disappearance and destruction in v. 8.

A recent interpretation builds on an alternative meaning for the key Greek word *katechein,* understanding it as "to oppress" rather than "to restrain." While the pagans and their leader thought they were "restraining" the Christians through persecution, they really were "oppressing" them. Thus the Christians who know the oppression now (v. 6) are being told that he who oppresses them will continue to do so until he is out of the way. The oppression meant is the mystery of lawlessness, which will be followed by the appearance of the man of lawlessness. This timetable is seen as the key to the refutation of the apocalyptic enthusiasts.[7] This interpretation assumes that the author of 2 Thessalonians borrowed his verb forms from his opponents and reformulated them in an ad hoc manner. Yet the primary meaning of *katechein* is "to restrain," "to hold back," not "to oppress." In addition, a number of early church fathers thought of "the restrainer" as a *positive* entity, adding "let him (further) restrain" after the masculine participle in v. 7b.[8] In this interpretation, however, the same figure is seen negatively, as "the oppressor."

My own proposal for the masculine and neuter participles of vv. 7 and 6 builds upon another interpretation made by two early church fathers. Theodore of Mopsuestia and Theodoret of Cyrus expressly state or assume that it is God who restrains in v. 7. There was also precedent in the Greek Old Testament (Isa. 40:22) for God to be described with this verbal participle (he who restrains). Having employed imagery from various verses of Isaiah 66 in Chapter 1, and being aware of the Jewish messianic interpretation of 66:7, Paul borrowed a term from the neighboring v. 9 in Hebrew, where God states that he will not "restrain" the birth of the son. This Hebrew verb can also be translated in the Greek Bible by *katechein*. If this proposal is accepted, then God is the one who graciously restrains the second advent of Jesus, the Day of the Lord, the end, until the gospel has been preached to all nations (Mark 13:10; 2 Peter 3:9). The universal proclamation of the gospel, then, would be the content of "that which restrains" in v. 6.

I also suggest that the **mystery of lawlessness** in v. 7a is the subject of **is out of the way** in 7b, even though the masculine verbal participle (**he who now restrains**) lies between them. Paul was not very careful with his grammar, as noted several times above. The point Paul makes is that when evil has reached its peak, its mysterious aspect will be removed or disappear. When it is most intense, apparent to all, God will cease his restraining, and the Messiah will come to wage the decisive battle with the lawless one (v. 8). The persecutions which the Thessalonians are presently enduring are thus not to be interpreted by them as the messianic woes; tribulation must increase even more before the Day of the Lord arrives, and the man of lawlessness must first be revealed.

No interpretation of vv. 6-7 can answer all the questions the text poses. In contrast to the Thessalonians, who knew the identities of the masculine and neuter participles, we today can only attempt "informed guessing."

2:8-10—These verses are one sentence in Greek. **The lawless one** in v. 8 may derive from the Greek text of Isa. 66:3. His being **revealed** takes up the same motif from vv. 3 and 6. Part of the background of this passage may be "the king of bold countenance" of Dan. 8:23-24, who will magnify himself and rise up against God. Dan. 8:25 states: "by no human hand, he shall be broken." This reference to supernatural destruction may account for the application of Isa. 11:4, another such reference, to Jesus here. This verse was often applied to the Messiah in Jewish sources. Jesus' slaying the lawless one **by his appearing and his coming** (v. 8, note the redundancy) also shows supernatural destruction. The author is not interested in portraying the adversary's defeat in broad colors. He could never, for example, have written the detailed description of hell in Dante's *L'Inferno*.

In v. 9 the **lawless one,** like Jesus, has his own **coming** (parousia). He is clearly differentiated from **Satan,** who lends him his power. As Jesus will come with the angels of his might in 1:7, so this figure will come with **all power.** Yet his **signs** and **wonders** are only specious.

In v. 10 **all wicked deception** recalls 2:3. The phrase **those who are to perish** does not imply militant predestination; rather, it expresses Paul's deep conviction of the righteous justice of God, who is in charge here. Those who did not **love the truth** (i.e., the gospel) will not be saved. The **refused** of RSV is overstatement. It is unbelief which results in the lack of salvation.

2:11-12—**Therefore God sends upon them a strong delusion**—but not if they had believed in Jesus as Lord. Again, God only reacts after a person's own negative action (see Rom. 1:28).

In contrast to those who **believe what is false** and are greatly "deceived," Paul's message of the gospel was not given with "guile" (1 Thess. 2:3). The fronts are clearly drawn: Everyone

who did not believe in the truth (of the gospel) but **had pleasure in unrighteousness** will be judged (negatively). In apocalyptic thought there are few grays; blacks and whites dominate.

Although the "man of lawlessness" is definitely not Satan, the only clues we have to his identity are to be found in Paul's descriptive words here, in part based on Antiochus IV Epiphanes in Daniel, as indicated in the commentary on 2:3-4. The wish by emperor Gaius Caligula to be considered a god, and his attempt to desecrate the Jerusalem Temple by having his own statue erected there in A.D. 38-39 (see Josephus, *Antiquities* 18.261 and *Wars* 2.184-85), certainly influenced the popularization of this motif, often called the "Antichrist." Christians in the 20th century have even identified him with Hitler or Stalin; yet these figures have come and gone and God still "restrains" the Day of the Lord Jesus. Perhaps the author intentionally left his characterization indefinite. That, too, would be typical of apocalyptic language.

■ Resumption of the Thanksgiving, Prayer for Comfort (2:13-17)

·**2:13-15**—These verses begin by taking up again the thanksgiving of 1:3. The **Lord** in **beloved by the Lord** is probably God, as in 1 Thess. 1:4. God showed his love to the addressees by choosing them as the "first fruits" or "first converts" in their area (see Rom. 16:5 and 1 Cor. 16:15; the RSV, preferring a different Greek text, reads **from the beginning**). The Spirit of God and of the Lord Jesus sanctified them (see 2 Cor. 3:17-18); their confidence/**belief in the truth** (of the gospel) led to their salvation. This salvation is not merely future (1 Thess. 5:9) but also partially present (see 1 Cor. 1:18 and 2 Cor. 2:15). Thus Paul reassures the persecuted Thessalonian community that God has *already* saved them. It was God who, through the good news brought by the missionaries, called them (see 1:11), resulting in their sharing in Jesus' glory. This is in part a present reality, anticipating a later, full sharing (1:10, 12).

Summing up all of what he has said in 2:1-14, Paul in v. 15 encourages the readers to stand firm in their persecutions (cf. Phil. 1:27-29; 1 Thess. 3:3-4, 8). He and his staff had taught them Christian **traditions** both personally and by **letter,** a reference to only one writing, 1 Thessalonians. This excludes a fraudulent letter, as in 2:2. These traditions are not merely to be observed (Mark 7:3, 9), but held fast (see 1 Thess. 4:1-2, 6, 11). The non-Pauline tradition which had resulted in the false belief that the Day of the Lord has already (started to) come and in idling (3:6-15) must be rejected.

2:16-17—These verses sound like the close of the letter, like the end of a contemporary pastor's sermon. God has *already* **loved** (2:13) the Christians and given them **eternal comfort and good hope** through the gracious gift of his Son Jesus. He who has already granted this foretaste of **eternal comfort** is asked to **comfort** the Thessalonians even further. They indeed need continuing comfort in light of the situation of present persecution. **Comfort** of the Thessalonians is revealed here as the main purpose of the letter. God is also asked to fortify their concrete love for one another (see 1:3-4, 11), as it manifests itself **in every good work and word.**

■ Prayer for the Author(s) and the Addressees (3:1-5)

3:1-2—Up to now Paul's concern has been exclusively with the recipients of his letter. Here, as at the end of Romans (15:30), he asks for their prayers. **Wicked and evil men** who do not recognize Jesus as their Lord impede the proclamation of the gospel by Paul and his staff. It cannot be brought to its glory if such hindrances prevail (see 1 Thess. 2:2, 14, 16, 18). The prayer that the gospel may **speed on and triumph** may reflect God's purpose in still restraining the Day of the Lord (Jesus).

3:3-5—The Thessalonians' lack of faith contrasts with the Lord's faithfulness. Since he has called and loved them, he will certainly grant them strength and protection in their persecutions. He will guard them from **evil,** which in Greek can also be the Evil One, Satan (2:9), as it can be in the Lord's Prayer.

Paul's **confidence in the Lord** concerning them in v. 4 is a pastoral measure (see 2 Cor. 7:16 and Phil. 1:14). Harsh language is not used by Paul because it would not effect their present and future doing of the things he **commands** (3:6, 10; in 12 it is coupled with exhorting). As an apostle of Christ (see 1 Thess. 2:7), however, he would have the authority to use such language.

In v. 5, language of Jesus and God is again mixed. **May the Lord** [Jesus] **direct your hearts to the love of God** does not fit well with **and to the steadfastness of Christ.** The Thessalonians' steadfastness, a cause for Paul's boasting (1:4), is to be modeled on Jesus' endurance of suffering on the cross (see 1 Cor. 1:5-6; Rom 5:3, 6).

■ Instructions Regarding the False Behavior of Some of the Recipients (3:6-15)

This is the third main section of the letter. Idleness, only one of the minor problems in 1 Thessalonians (5:14), has increased to such an extent that it now deserves extensive consideration. The only convincing reason for this behavior offered up to now is that belief in the Day of the Lord's having (started to) come in 2:2 produced resignation on the part of some. "Why continue to strive and toil if the end, Jesus' second coming, is so near? Living off one's savings, or off those of fellow Christians, will do for that short period!"

215

In his commentary on the apocalyptic book of Daniel (4:19), Hippolytus writes of the leader of a church in Pontus in Asia Minor (now northern Turkey) at the end of the second century A.D. On the basis of repeated dreams, he had prophesied that the final judgment would come at the end of the year, indeed, that "the Day of the Lord had come." Because the Christians of that area greatly feared the imminent arrival of that day, they abandoned their lands and fields and sold all their personal possessions. As in 2 Thessalonians, they probably asked themselves why they should work if the Day of the Lord, synonymous in intertestamental writings with the Day of Judgment, was about to come.

3:6-13—Paul's commanding the Thessalonians **in the name of our Lord Jesus Christ** in v. 6 adds authority to his words. The advice to avoid a misbehaving fellow Christian recalls various cases in 1 Corinthians 5.

The phrase **you yourselves know** in v. 7 is reminiscent of similar terminology in 2:6-7 and 1 Thess. 3:3 and 2:1. The tone here is one of gentle chiding, admonishing. Paul encourages them to **imitate us,** a theme which occurs in Phil. 3:17; 1 Cor. 4:16 and 11:1 (see also 1 Thess. 1:6 and 2:14, as well as v. 9 here). The apostle to the Gentiles did not suffer from low self-esteem, even claiming a pure conscience elsewhere (1 Cor. 4:4 and Phil. 3:6). In contrast to the idlers, Paul worked with his own hands (1 Thess. 2:9; 1 Cor. 4:12; see also Acts 18:2-3). He did this in order to avoid any false interpretation of his missionary motives and in order not to burden his very small congregations. He worked even though he expected Jesus' return from heaven during his own lifetime (see the references cited on 2:7). A rabbinic saying also stresses the continuation of work even though the Messiah is thought to arrive soon: "If there was a plant in your hand and they should say to you, 'Look, the Messiah is here!' Go and plant your plant and after that go forth to receive him." [9]

After the long eschatological passage concerning the resurrection in 1 Corinthians 15, Paul closes in v. 58 with an admonition to continue to work, for this is "not in vain." All work is work "in the Lord." The right to financial support as a missionary in 3:9 is also maintained in Luke 10:7 and 1 Cor. 9:4-15 (see also 1 Thess. 2:5-6). Paul and his helpers are an **example** to the congregations founded by them (Phil. 3:17). The Greek imperfect tense behind **we gave you this command** in v. 10 indicates it was done several times (see 1 Thess. 4:11).

Idleness was not a minor matter, perhaps in part because the culture of the Greek majorities in the congregations considered physical labor to be the menial task of slaves. Only *some* of the addressees in v. 11 are not busy working. They are **busybodies,** probably trying to convince the others that the Day of the Lord is already in the process of coming, so there is no point in further labor. Paul's adjuration of such persons **in the Lord Jesus** in v. 12, as in v. 6, imparts solemnity to the command. The idlers should rather return to their trades (v. 12), for the end has not yet come (2:3-12). In the meantime they should set aside their false excitement (2:2) and live quietly, settling down to "business as usual" (1 Thess. 4:11).

Verse 13 begins with an emphatic contrast: "But *you,* brethren . . ." (omitted in RSV). These brethren are thought of as the great majority in the addressees' congregation. Their not growing **weary in well-doing** has an exact parallel in Gal. 6:9. Paul himself refuses to grow weary in promoting the gospel (1 Cor. 4:1, 16).

3:14-15—Shaming a disobedient member of the congregation, one who refuses to return to normal tasks and to help others (1 Thess. 5:14), is done by ostracizing that person. Much severer cases of church discipline are found in 1 Cor. 5:2, 9 and 11, as well as Matt. 18:15-17; see also 1 Cor. 7:9. The ostracized people are not *enemies* simply because their eschatological views are wrong. They are still fellow Christians and should be warned in a fraternal manner.

■ Final Prayer, Personal Remark, and Benediction (3:16-18)

3:16—The closing double emphasis on peace is very appropriate (see 1 Thess. 5:13). Eschatological fervor had led to the Thessalonians being shaken up and excited, with some of them consequently abandoning their occupations. They need to settle down, to become peaceful again. **The Lord of peace** here can be either Jesus or God, yet in light of 1 Thess. 5:23; Rom. 15:33; and Num. 6:23 (the Aaronic benediction often used in today's worship services), it is more probably God.

3:17-18—To exclude the possibility of another false letter, Paul himself signs the epistle (dictated to a scribe), saying this is his custom (see 1 Cor. 16:21). The benediction in v. 18, **The grace of our Lord Jesus Christ be with you all,** is identical to 1 Thess. 5:28, with the addition of **all.** Although a standard liturgical phrase (Rom. 16:20; 1 Cor. 16:23), it is meant inclusively here, even for those who believe the Day of the Lord has already (started to) come and have therefore given up their trades (see 2 Cor. 13:14, also written in a context of congregational disunity, which likewise contains a blessing for **all**).

SELECTED BIBLIOGRAPHY

Aus, Roger. *Comfort in Judgment: The Use of Day of the Lord and Theophany Traditions in Second Thessalonians 1* (1971 Yale dissertation).

Best, Ernest. *The First and Second Epistles to the Thessalonians* (Black's; London: Black, 1972). The best recent commentary in English on 2 Thessalonians, it also surveys the views of others fairly.

Filson, Floyd. *St. Paul's Conception of Recompense* (Leipzig: Hinrichs, 1931). Explains what is often falsely thought of as a negative aspect of the apostle's theology.

Frame, James E. *Epistles of St. Paul to the Thessalonians* (ICC; New York: Scribner's, 1912). Strong on the Hellenistic side, it is solid philological work.

Giblin, Charles H. *The Threat to Faith. An Exegetical and Theological Re-examination of 2 Thessalonians 2* (Rome: Pontifical Biblical Institute, 1967). Advocates a "seizing force" and an (unknown) individual incorporating this force for 2 Thess. 2:6-7.

Glasson, T. Francis. *The Second Advent. The Origin of the New Testament Doctrine* (London: Epworth, 1963 [3]). Maintains that Jesus' parousia was taken over directly from Old Testament language of theophany and Day of the Lord.

Morris, Leon. *The First and Second Epistles to the Thessalonians* (NICNT; Grand Rapids, Michigan: Eerdmans,

1959). Representing conservative New Testament scholarship, the volume can also be appreciated by laypersons since it is entirely in English.

Robinson, John A. T. *Jesus and His Coming. The Emergence of a Doctrine* (London: SCM, 1957). Modifies Glasson's views to include the coming of the Son of man.

Sanders, Jim A. *Suffering as Divine Discipline in the Old Testament and Postbiblical Judaism* (Special issue of the *Colgate Rochester Divinity School Bulletin,* number 28 of 1955). Aids in understanding a Jewish "theology of suffering," employed in part by Paul.

NOTES

1. Cf. G. Krodel, *Ephesians, Colossians, 2 Thessalonians, The Pastoral Epistles*, ed. G. Krodel (Proclamation Commentaries; Philadelphia: Fortress, 1978) 87.
2. Cf. "The Relevance of Isa. 66:7 to Revelation 12 and 2 Thessalonians 1" in *ZNW* 67 (1976) 252-68, and "God's Plan and God's Power: Isaiah 66 and the Restraining Factors of 2 Thess. 2:6-7" in *JBL* 96 (1977) 537-53.
3. Cf. "The Liturgical Background of the Necessity and Propriety of Giving Thanks According to 2 Thess. 1:3" in *JBL* 92 (1973) 432-38.
4. Cf. the sources cited in the first article in n. 2 above, as well as the Jewish commentary Bereshit Rabbati Vayetze on Gen. 30:41 (ed. Ch. Albeck, *Midraš Berešit Rabbati ex libro R. Mosis Haddaršan*. Jerusalem: Mekize Nirdamim, 1940), p. 131. This applies Isa. 66:7 to the birth of the Messiah in Bethlehem.
5. On the "day" of the King Messiah see Targum Neofiti Gen. 3:15. It reads: "For her son, however, there will be a remedy, but for you, serpent, there will be no remedy, for they will make peace in the future, in the day of King Messiah." See A. Diez Macho, *Neophyti 1*. Tomo I, Génesis (Madrid-Barcelona: Consejo superior de investigaciones cientificas, 1968) 17 and 503-04. See also 4 Ezra 13:52.
6. The phrase "disappears," "is removed," has a Hebrew equivalent in Dan. 11:31 and 12:11, part of the Antiochus IV Epiphanes narrative alluded to earlier.
7. Cf. G. Krodel, *Ephesians* 93.
8. Cf. the sources cited in E. Nestle and K. Aland's edition of the Greek New Testament on this verse.
9. Cf. *The Fathers According to Rabbi Nathan, Version B*, Chap. 31, trans. A. Saldarini (Leiden: Brill, 1975) 182. There is a similar saying attributed to Martin Luther: "And even if the world came to an end tomorrow, I would still plant an apple tree today!"

ABOUT THE AUTHOR

Roger David Aus studied at St. Olaf College, Harvard Divinity School, Luther Theological Seminary, and Yale University, from which he received the Ph.D. degree in 1971. An ordained Lutheran clergyman, he has since served a German-speaking congregation in West Berlin, Germany, which granted him a short study leave in Jerusalem, Israel, in 1981. His numerous articles on New Testament themes reflect his great interest in, and appreciation of, the Jewish roots of the Christian faith.